Stain & Spot Removal Handbook

Beekman House
New York

Manufactured in the United States of America
' 2 3 4 5 6 7 8 9 10

Library of Congress Catalog Card Number: 80-84042
ISBN: 0-517-316838

This edition published by:
Beekman House
A Division of Crown Publishers, Inc.
One Park Avenue
New York, N.Y. 10016
By arrangement with Publications International, Ltd.

Cover Design: Frank E. Peiler
Illustrations: Steven Boswick

Contents

Chapter 1

How to Master Stains & Spots

It seems that in every household, there's at least one person who leaves behind a trail of stains and spots like a path of gingerbread crumbs: the home handyman who scatters grease spots from garage to attic, the toddler who expresses independence by painting with peanut butter on the wallpaper; the enthusiastic cook who splatters spaghetti sauce from ceiling to carpet; the new puppy that pointedly demonstrates its need for house-training. Grass spots on jeans, wine spots on tablecloths, oil stains on the driveway—and what makes it worse is that each stain calls for a different treatment. Catsup on carpet is not treated in the same way as catsup on concrete, and on top of having to identify both the staining agent and the stained surface, you have to work fast. The longer most stains set, the harder they are to remove without damage to the stained surface. If you haven't identified the stain correctly, or if you use an improper stain-removing agent or technique, you may make the stain permanent and cause additional damage to the stained object.

Three Types of Stains on Fabrics

Generally, stains can be divided into three types. Each type dictates certain general treatment procedures.

Greasy Stains. Lubricating and cooking oils, butter, machine grease, and similar substances produce greasy stains. Grease spots are sometimes removed from washable fabrics by hand or machine laundering. Pretreating by rubbing a little detergent directly into the spot often helps, as does using a dry-cleaning solvent on the stain. If you are treating an old stain or one that has been ironed, a yellow stain may remain after treatment with a solvent. Bleach is often effective at eliminating this yellow residue.

To remove grease spots from nonwashable fabrics, sponge the stain from center to edge with dry-cleaning solvent. Removal may take several applications, and the spot should be allowed to dry completely before each sponging. Greasy stains may also be removed from nonwashable fabrics by using an absorbent substance such as cornstarch, cornmeal, French chalk, or fuller's earth. Absorbents are dusted on greasy spots to pick up the grease. When the absorbent material begins to look caked, it should be shaken or brushed off. Repeat this procedure until most of the stain is gone.

Absorbents are easy to use and will not harm fabrics. However, the other stain removal agents (detergent, dry-cleaning solvent, and bleach) can damage fibers; before using them you should carefully read the care label on the stained item and the label on the product container.

Nongreasy Stains. Nongreasy stains are produced by materials such as tea, coffee, fruit juice, food coloring, and ink. If you have such a stain on a washable fabric, the best treatment is to sponge the stain with cool water as soon as possible. If this doesn't work, try soaking the fabric in cool water. The stain may soak out within half an hour, or you may need to leave the item in the water overnight. If some stain still remains, gently rub liquid detergent into it and rinse with cool water. The last resort is to use bleach, but read the fabric care label first. If the stain is old or has been ironed, it may be impossible to remove it completely.

A nongreasy stain on a nonwashable fabric can also be sponged with cool water. Or, you can place a disposable diaper or other absorbent pad beneath the stained area and slowly and carefully flush the stain by pouring water onto it using a mister or eyedropper. You must control the amount of water and the rate at which it is poured to avoid spreading the stain. This may be sufficient to remove some stains, especially if treatment is started promptly. If not, work liquid detergent into the stain as described above and rinse by flushing or sponging with cool water. Sponge the stain with rubbing alcohol after rinsing to remove detergent residue and to speed drying. (**Caution:** If treating acetate, acrylic, modacrylic, rayon, triacetate, or vinyl, dilute 1 part alcohol with 2 parts water.)

Combination Stains. Coffee with cream, Thousand Island salad dressing, and lipstick are items that cause combination stains; that is, they combine greasy and nongreasy elements. Such stains may require double treatment—first the nongreasy elements of the stain should be treated, then the greasy residue should be removed. The first step in treating such stains is to sponge with cool water as described above, then work liquid detergent into the stain and rinse thoroughly. After the fabric has dried, apply dry-cleaning fluid to any remaining greasy portion of the stain with a sponge. Allow the fabric to dry. Repeat applications of cleaning fluid if necessary.

The Ground Rules

Once you understand the basic rules about treating stains and spots, you'll be able to deal with them more effectively—no more wasting time trying to rinse away a stain with tap water when what it needs is to be treated with dry-cleaning solvent. The following rules apply to almost every spot and stain. Rules number one and two are cardinal in treating every spot and stain across the board.

1. The quicker, the better. The optimum time to treat a stain is within moments of its occurrence. The longer a stain sets, the more likely it is to become permanent.

2. Identify or try to identify both the staining agent and the stained surface before you begin treatment. Both factors affect how you treat the stain. Cotton is treated differently than rayon or silk. Knowing what the stained surface is helps you choose the proper treatment technique and avoid damaging the surface.

3. Remove as much as possible of the staining agent before treating with a stain-removal product. The less mayonnaise you have to deal with on the blouse front, the better; so scrape off as much as possible. Excess liquids can be blotted. (If there is enough liquid to form a puddle, spoon it out or remove it by dipping the corner of a clean, white cloth or paper towel into it and allowing the cloth to draw up the liquid.) If the staining agent is a solid, scrape off excess with a dull knife, spoon, or spatula. Powders can be shaken or brushed off. Be careful not to spread the stain when removing the excess staining material.

4. Handle stained items gently. Rubbing, folding, wringing, or squeezing can cause the stain to penetrate more deeply and may damage delicate fibers.

5. Avoid using heat. Don't use hot water on stains, don't dry stained articles with heat, and never iron stained fabrics. Heat can make a stain impossible to remove. (Heat, however, is used to remove wax from certain fibers.)

6. Pretest any stain-removing agent. Even water may damage some surfaces, so always run a sample test on some inconspicuous spot—the seam allowance or under the hem of a garment, the part of the rug that's hidden under a table or chair, the part of the upholstery that faces the wall—to avoid costly mistakes.

7. Follow directions to the letter. Read all the manufacturer's directions on the product container. If you make your own cleaning supplies, be sure you're using the proper ingredients and that you are using the cleaning agent exactly as described.

8. Work from the center of the stain outward. Most stains are

best treated with movements that are directed outward. Such movements help avoid leaving a ring around the cleaned area.

How to Use This Book

Being educated in the treatment of stains, you will save on costly cleaning bills and lengthen the life of your clothes and other possessions. Precautions must be taken during the cleaning process, as some dry-cleaning solvents and homemade formulas can damage fibers if allowed to remain on the stain or if directions are not carefully followed.

With the newer flame-retardant finishes and synthetic blends, manufacturers no longer take the care and cleaning of a garment for granted. Care labels, which are explained in Chapter 2, not only tell you how to launder an article, but state the fiber content, usually by percentage. This knowledge is helpful in determining which particular solvent to use. For example, a 100% wool garment will shrink when exposed to a large amount of water, whereas wool blended with synthetic fabrics often can be washed. Fabric stores now also include the manufacturers' care instructions and fiber content specifications with purchase of a fabric so the sewer can care for the finished garment properly.

All of the commerical products and homemade mixtures you should stock at home for quick stain removal are listed in Chapter 3. As many of these products are toxic or flammable, you'll find warnings about the correct use and storage of these stain-removing agents. All poisonous or caustic materials are so indicated so you can take precautions as you use and store them.

Techniques used in stain removal are nearly as varied as the stains themselves. Tamping may work well on one fabric and stain, while flushing would be better for another. Chapter 4 describes stain-removing methods and illustrates them.

Chapter 5 contains a chart of common stains and the procedures for their removal. Arranged alphabetically according to the specific stain, each entry is followed by individual groupings, also alphabetical, of stained materials that can be treated with a similar method, as well as the technique for removing the stain.

For a list of trademarked names for the generic synthetic fibers included in the stain-removal chart, see Chapter 6.

To get the most from this book, become familiar with its contents before stains occur. Learn the techniques and keep the most-often-used preparations on hand, along with utensils, such as a toothbrush or an absorbent pad. Refer to the specific stain for its treatment and learn how to cope with the "unknown stain."

Chapter 2
Understanding Fabric Care Labels

Permanently attached care labels have been required on almost all garments manufactured or sold in the United States since 1972. Care labels are also required on garments made of suede and leather, upholstered furniture, draperies, most bed linens, tablecloths, towels, and slipcovers. Fabric stores must supply care labels whenever a consumer purchases fabric, other than remnants less than 10 yards long. These labels can be of enormous help in determining exactly how you should go about removing stains, because, in addition to giving care instructions, they identify fiber content.

Certain information is not required under the 1972 regulation. For example, neither the manufacturer nor the retailer is required to inform a consumer that a certain fabric will shrink. It is assumed that consumers know the fundamentals of laundering clothing; it is also assumed that the purchaser knows that an item labeled "Hand wash" should be washed in lukewarm water and that all nonwhite articles should not be treated with chlorine bleach. Therefore, care labels do not have to specify such information. (If, however, an all-white garment should not be bleached, it should be labeled "Do not bleach.") The chart that follows explains the instructions found on care labels.

Another important piece of information contained on garment care labels is the fiber content of the fabric. This is especially important in light of the widespread use of blends in modern garments. A blend is a combination of fibers, such as cotton and wool, cotton and polyester, or wool and acrylic. Generally, it is suggested that blends be cared for in the same way you would care for the fiber with the highest percentage in the blend. A blend of 60% cotton and 40% polyester should be cleaned as though it were 100% cotton. However, when removing spots and stains, *you should follow procedures recommended for the most delicate fiber in the blend.* To remove stains from a blend of cotton and silk, use the procedure recommended for silk. If after such treatment, the stain is still apparent, follow the procedure for cotton, the more durable fiber in this blend.

Machine Washable

When label reads:	It means:
Machine wash	Wash, bleach, dry, and press by any customary method, including commercial laundering and dry-cleaning.
Home launder only	Same as above but do not use commercial laundering.
No chlorine bleach	Do not use chlorine bleach. Oxygen bleach may be used.
No bleach	Do not use any type of bleach.
Cold wash Cold rinse	Use cold water from tap or cold washing machine setting.
Warm wash Warm rinse	Use warm water or warm washing machine setting.
Hot wash	Use hot water or hot washing machine setting.
No spin	Remove wash load before final machine spin cycle.
Delicate cycle Gentle cycle	Use appropriate machine setting; otherwise wash by hand.
Durable press cycle Permanent press cycle	Use appropriate machine setting; otherwise use warm wash, cold rinse, and short spin cycle.
Wash separately	Wash alone or with like colors.

Nonmachine Washing

When label reads:	It means:
Hand wash	Launder only by hand in lukewarm (hand comfortable) water. May be bleached. May be dry-cleaned.
Hand wash only	Same as above, but *do not* dry-clean.
Hand wash separately	Hand wash alone or with like colors.
No bleach	Do not use bleach.
Damp wipe	Surface clean with damp cloth or sponge.

Home Drying

When label reads:	It means:
Tumble dry	Dry in tumble dryer at specified setting—high, medium, low, or no heat.
Tumble dry Remove promptly	Same as above, but in absence of cool-down cycle remove at once when tumbling stops.
Drip dry	Hang wet and allow to dry with hand shaping only.
Line dry	Hang damp and allow to dry.
No wring No twist	Hang dry, drip dry, or dry flat only. Handle to prevent wrinkles and distortion.
Dry flat	Lay garment on flat surface.
Block to dry	Maintain original size and shape while drying.

Ironing or Pressing

When label reads:	It means:
Cool iron	Set iron at lowest setting.
Warm iron	Set iron at medium setting.
Hot iron	Set iron at hot setting.
Do not iron	Do not iron or press with heat.
Steam iron	Iron or press with steam.
Iron damp	Dampen garment before ironing.

Miscellaneous

When label reads:	It means:
Dry-clean only	Garment should be dry-cleaned only, including self-service.
Professionally dry-clean only	Do not use self-service dry cleaning.
No dry-clean'	Use recommended care instructions. No dry-cleaning materials to be used.

Reprinted with permission of the Consumer Affairs Committee, American Apparel Manufacturers Association.

Chapter 3
What to Have on Hand

In order to treat stains and spots as soon as they occur, you have to be prepared. You should always have on hand the cleaning supplies and household products appropriate for treating the stains likely to occur in your home. This chapter lists stain-removing agents by category. It tells you where to purchase these supplies and for what they are used. Because many of these products are flammable or toxic, certain safety tips should be kept in mind when storing and using them.

- Store stain-removing products carefully, out of the reach of children. The storage area should be cool, dry, and apart from food storage areas. Keep bottles tightly capped, boxes closed.
- Do not transfer cleaning products to new containers. Keep them in their original containers so that you never have to search for directions for their proper use and so that they are always clearly labeled.
- Follow the directions on the product label and heed all warnings.
- Glass or unchipped porcelain containers are preferable to metal or plastic when working with stain-removal agents. Never use plastic with solvents. Never use any container that is rusty. Clean all containers thoroughly after use.
- Protect your hands with rubber gloves and don't touch your eyes or skin while handling stain-removal chemicals. If you do accidentally touch your eyes, or spill chemicals on your skin, flush immediately with clear water.
- Remember that the fumes of solvents are toxic; work in a well-ventilated area.
- Do not use chemicals near an open flame or electrical outlet. Do not smoke while using chemicals.
- Do not use a solvent as a laundry additive.
- When using a solvent on a washable fabric, be sure to rinse all traces of the solvent out of the fabric.
- Don't experiment with mixtures of stain-removal agents. Never combine products unless specifically directed to do so. (See Chapter 5.) Such combinations can be dangerous.

● If the cleaning process requires the use of more than one stain-removal agent, rinse each out before applying the next.

In addition to the solvents, bleaches, detergents, and chemicals you'll probably need, there are certain items you should have ready for a spot or stain catastrophe. The following are the basic tools used in treating most stains:

Clean white cotton cloths

Disposable diapers, white blotting paper or paper towels

Spoon, blunt knife, or spatula

Eyedropper, trigger spray bottle, or mister (the kind used for misting houseplants)

Small brush

Several colorfast weights

Stain-Removal Agents

Check through the listing of stains in Chapter 5 for the stains that occur most frequently in your household. Read the treatment to find which of the following stain-removing agents you're most likely to need. Most are available at grocery stores, hardware stores, or pharmacies.

Absorbents

Substances used as absorbents "soak up" stains, especially grease stains. Materials used as absorbents include cornstarch, cornmeal (usually considered the best for lighter colors), white talcum powder, or fuller's earth (best for use on darker colors, available at pharmacies and garden supply stores). Absorbents are used on light or new stains; they will damage neither fabrics nor other surfaces and they are easy to use. The absorbent material is spread on the stained area and allowed to work. As the grease is soaked up, the absorbent material will cake or become gummy. It should then be shaken or brushed off. The process should be repeated until most of the stain has been removed. Some light stains may be completely removed if the absorbent is left on for 8 hours or more.

Bleaches

Chlorine.   Commonly used to bleach white cotton, linen, and synthetic fabrics, chlorine bleach can also be used as a disinfectant and stain remover. Chlorine bleach is potent and can weaken fibers. If allowed to soak in a bleach solution too long, even cotton and linen will be weakened. Chlorine bleach should not be used on silk, wool, or fabrics exposed to sunlight (curtains, for example). To avoid damaging your fabric, always pretest bleach on a hidden area and rinse all bleached items thoroughly. **Caution:** Chlorine bleach is poisonous. If it comes in contact with the skin or eyes, it will cause burns and irritation. Read all warnings on the label.

Color Remover.   Color removers contain hydrosulfite chemicals and are used both for stain removal and to lighten the color of fabrics before they are redyed a lighter color. They are safe for colorfast fibers, but they fade or remove many dyes. Always pretest color removers on an inconspicuous corner of the article you are treating. If the product causes a distinct color change rather than fading, rinse with water immediately and you may be able to restore the original color. However, if the colors fade when the color remover is applied, the original color cannot be restored. Color remover should not be used or stored in metal containers. **Rit Color Remover** (Special Products, an Affiliate of CPC North America) is a good product and can be found in drug, grocery, and variety stores. **Caution:** Color removers are poisonous. Avoid prolonged contact with skin. Observe all precautions on the label.

Hydrogen Peroxide.   The 3% solution of hydrogen peroxide sold in drugstores as a mild antiseptic is a good bleach, safe for most surfaces and all fibers (though dyed fabrics should be pretested for colorfastness). Be careful not to purchase the stronger solution sold for bleaching hair. Peroxide should be stored in a cool, dark place. Buy small quantities; it loses strength if stored for a long time. Do not use or store peroxide in metal containers. If you pour out too much peroxide, do not pour the excess back in the bottle as peroxide is easily contaminated.

Sodium Perborate.   You can purchase sodium perborate under trade names or generically at drugstores. Sold in crystal form, sodium perborate is safe for all fabrics and surfaces, although, once again, pretesting is recommended to assure that your fabric is colorfast. This oxygen-type bleach is slower-acting than hydrogen peroxide. When using this bleach, be sure to rinse treated articles thoroughly.

Chemicals

Acetic Acid.   A 10% solution of acetic acid can be purchased generically at pharmacies. (White vinegar is 5% acetic acid and can be used as a substitute for the stronger solution.) It is a clear fluid that can be used to remove stains on silk and wool. It must be diluted with 2 parts water for use on cotton and linen (a pretest is recommended). It should not be used on acetate. If acetic acid causes a color change, sponge the affected area with ammonia.

Acetone.   Acetone can be purchased generically at pharmacies and hobby shops. A colorless liquid that smells like peppermint, it can be used on stains caused by substances such as fingernail polish or household cement. Although it will not damage either natural fibers or most synthetics, it should be pretested to make sure that dyed fabrics will not be harmed. It should not be used on fabrics containing acetate. Use only pure acetone on stains; although most nail polish removers contain acetone, the other ingredients included in these products can worsen stains. **Caution:** Acetone is flammable and evaporates rapidly, producing toxic fumes. When using acetone, work outside or in a well-ventilated place. Avoid inhaling fumes. Store in a tightly capped container in a cool place.

Alcohol.   Common isopropyl alcohol (70%), which can be purchased generically at drugstores, is sufficient for most stain-removal jobs that call for alcohol, although the stronger denatured alcohol (90%) can also be used. Be sure you don't buy alcohol with added color or fragrance. Alcohol will fade some dyes; pretest before using it. Alcohol will damage acetate, triacetate, modacrylic, and acrylic fibers. If you must use it on fibers in the acetate family, dilute the alcohol with two parts water. **Caution:** Alcohol is poisonous and flammable. Observe all label precautions.

Ammonia.   For stain removal, purchase plain household ammonia without added color or fragrance. It is sold at grocery stores. Because ammonia affects some dyes, always pretest on a hidden corner of the stained article. To restore color changed by ammonia, rinse the affected area with water and apply a few drops of white vinegar. Rinse with clear water again. Ammonia damages silk and wool; if you must use it on these fibers, dilute it with an equal amount of water and use as sparingly as possible. **Caution:** Ammonia is poisonous. Avoid inhaling its fumes. It will cause burns or irritation if it comes in contact with the skin or eyes. Observe all label precautions.

Amyl Acetate.   Buy chemically pure amyl acetate (banana oil) for use in stain removal. It is available at drugstores. It is safe for use on fibers that could be damaged by acetone, but it should not be allowed to come in contact with plastics or furniture finishes. **Caution:** Amyl acetate is poisonous and flammable. Avoid contact with the skin and inhaling the vapors.

Coconut Oil.   Coconut oil is sold in drug and health food stores. It is used in the preparation of a Dry Spotter (see How to Make Dry and Wet Spotters in this chapter), which is used to remove many kinds of stains. If you cannot obtain coconut oil, you may substitute mineral oil which is almost as effective.

Glycerine.   Glycerine is sold generically in pharmacies. It is used in the preparation of the Wet Spotter (see How to Make Dry and Wet Spotters in this chapter), which is used to remove many kinds of stains.

Oxalic Acid.   Effective in treating ink and rust stains, oxalic acid crystals are sold in many pharmacies. Before using them, you must dissolve the crystals in water (1 tablespoon crystals to 1 cup warm water). Pretest the solution on a hidden corner before using it on the stain. Moisten the stained area with the solution. Allow to dry, then reapply, keeping the area moist until the stain is removed. Be sure all traces of the solution are rinsed out. **Caution:** Oxalic acid is poisonous. Avoid all contact with the skin and eyes and wear rubber gloves when working with it.

Sodium Thiosulfate.   Available in crystal form at drugstores and photo supply houses, sodium thiosulfate is also known as photographic "hypo" or fixer. Although considered safe for all fibers and harmless to dyes, it should be tested on an inconspicuous area of fabric before use.

Turpentine.   Turpentine is commonly found in paint and hardware stores and in art supply houses. Most often used as a thinner for oil-base paints, it is effective on paint and grease stains, but it must be used carefully. **Caution:** Turpentine is flammable and poisonous. Observe all label precautions.

Vinegar.   Only white vinegar should be used for stain removal. Cider and wine vinegar have color that can leave a stain. Vinegar can be purchased at grocery stores and pharmacies. It contains a 5% acetic acid solution and should be diluted if you must use it on cotton or linen. Vinegar is safe for all other colorfast fibers, but can change the color of some dyes, so always test its effects on an inconspicuous area first. If a dye changes color, rinse the affected area with water and add a few drops of ammonia. Rinse thoroughly with water again.

Dry-cleaning Solvents

Perchloroethylene, trichloroethane, and trichloroethylene are three of the most common and effective ingredients in the dry-cleaning solvents found on the market today. Most of these solvents are nonflammable, but their fumes are toxic and should not be inhaled. Not all spot removers/dry-cleaning solvents can be used on all surfaces, nor will all products remove all stains, so be sure to read the labels before using. Dry-cleaning solvents are available at pharmacy, grocery, variety, and hardware stores. A few exceptional products are **Carbona No. 10 Special Spot Remover, Carbona Cleaning Fluid,** and **Carbona Spray Spot Remover** (Carbona Products Company), **K2r Spot-lifter** (Texize) (tube and aerosol forms), **Brush Top Spot Remover** (Scot Laboratories Division of Scott & Fetzer), **Afta Cleaning Fluid** and **Afta Spot Wipes** (Afta Solvents Corporation), and **Amway Remove Fabric Spot Cleaner** (Amway Corp.).

Note: Carbona No. 10 Special Spot Remover and Carbona Cleaning Fluid are chemically identical. Carbona No. 10 Special Spot Remover is sold in a bottle with a built-in fabric applicator top, while the cleaning fluid is packaged in a can. The former is more convenient to use for many spots, but the cleaning fluid usually is substantially cheaper and can be applied with a sponge or absorbent pad. The two are listed interchangeably on the chart in Chapter 5.

Shampoos and Stain Removers for Carpets

To use a foam carpet shampoo, simply spray it on, rub or sponge it in if instructions require it, then vacuum when dry. Follow the manufacturer's directions and always pretest in an inconspicuous corner to be certain the fiber is colorfast. You may have to shampoo the entire carpet if removing the spot leaves a brighter patch. Some very good carpet shampoos are **Carbona 1 Hour Rug Cleaner** (Carbona Products Company), **Glory Professional Strength Rug Cleaner** (S. C. Johnson & Son, Inc.), and **Lestoil Deodorizing Rug Shampoo** (Noxell Corporation).

To remove small spots, apply a carpet stain-removing product such as **Afta Carpet Stain Remover** (Afta Solvents Corporation), **Spot Shot Carpet Stain Remover** (Sifers Chemicals, Inc.), **Stain-X Carpet Stain Remover** (Positive Products Laboratories, Inc.) or **Up & Out** (Trewax Company). Up & Out is not for use on wool carpets.

Specialty Products

For almost everything that can get stained, there is a product made specifically for that job. In most cases, a substitute will work as well, but a few products listed below are exceptional for removing specific stains.

Leather and Vinyl Conditioners. The Tannery (Missouri Hickory Corp.) can remove many stains from leather and vinyl, while conditioning the surface at the same time. It is easy to use and in many cases restores the luster and suppleness on poorly maintained leathers. Be sure to read the label carefully. **Fieb-**

ing's **Saddle Soap** (Fiebing Company, Inc.) and **Vinyl Magic** (Magic American Chemical Corp.) also are good leather and vinyl cleaners/conditioners.

Mildew Removers. **X-14 Instant Mildew Stain Remover** (White Laboratories, Inc.) is a very good mildew remover for most surfaces. It is not recommended for fabrics. It kills the mildew spores on contact and prevents restaining. Be sure to read the label carefully. Using **Afta Mildew Stop** (Afta Solvents Corporation), available in aerosol and dry packet forms, is a good preventive measure for mildew-prone areas.

Rust Removers. **Bar Keepers Friend Cleanser & Polish** (SerVaas Laboratories, Inc.) is an abrasive that works very well on rust stains. It is safe for most fabrics, though be sure to read the label. It will also remove tarnish, coffee and tea stains, fruit and vegetable stains, and smoke. **Pumie Scouring Stick** (United States Pumice Company) and **Whink Rust Stain Remover** (Whink Products Company) also are effective.

Suede Cleaners. **Suede Stone** (Canden Company) is a product for rubbing marks from suede. Usually, rubbing is all that is needed to remove grime, dirt, and oil stains; however, it can be dampened for tougher stains. It will also remove some types of marks from wallpaper, much like an eraser. Be sure to read label directions and restrictions carefully. **Child Life Suede & Fabric Cleaner** is an excellent all-around cleaner and conditioner.

Tile and Grout Cleaners. For removing stains from grout without chipping, use **Afta Tile & Grout Cleaner** (Afta Solvents Corporation), baking soda, or powdered cleanser. For mildew stains, apply **Carbona Tile and Bath Cleaner** (Carbona Products Company) to the grout and ceramic tile to kill all mildew.

Wallpaper Cleaner. Crayon marks and graphite can be removed from wallpaper, woodwork, linoleum, marble, and brick with **Crayerase** (Canden Company), a nontoxic cleaning bar.

Washing Agents

Detergents. When stain-removal directions call for mild detergent, choose a white dishwashing liquid detergent; the dyes in nonwhite detergents may worsen your stain. If instructions call for a pretreating paste made of detergent and water, use a powdered detergent that does not contain bleach. If the stain-removal directions specify that you should apply a liquid laundry detergent directly to the spot or stain, be sure to read label directions carefully. Some products cannot safely be used in this manner. Other detergent products (those used in automatic dishwashers or for heavy household cleaning, and certain laundry products) may contain alkalies that could set stains such as ammonia, soap, and oven cleaner.

Enzyme Presoaks.　Most effective on protein stains (meat juices, eggs, blood, and the like), enzyme presoaks may harm silk and wool. Make sure you've exhausted every alternative before you use enzyme presoaks on these two fabrics. Use as soon as possible after mixing in solution; enzyme presoak solutions become inactive in storage. Two very good enzyme products are **Axion** (Colgate-Palmolive Company) and **Biz** (Procter & Gamble). Be sure to read and observe all label directions.

Powdered Cleansers.　Scouring powders and baking soda can be used to remove stains on surfaces that won't be harmed by abrasives. However, you should be aware that prolonged or overly vigorous scrubbing with these products can scratch the most durable surface. Make sure you rinse away all of the powder when the job is completed.

Pretreaters.　Pretreaters are used on spots and stains that might not respond to normal laundering procedures. They start the cleaning process before the stained item is put in the washer. Pretreaters must be used in conjunction with the rest of the laundering process; do not try to use them alone as though they were spot removers. After applying a pretreater, do not allow the fabric to dry before washing. Follow label directions. Some good brands are **Shout Laundry Soil & Stain Remover** (S. C. Johnson & Son, Inc.), **Spray 'n Wash** (Texize), **Magic Pre-Wash** (Armour-Dial Inc.), and **Miracle White Laundry Soil & Stain Remover** (The Drackett Company).

Soaps.　Do not use bath soaps with added moisturizers, fragrance, dyes, or deodorant to treat spots and stains. Purchase either laundry soap or pure white soap.

How to Make Dry and Wet Spotters

To mix a Dry Spotter, combine 1 part coconut oil (available at pharmacies and health food stores) and 8 parts liquid dry-cleaning solvent. This solution may be stored if the container is tightly capped to prevent evaporation of the solvent. Mineral oil may be substituted for the coconut oil, but is not quite as effective. **Caution:** Dry-cleaning solvents are poisonous and may be flammable. Follow all of the precautions given under Dry-cleaning Solvents in this chapter.

To prepare a Wet Spotter, mix 1 part glycerine, 1 part white dishwashing detergent, and 8 parts water. Shake well before each use. Store Wet Spotter in a plastic squeeze bottle.

Chapter 4
Special Techniques

Basically, there are two approaches to removing spots and stains. You can use a stain-removal agent (see Chapter 3) that interacts with the stain chemically, or you can physically loosen or remove the stain from the surface. Many stubborn stains require both chemical and physical treatment. In this chapter, we discuss eight physical stain-removal techniques: brushing, flushing, freezing, presoaking, pretreating, scraping, sponging, and tamping.

Which technique to use in treating a particular spot or stain depends upon both the nature of the stain and the type of surface stained. For example, a stain may be wet or dry, semisolid or hardened. On a very delicate surface, you may not be able to use such techniques as scraping and tamping. A stain may be flushed more easily from a loosely woven fabric than from one that is tightly woven; but a tightly woven fabric can withstand a treatment such as tamping more successfully.

Following is a list of special techniques with directions for their use. Follow these directions carefully to assure successful stain removal without harm to the stained article. Note that whenever you use absorbent pads (when you flush or sponge a stain) you should check the pad frequently and change it as soon as any of the stain is deposited. This will prevent reapplication of the stain to the treated article. Remember, too, that to avoid fabric damage you should never apply heavy pressure when using techniques such as brushing, tamping, or scraping.

Brushing

Brushing is used to remove dried stains and spots. Some spots, such as those formed of dried mud, may be completely removed by brushing. In treating other types of dry stains (for example, face powder), brushing is just the first step in treating the stain. In treating some stains, brushing may be one of the last steps, as when you want to remove an absorbent or a dried stain-removing paste from a surface.

Use a small, stiff-bristled brush for this technique. A toothbrush works well on small stains. When working on a fabric, stretch the piece on a firm, clean working surface. Hold a clean

Use a stiff-bristled brush to brush stain up and onto the paper.

sheet of paper next to the stain (on walls, hold the paper beneath the stain) so that you can brush the staining material onto the paper. Use a gentle motion to brush the stain up off the surface and onto the paper. It may help to blow softly on the spot as you brush.

Flushing

Flushing is used to remove loosened staining materials and any residue from the stain-removal agent. This is an important step in the process, for if any chemicals are left in the material, they may cause additional staining or they may damage the treated article.

When flushing a stain, especially one on a nonwashable fabric, you need to control the flow of water carefully. To apply a measured amount of flushing liquid, use a device such as an eyedropper or plant mister, or a plastic trigger spray bottle that can be adjusted to spray a fine stream. Before you begin the

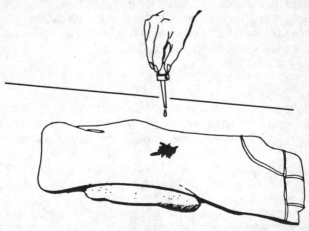

Apply flushing liquid to only the stain with an eyedropper or mister.

treatment, place a clean absorbent pad beneath the spot, then slowly and carefully apply the recommended stain remover to the stain. If you decide to use a mister, place the tip against the stained area and depress the plunger or pump the trigger slowly. In this way, you can force out a thin stream of fluid without wetting a large area. You must work slowly; do not apply the liquid faster than the pad beneath can absorb it and do not spread the stain. Replace the absorbent pad frequently so that the deposited staining material does not restain the fabric.

Stains on area rugs may be flushed following the directions above. In fact, any rug under which you can place an absorbent pad can be treated by flushing. If, however, your rug is too large to lift or if the stain is on tacked-down rugs or carpeting, you may have to sponge the stain-removal agent onto the spot instead. Then sponge with clear water to remove chemical residues. Remember, the pad or cloth used for sponging must be changed frequently.

If you are treating a washable fabric and directions call for flushing with water, you may rinse the stained article. To rinse out a stain, dip the article up and down repeatedly in a container of warm water. Change the rinse water frequently.

Pretreating

Pretreating is used to ease the removal of small stains, espe-cially those that are oily or greasy. Stubborn soil, such as the ground-in dirt on collars, cuffs, and socks, is easier to remove after it's been pretreated. When you are pretreating a stain, you apply the stain-removing agent directly to the stained area. To pretreat a stain, you may use a liquid detergent, a soil-and-stain-removing pretreat spray, bar soap, or a pretreating paste made of powdered detergent (do not use one that contains bleach) and water.

Liquid detergent and pretreating sprays should be applied directly onto the dry stain. If you are using bar soap or have prepared a paste of powdered or granular detergent and water, dampen the fabric slightly before applying the pretreating agent. After its application, rub the pretreater into the stain gently, then wash the item as you normally do.

To use pretreating sprays successfully, you should keep a few points in mind. Pretest the spray by applying it to an inconspicu-ous part of the garment before using it on the stain. Most of these sprays are perfectly safe on all washable fabrics, but some contain an oxygen-type bleach ingredient that could harm some dyes. Apply the product according to package directions, wait 5 minutes, and then rinse the pretest area carefully. If no color change is apparent, you can safely treat the stain. After using one of these sprays, it is essential that you wash the treated article thoroughly to remove both the rest of the stain and any residue from the pretreat spray. Allowing the residue to set may cause a new stain.

Presoaking

Presoaking is a useful and effective treatment for washable articles that are grayed, yellowed, or heavily stained. You can presoak laundry in the washer or in a sink or tub. Use warm water. Sort the soiled items before presoaking; noncolorfast items should be soaked separately or with similar colors and for only a short time.

How long you should presoak stained articles depends upon the stain and the fiber. For most stains, 30 minutes should be adequate. Noncolorfast items should be soaked only briefly. Heavily stained items or stains that have set for a long time may require overnight soaking.

You may want to add bleach, laundry detergent, or an enzyme presoak product to the soaking water. However, avoid using enzyme products on silk or wool, and do not use chlorine bleach and an enzyme product at the same time. Whenever you add anything to the water used for presoaking, make sure that the item is then thoroughly rinsed before you launder it. There should not be any residue from the presoak product left in the item when it is washed.

Scraping

Scraping can be used to lift off excess semisold staining material and to loosen caked-on stains. Removal of as much of such material as possible makes it easier for the stain-removing agent to reach the surface, and although scraping may not remove a stain completely, it is often a necessary step before applying a stain remover.

Do not use an absorbent pad beneath an item you are going to scrape. For your scraping tool use a dull knife, spoon, or spatula. Don't press hard, but move the edge of your scraping tool back and forth across the stain in short strokes. Be gentle to avoid damaging the stained surface. To remove some stains you must add liquid as you scrape, working the liquid into the stain as you remove excess material.

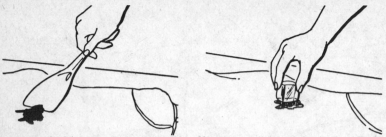

Scraping (left) is used to gently lift off excess solid or caked-on stains. Freezing is accomplished by holding ice against the stain (right).

Freezing

Some staining substances, such as candle wax and gum, can be hardened by the application of cold so that they are easier to remove. Work fast when treating a spill that is still semisolid. You may be able to limit the area stained by quickly hardening the staining material. To freeze a stain, hold one or more ice cubes against it. If the stained item is not washable, place the ice in a plastic bag. If the stained item is portable and the stain is large, you may put the article into a plastic bag and place it in the freezer. Take the item out when the staining material solidifies.

After the stain has solidified, it can usually be gently lifted or scraped from the surface. Any residue may require further stain-removal treatment.

Sponging

Sponging is one of the most frequently used methods of applying many stain-removing agents, including water. Sponging is another technique in which clean absorbent pads are used. The stained item should be laid on a pad, stainside down, if possible. You may have to sponge stains on carpets without any absorbent pad beneath, in which case you must be especially careful to wet the carpet as little as possible.

Use another clean pad or a clean sponge to apply the stain-removing agent. Dampen this pad with the agent specified in the stain-removal directions and sponge the stain gently. Use light strokes and work outward from the center of the stain. Try to keep your sponging strokes as close to the stain as possible. Use only enough stain remover to dampen the sponge and move in an irregular pattern. By following these directions, you are less likely to cause rings to form.

Check the pad beneath the stain at frequent intervals and

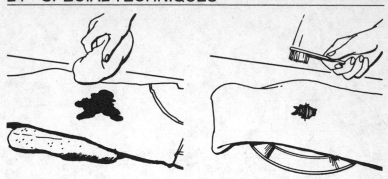

To sponge on a stain-removing agent (left), work outward from the center. To tamp (right), bring the brush down directly onto the stain.

examine the sponging pad as well. Change the pad as soon as any stain is deposited on it. In this way, the staining agent will not be reapplied to the fabric.

Certain fabrics, including acetate, triacetate, and rayon, are more likely than others to develop rings when treated with this technique. So, when sponging stains on these fabrics, you must be even more careful. Barely wet the sponge with stain remover and touch the fabric lightly so that the stain remover is absorbed as slowly as possible. Limit your strokes to the immediate stained area to keep the moistened area as small as possible and avoid spreading the stain. After the stain is removed, dry the fabric as quickly as possible. Blot the treated area gently between clean, dry absorbent pads; then allow it to dry. Unless you have used only water as the stain-removal agent, do not use heat in drying.

Tamping

Tamping is a stain-removal technique that is effective on durable, tightly woven fabrics, but it may damage more delicate materials. When stain-removal directions call for tamping, the only tool you need is a small brush (a soft-bristled toothbrush is usually fine). Place the stained article on the work surface—no need for an absorbent pad. Hold the brush 2 or 3 inches above the stain and bring it down directly on the stain repeatedly in light strokes. You are using too much pressure if the bristles bend. Try to hit the stained area squarely with the tips of the bristles. You are more likely to damage the fabric if you hit it with the side of the brush. To avoid harming the fabric, stop tamping as soon as the spot is removed. Tightly woven fabrics of high-twist yarn are able to withstand more tamping than loosely woven fabrics of slight- or moderate-twist yarn.

Chapter 5
Removing Stains & Spots

The key to successful removal of spots and stains is using the proper techniques and stain-removing agents. Some techniques will work only on certain types of stains and fabrics, and the use of improper chemicals and techniques can make some stains worse. Procedures and products listed on this chart have been carefully tested. To use the chart, first locate the "staining agent," or the substance that created the stain; these staining substances are listed in alphabetical order. Next, find the type of surface that the stain is on in the listing (also alphabetized) in the left column. Then read the procedure listed on the right for removing the staining agent from the target. For example, when you take down a poster and find a gummy residue from the tape on your wallpaper, look up the staining agent, "Adhesive Tape," on the chart. Then look for the stained surface, "Wallpaper," in the left column. The column to the right describes the steps to take to remove the residue.

All fabrics are listed by generic fiber in the chart. If you are unsure what fiber a synthetic trademarked fabric is made of, see Chapter 6, which lists many common fiber trademarks.

Specific stain-removal techniques, including brushing, flushing, freezing, presoaking, pretreating, scraping, sponging, and tamping, are not described in detail each time they are listed on the chart. Refer to Chapter 4 for explanations of how to use these techniques properly.

For complete instructions for preparing stain-removing mixtures, such as Dry Spotter and Wet Spotter, and for descriptions of commercial products, refer to Chapter 3. If stores in your area don't stock the products recommended here, consult the Directory of Manufacturers for ways to contact the companies that market the products.

Unless you know a surface is colorfast, can accurately identify the stain, and know which products are safe to use on the stain target, *always* pretest cleaning products on a hidden portion of the stained item. Even a common agent like water can leave marks that are impossible to remove. When using any stain-removing product, it is better to read the manufacturer's cautions and test the product's action on an inconspicuous spot (a hem, a hidden portion of carpet, etc.) than to ruin the stained surface.

Note: In most instances, the first few steps listed on the chart should completely remove a fresh stain, making the remaining steps unnecessary. However, be sure to follow the procedures in sequence until the stain is removed.

Adhesive Tape

- Acetate
- Carpet/Synthetic
- Carpet/Wool
- Fiberglass Rayon
- Silk Triacetate
- Wool

Scrape* gummy matter from the material very gently. Use either **Afta Cleaning Fluid, Carbona No. 10 Special Spot Remover/Carbona Cleaning Fluid,** or **K2r Spot-Lifter** (tube) dry-cleaning solvents. If stain persists, apply a Dry Spotter to the stain and cover with an absorbent pad dampened with the spotter. Change the pad as it picks up the stain. Let it stand as long as any stain is being removed, keeping both the stain and pad moist. Sponge* the area with a dry-cleaning solvent. Allow surface to dry completely.

- Acrylic Fabric
- Burlap Nylon
- Olefin Polyester
- Spandex

Gently scrape* the excess. Very carefully, apply **Afta Cleaning Fluid** to the stain. If any remains, apply a Wet Spotter, with a few drops of ammonia added, to the stain. Tamp* and blot occasionally with an absorbent pad. Flush* with water and dry thoroughly.

- Acrylic Plastic
- Alabaster
- Asphalt
- Chromium
- Copper Enamel
- Glass Linoleum
- Marble Pewter

Scrape* to remove any excess. Do not use an abrasive product. Dip a clean sponge or cloth into warm sudsy water and rub the gummy matter. The warm water will soften the tape so it can be removed with the sponge or cloth. Rinse with warm water and wipe dry with a clean cloth.

(continued)

See Chapter 4 for specific technique instructions.

- **Platinum**   *(see base of preceding page)*
- **Plexiglas**
- **Vinyl Clothing**
- **Vinyl Tile**
- **Vinyl Wallcovering**

- **Aluminum** •**Iron**
- **Stainless Steel**

Pick off as much tape as possible with your fingertips or tweezers. If possible, soak the stain in warm to hot sudsy water. This should loosen the sticky substance enough that it can be wiped off. Should any remain, gently rub the area in one direction only with a soft scouring pad to remove any traces.

- **Bamboo** •**Cane**
- **Ceramic Glass/Tile**
- **Polyurethane**

Rub the gummy area with a cloth or sponge dipped in warm, mild soapy water to which a few drops of ammonia have been added. Rinse with clear water. Dry thoroughly.

- **Bluestone** •**Brick**
- **Concrete**
- **Flagstone**
- **Granite**
- **Limestone**
- **Masonry Tile**
- **Sandstone** •**Slate**
- **Terrazzo**

Mix a solution of washing soda or laundry detergent and warm water. Do not use soap; it will leave a hard-to-remove scum. With a soft brush—a toothbrush is good for small areas—gently spread the solution over the gummy portion until it is removed. Rinse with clear warm water.

- **Brass** •**Bronze**
- **Ivory** •**Jade**
- **Porcelain** •**Tin**
- **Zinc**

Remove any excess matter with your fingertips or tweezers. Mix a solution of hot water and a mild soap. With a soft cloth dipped in the solution, rub until the gummy substance is softened and removed. Rinse with clear water and wipe dry.

- **Cork**

Scrape* to remove excess, taking care not to gouge the soft surface. Gently rub any remaining gummy matter with a piece of fine steel wool
(continued)

---

*See Chapter 4 for specific technique instructions.

(continued from preceding page) dipped in liquid or paste polishing wax. Wipe away soiled wax as you work.

•Cotton •Linen	Scrape* to remove excess. Place face down on an absorbent pad and sponge* area with **Carbona No. 10 Special Spot Remover/Carbona Cleaning Fluid** or **Afta Cleaning Fluid.** Allow fluid to dry thoroughly; launder soon to remove all traces of fluid.
•Felt	Remove excess carefully to avoid shredding the fiber. Freeze* to harden remainder and gently brush* with a sponge or fine-bristled brush. This should remove any remaining adhesive. In extreme cases, rub the surface carefully, using a razor blade with the direction of the nap; however, this removes some felt fiber.
•Fur/Natural •Fur/Synthetic	Take care not to remove the fur when removing excess adhesive. With ice cubes in a plastic bag, freeze* to harden the remainder. Gently brush* with a fine-bristled brush or a damp sponge. Take care not to soak backing or pelt. If a gummy residue remains, scrape* it carefully in the direction of the nap with a razor blade. In extreme cases, the gummy matter can be *carefully* cut away with a pair of scissors if it is at the very tips of the hairs.
•Gold	Mix some hot sudsy water to which a few drops of ammonia have been added. Immerse the stained area if it is small, or use a brush, such as a toothbrush, to apply the solution. Rinse in clear hot water and dry with a soft cloth.

See Chapter 4 for specific technique instructions.

•Grout

Remove as much of the gummy matter as possible. Apply **Afta Tile & Grout Cleaner.** Or dip a wet toothbrush into a little powdered cleanser and gently scrub. Rinse with clear water and dry.

•Leather

Carefully scrape* to remove excess. Dip a cloth or sponge into the suds of a mild soap and gently scrub until the remaining matter is removed. Dry with a clean cloth. Condition the leather with **The Tannery** or **Fiebing's Saddle Soap.**

•Paint/Flat
•Paint/Gloss

Remove excess gum carefully to avoid removing any paint. Mix dishwashing detergent in hot water and swish to make a great volume of suds. Dip a cloth in only the foam and apply to the stain. Do not allow the water to run as it will cause hard-to-remove streaks. Rinse with clear water. Dry thoroughly.

•Photographs

With your fingertip and a very gentle touch, rub the gummy matter in one direction toward the edge of the photo. It should ball up as you rub and should roll off the photo. Continue until no more adhesive is removed.

•Silver

Pick off as much excess as possible with your fingertips or tweezers. Rub the remaining portion using hot suds and a soft cloth. Rinse with hot water and dry immediately and thoroughly to prevent tarnish.

•Suede

Carefully pick off as much excess as possible with your fingertips. Gently rub an artgum eraser over the remaining gummy substance.Or apply **Child Life Suede & Fabric Cleaner.**

(continued)

See Chapter 4 for specific technique instructions.

(continued from preceding page) If that doesn't work, cautiously rub the spot with an emery board or very fine (grade 6/0–8/0) sandpaper. You are attempting to remove a fine layer of the suede, so work carefully.

●**Wallpaper**

Put a white blotter against the tape and press through the blotter with a warm iron. Repeat if necessary with a clean portion of the blotter.

●**Wood**

Remove excess gently so the finish will not be marred. Rub gently with a cloth dipped in the suds of hot soapy water. Rub only on the portion stained. Rinse with clear water, wipe dry immediately, and polish.

Alcoholic Beverages

●**Acetate** ●**Burlap**
●**Felt** ●**Fiberglass**
●**Rayon** ●**Rope**
●**Silk** ●**Triacetate**
●**Wool**

Blot up any excess liquid. Spray on **Amway Remove Fabric Spot Cleaner.** Or, flush* area with cool water. Apply a Wet Spotter and a few drops of white vinegar. Cover with an absorbent pad dampened with the Wet Spotter and let stand as long as any stain is being removed. Keep the stain and pad moist, changing the pad as it picks up the stain. Flush with cool water, blotting excess liquid with a clean absorbent pad. Dry thoroughly.

●**Acrylic Fabric**
●**Cotton** ●**Linen**
●**Nylon** ●**Olefin**
●**Polyester**
●**Spandex**

Apply **Amway Remove Fabric Spot Cleaner.** Or, sponge* stain promptly with cool water. If possible, presoak* the stain in cool water for at least 30 minutes or overnight. Work undiluted dishwashing or liquid laundry detergent into stain. Rinse well. Launder as soon as possible. Old or ironed-in stains may be impossible to remove.

*See Chapter 4 for specific technique instructions.

- Acrylic Plastic
- Aluminum
- Asphalt
- Chromium
- Copper •Cork
- Enamel •Glass
- Iron •Ivory •Jade
- Linoleum
- Paint/Flat
- Paint/Gloss
- Pearls •Platinum
- Plexiglas
- Polyurethane
- Stainless Steel
- Tin •Vinyl Clothing
- Vinyl Tile
- Vinyl Wallcovering
- Zinc

Wipe spill immediately with a cloth or sponge moistened with warm sudsy water. Rinse well and wipe dry.

- Alabaster •Marble

Wipe immediately and thoroughly with a damp cloth. If a stain remains, make a poultice of water, chlorine bleach, and a mild powder laundry detergent and put it on the stain. Cover with a damp cloth. Let it stand until the stain is bleached out. Rinse thoroughly and dry.

- Bamboo •Cane
- Ceramic Glass/Tile
- Gold

Wipe up spill immediately. Wash with a cloth dipped in a solution of warm water and mild pure soap with a few drops of ammonia added. Rinse with clear water and dry thoroughly.

- Bluestone •Brick
- Concrete
- Flagstone
- Granite
- Limestone
- Masonry Tile
- Sandstone •Slate
- Terrazzo

Wipe spill immediately. Clean any residue with a solution of washing soda or all-purpose laundry detergent (do not use soap) and water. Rinse well. Allow to dry thoroughly.

•Brass •Bronze

Wipe up spill immediately. Wash with a cloth dipped in a solution of hot water and a mild soap. Rinse with clear water and wipe thoroughly dry.

•Carpet/Synthetic
•Carpet/Wool
•Foam Rubber

After blotting up excess, apply **Afta Carpet Stain Remover, Spot Shot Carpet Stain Remover,** or **Stain-X Carpet Stain Remover.** An alternate technique is to blot up excess moisture, working from the outside of the spill inward. Spray with a rug shampoo or mix 1 teaspoon of a mild, non-alkali detergent in ½ pint lukewarm water. Add a small amount to the stain and blot until no more is removed. Mix 1 part white vinegar to 2 parts lukewarm water. Apply a small amount of the mixture and blot to neutralize any of the remaining stain. Place an absorbent pad over the stained area and weight it down for several hours. Allow to dry thoroughly.

•Fur/Natural
•Fur/Synthetic

For quick spot removal, use **Afta Spot Wipes,** disposable cleaning cloths. Or, blot up spill immediately with a clean dry cloth. Try to prevent the hide or backing from getting wet. Mix dishwashing detergent in hot water and swish to make a great volume of suds. Dip a cloth in only the foam and gently rub with the nap. Rinse with another cloth dipped in clear water and wrung nearly dry. Allow to air dry away from heat.

•Grout

Wipe spill immediately. This should be all that is needed, but if the sealer on the grout is gone or old, try dipping a wet toothbrush into a little powdered cleanser or apply **Afta Tile & Grout Cleaner.** Gently scrub. Rinse thoroughly and allow to dry.

•Leather •Suede	Blot up spill immediately. On leather, spray on **The Tannery.** Or mix a solution of mild soap in lukewarm water. Swish to make a great volume of suds. Apply only the suds to suede or leather with a slightly damp cloth. Rub gently, but with vigor. Rub dry with a clean cloth. On leather only, condition with **The Tannery** or **Fiebing's Saddle Soap.**
•Silver	Wipe up excess immediately. Wash silver in hot sudsy water with a soft cloth. Rinse well in clear hot water. Wipe dry immediately to prevent tarnish.
•Wallpaper	Blot up excess immediately. Wipe stained area very gently with clear warm water—do not use detergent or soap—without over-wetting the paper. Strokes should overlap or wall may become streaked. Carefully pat dry.
•Wood	Wipe up spill immediately. Rub stained area with a liquid or paste wax, boiled linseed oil, or a cloth dampened in water and a few drops of ammonia. Rewax the stained area.

Alkalies (*See* Ammonia, Oven Cleaner, Soap.)

Ammonia

•Acetate **•Acrylic Fabric** **•Burlap** **•Carpet/Synthetic** **•Carpet/Wool**	Sponge* with cool water. If stain persists, thoroughly flush* it with cool water. If the color has been altered, or to prevent fading or bleeding, neutralize the spot with a few drops of a mild acid such as lemon juice, white

(continued)

*See Chapter 4 for specific technique instructions.

(continued from preceding page)

- Nylon ●Olefin
- Polyester ●Rayon
- Silk ●Spandex
- Triacetate ●Wool

vinegar, or 10% acetic acid solution. Sponge thoroughly with cool water. Silk and wool are weakened and sometimes destroyed by alkalies such as ammonia, so be especially prompt in treatment.

- Acrylic Plastic
- Alabaster
- Aluminum
- Asphalt ●Bamboo
- Brass ●Bronze
- Cane
- Ceramic Glass/Tile
- Chromium
- Copper ●Coral
- Cork ●Fiberglass
- Glass ●Gold
- Grout ●Iron
- Ivory ●Jade
- Linoleum ●Marble
- Opal ●Paint/Flat
- Paint/Gloss
- Pearls ●Pewter
- Platinum
- Plexiglas
- Polyurethane
- Porcelain ●Rope
- Stainless Steel
- Tin ●Vinyl Clothing
- Vinyl Tile
- Vinyl Wallcovering
- Zinc

Rinse well with a sponge dipped in cool water. Wipe dry with a clean soft cloth. Treat pearls stained with an alkali such as ammonia immediately; they are permanently damaged by alkalies.

- Bluestone ●Brick
- Concrete
- Flagstone
- Granite
- Limestone
- Masonry Tile

Scrub with a solution of washing soda or detergent—not soap—and water. Rinse well and dry.

(continued)

•Sandstone •Slate •Terrazzo	*(see base of preceding page)*
•Cotton •Linen	Flush* area with cool water until all trace of ammonia is gone. Launder as soon as possible. The acid treatment recommended for other fabrics cannot be used on cotton or linen, as they may be permanently damaged by acids.
•Felt	With a sponge dipped in cool water and wrung out, gently brush* in the direction of the nap. If any stain remains, neutralize it with a few drops of lemon juice, white vinegar, or 10% acetic acid solution. Sponge* thoroughly with cool water. Since felt is composed mainly of wool fibers, an ammonia stain may damage it permanently.
•Fur/Natural •Fur/Synthetic	Dip a cloth or sponge in cool water and remove as much of the water as possible. Gently rub with the nap; do not over-wet the pelt or backing. Air dry away from heat.
•Leather •Suede	Mix dishwashing detergent in hot water and swish to make a great volume of suds. Dip a cloth in only the foam and gently wipe away any ammonia residue. Rinse with a clean dry cloth. Dry away from heat. To leather only, apply a conditioner like **The Tannery** or **Fiebing's Saddle Soap.**
•Silver	Wash silver in hot sudsy water with a soft cloth. Rinse in hot water and dry immediately with a soft cloth.
•Wallpaper	Take special care here, as an alkali like ammonia may dissolve the adhe- *(continued)*

*See Chapter 4 for specific technique instructions.

(continued from preceding page) sive behind the paper. Dip a sponge in clear warm water, wring until sponge is damp, then gently stroke the stain, overlapping strokes. Pat dry with a clean cloth.

•Wood

Ammonia may dissolve wood polishes. With a sponge dipped in cool water, then wrung out until damp, wipe the area making sure not to spread the stain. Wipe dry with a soft cloth. Polish or wax immediately to prevent permanent wood damage.

Antiperspirant
(Follow procedures for Deodorant.)

Apple

•Acetate
•Carpet/Synthetic
•Carpet/Wool
•Fiberglass •Rayon
•Silk •Triacetate
•Wool

Spray on **Amway Remove Fabric Spot Cleaner.** If stain remains, sponge* area with cool water, then apply a Wet Spotter and a few drops of white vinegar. Cover stain with an absorbent pad dampened with Wet Spotter. Let stand as long as any stain is being removed. Keep both the stain and pad moist with Wet Spotter and vinegar. Flush* with water and repeat if necessary. If stain persists, moisten the area with a solution of 1 cup warm water and 1 teaspoon **Axion,** an enzyme presoak product—do not use on silk or wool. Cover with a clean pad moistened with the solution. Let it stand 30 minutes. Add more solution, if needed, to keep the area warm and moist, but do not allow the wet area to spread. When no more stain is being lifted, flush with water.

*See Chapter 4 for specific technique instructions.

●**Acrylic Fabric**
●**Cotton** ●**Linen**
●**Modacrylic** ●**Nylon**
●**Olefin** ●**Polyester**
●**Spandex**

Spray on **Amway Remove Fabric Spot Cleaner.** If stain remains, presoak* in a solution of 1 quart warm water, ½ teaspoon liquid dishwashing or laundry detergent, and 1 tablespoon white vinegar for 15 minutes. Rinse with water and launder if possible. If not, presoak in a solution of 1 quart warm water and 1 tablespoon **Axion** or **Biz** (enzyme presoak products) for 30 minutes. Rinse well with water and launder as soon as possible.

●**Acrylic Plastic**
●**Aluminum**
●**Asphalt** ●**Brass**
●**Bronze**
●**Ceramic Glass/Tile**
●**Copper** ●**Cork**
●**Enamel** ●**Glass**
●**Grout** ●**Iron**
●**Linoleum**
●**Masonry Tile**
●**Paint/Flat**
●**Paint/Gloss**
●**Plexiglas**
●**Polyurethane**
●**Porcelain Dishes**
●**Stainless Steel**
●**Tin** ●**Vinyl Clothing**
●**Vinyl Tile**
●**Vinyl Wallcovering**

Wipe up the excess spill. Then wipe the surface with a cloth or sponge dipped in warm sudsy water. Rinse well and wipe dry.

●**Bluestone** ●**Brick**
●**Concrete**
●**Flagstone**
●**Granite**
●**Limestone**
●**Sandstone**
●**Slate**
●**Terrazzo**

Wipe up any excess. Wash with a solution of washing soda or detergent (never soap) and water. Use a soft cloth or soft-bristled brush. Rinse thoroughly with clear water and allow to dry.

*See Chapter 4 for specific technique instructions.

•**Leather** •**Suede**	Blot up any excess spill. Mix a solution of mild soap in lukewarm water. Swish to create a great volume of suds. Apply only the foam with a sponge. Wipe with a clean dry cloth. On leather only, follow with **The Tannery** or **Fiebing's Saddle Soap** to condition the leather.
•**Silver**	Wash as soon as possible in hot sudsy water. Rinse in hot water and dry immediately with a soft cloth.
•**Wood**	Mix dishwashing detergent in hot water and swish to make a great volume of suds. Dip a cloth in only the foam and wipe up the excess spill. Rinse with a clean cloth dampened with clear water. Polish or wax as soon as possible.

Baby Food/Formula

•**Acetate** •**Burlap** •**Carpet/Synthetic** •**Carpet/Wool** •**Fiberglass** •**Rayon** •**Rope** •**Silk** •**Triacetate** •**Wool**	Blot up excess liquid or scrape* excess solids from fabric. Sponge* with a dry-cleaning solvent—**Afta Cleaning Fluid** or **Carbona No. 10 Special Spot Remover/Carbona Cleaning Fluid**—or apply **K2r Spot-lifter** (tube). Or, apply a Dry Spotter to the stain and cover with an absorbent pad dampened with the Dry Spotter. Let it stand as long as any stain is being removed. Keep pad and stain moist, changing the pad as it picks up the stain. Flush* with one of the recommended liquid solvents. Allow to dry completely.
•**Acrylic Fabric** •**Cotton** •**Linen** •**Nylon** •**Olefin** •**Polyester** *(continued)*	Blot up or scrape* excess material and rinse stain in cool water. Presoak* for 30 minutes in an enzyme presoak—**Axion** or **Biz.** Launder im-

See Chapter 4 for specific technique instructions.

(continued from preceding page)

●**Spandex**

mediately if possible. If not, flush* with cool water and allow to dry thoroughly. If stain has dried, repeated laundering may be necessary.

●**Acrylic Plastic**
●**Aluminum**
●**Asphalt** ●**Bamboo**
●**Cane**
●**Ceramic Glass/Tile**
●**Chromium** ●**Cork**
●**Enamel** ●**Glass**
●**Iron** ●**Linoleum**
●**Marble** ●**Paint/Flat**
●**Paint/Gloss**
●**Plexiglas**
●**Polyurethane**
●**Porcelain**
●**Stainless Steel**
●**Tin** ●**Vinyl Clothing**
●**Vinyl Tile**
●**Vinyl Wallcovering**

Wipe up spills or excess matter immediately with a sponge dipped in warm sudsy water. Rinse with clear water. Some baby foods contain dyes that will stain the surface if allowed to remain on these surfaces.

●**Grout**

Wipe up excess liquid or solids from grouting. If any stain remains, dip a wet toothbrush into a little powdered cleanser or apply **Afta Tile & Grout Cleaner.** Gently scrub the grout. Rinse with clear water.

●**Leather** ●**Suede**

Carefully blot up liquid or scrape* excess matter from surface immediately. Mix a solution of mild soap in lukewarm water. Swish to create a great volume of suds. Apply only the foam with a sponge. Blot dry with a clean cloth. If stain persists, file gently with an emery board or very fine (grade 6/0–8/0) sandpaper. Work slowly and carefully, because the procedure removes a fine layer of
(continued)

---

*See Chapter 4 for specific technique instructions.

(continued from preceding page) the hide. To leather only, apply **The Tannery** or **Fiebing's Saddle Soap** to condition the leather.

•Silver

Wash silver immediately in hot sudsy water. Rinse in hot water and dry immediately with a soft cloth or silver polishing cloth to prevent tarnish.

•Wallpaper

Carefully blot up excess liquid or scrape* excess solids. Try wiping with a cool damp cloth in even, overlapping strokes. Pat dry. If stain persists, try rubbing very gently with an artgum eraser or a stale piece of rye bread to soak up the oily residue.

•Wood

Immediately wipe excess liquid or matter with a damp sponge. Follow with a coat of wood cleaner, then apply a polish or wax.

Beer *(Follow procedures for Alcoholic Beverages.)*

Beets *(Follow procedures for Berries.)*

Berries (Blueberry, Cranberry, Raspberry, Strawberry)

•Acetate
•Carpet/Synthetic
•Carpet/Wool
•Fiberglass •Rayon
•Rope •Triacetate
•Wool

Spray on **Amway Remove Fabric Spot Cleaner.** If stain remains, sponge* with cool water. Then sponge the area with lemon juice (or rub the cut sides of a slice of lemon over the stain). Flush* with water. Blot as much excess liquid as possible and allow to dry. If stain still persists, apply a Wet Spotter. Cover
(continued)

---

*See Chapter 4 for specific technique instructions.

(continued from preceding page) with an absorbent pad moistened with Wet Spotter. Let stand as long as any stain is being removed. Change the pad as it picks up the stain. Keep the pad and stained area moist with Wet Spotter. Flush with water. If any trace of stain still appears, moisten the area with a solution of 1 cup warm water and 1 teaspoon **Axion,** an enzyme presoak product—do not use on silk or wool. Cover with a clean absorbent pad that has been dipped in the solution and wrung almost dry. Let it stand for 30 minutes. Add enough solution to keep the stain and pad moist, but do not allow the wet area to spread. When no more stain is visible, flush thoroughly with water and allow to air dry.

●**Acrylic Fabric**
●**Modacrylic** ●**Nylon**
●**Olefin** ●**Polyester**
●**Spandex**

Spray on **Amway Remove Fabric Spot Cleaner.** If stain remains, sponge* with cool water immediately. Then sponge with lemon juice or rub a lemon slice over the stain. Flush* with water. Blot as much excess liquid as possible and allow to dry. If any trace of stain still exists, presoak* in a solution of 1 quart warm water, ½ teaspoon liquid dishwashing or laundry detergent, and 1 tablespoon white vinegar for 15 minutes. Rinse with water and launder if possible. If not, presoak in a solution of 1 quart warm water and 1 tablespoon **Axion,** an enzyme presoak product, for 30 minutes. Rinse well with water and launder as soon as possible.

●**Acrylic Plastic**
●**Aluminum**
●**Asphalt**
●**Bamboo** ●**Brass**
●**Bronze** ●**Cane**
(continued)

Wipe up any excess spill with a cloth or sponge dipped in warm sudsy water. Rinse well and wipe dry.

See Chapter 4 for specific technique instructions.

●**Ceramic Glass/Tile**   *(see base of preceding page)*
●**Copper**
●**Enamel**
●**Glass** ●**Grout**
●**Iron**
●**Paint/Flat**
●**Paint/Gloss**
●**Plexiglas**
●**Polyurethane**
●**Porcelain Dishes**
●**Porcelain Fixtures**
●**Stainless Steel**
●**Vinyl Clothing**
●**Vinyl Wallcovering**

●**Bluestone** ●**Brick**
●**Concrete**
●**Flagstone**
●**Granite**
●**Masonry Tile**
●**Slate** ●**Terrazzo**

Wipe up excess spill. Wash area with a solution of washing soda or detergent (not soap) and water. Use a soft cloth or soft-bristled brush. Rinse thoroughly with clear water and allow to dry.

●**Cork** ●**Linoleum**
●**Vinyl Tile**

Wipe up excess spill and wash the area with a solution of washing soda or detergent and water. Use a soft-bristled brush or cloth to scrub gently. Rinse thoroughly with clear water and allow to dry. If stain persists, wipe area with a cloth dampened in a solution of 1 tablespoon oxalic acid and 1 pint water. Rinse well and wipe dry. Repolish the surface if necessary.

●**Cotton** ●**Linen**

Test fabric for colorfastness. If color doesn't change, stretch the stain over a bowl; fasten in place with a rubber band. Pour boiling water through the fabric from the height of 2 or 3 feet. Avoid splatters. This procedure must be done immediately. If stain persists, soak in a solution of 1 quart warm water and ½ teaspoon

(continued)

(continued from preceding page) detergent for 15 minutes. Rinse with water. Sponge* the area with rubbing alcohol and launder if possible. If not, presoak* in a solution of 1 quart warm water and 1 tablespoon **Axion** or **Biz** (enzyme presoak products) for 30 minutes. Rinse well and launder.

●Leather ●Suede

Blot up any excess liquid. Mix a solution of mild soap in lukewarm water. Swish to create a great volume of suds. Apply only the foam with a sponge. Wipe with a clean dry cloth. On leather only, follow with **The Tannery** or **Fiebing's Saddle Soap** to condition the leather.

●Marble

After wiping up any excess liquid, wipe surface with a cloth or sponge dipped in warm sudsy water. Rinse well and wipe dry. If any stain or discoloration remains, mix a poultice of water, powdered detergent, and chlorine bleach. Apply a thick paste to the stain and cover with a damp cloth to retard evaporation. When the stain has been bleached out, rinse thoroughly and dry.

●Silver

Wash silver as soon as possible in hot sudsy water. Rinse in hot water and dry immediately with a soft cloth to prevent tarnish.

●Wood

Mix dishwashing detergent in hot water and swish to make a great volume of suds. Dip a cloth in only the foam and apply to berry stain. Rinse with a clean cloth dampened with clear water. If any stain remains, rub the area with a cloth dampened in a solution of 1 tablespoon oxalic acid to 1 pint water. Rinse well and wipe dry. Wax or polish as soon as possible.

*See Chapter 4 for specific technique instructions.

Blood

● Acetate ● Burlap
● Fiberglass ● Rayon
● Rope ● Silk
● Triacetate ● Wool

Treat the stain as soon as possible, as set blood stains can be extremely difficult to remove. Sponge* the stain with cold water. If the blood is still wet, this step should remove it. If any stain remains, apply a Wet Spotter and a few drops of ammonia (but do not use ammonia on silk and wool). Cover with an absorbent pad dampened with the Wet Spotter and ammonia. Let it stand as long as any stain is being removed, changing the pad as it picks up the stain. Keep the stain and pad moist with the Wet Spotter and ammonia. Flush* thoroughly with cool water, making sure to remove all traces of the ammonia. If stain persists, moisten it with a solution of ½ teaspoon of the enzyme presoak **Axion**—except on silk or wool—and ½ cup warm water. Cover the stain with an absorbent pad dampened slightly with the enzyme solution. Let it stand for 30 minutes. Add more solution to keep the stain moist and warm, but do not let the wet area spread. Flush with water and dry thoroughly.

● Acrylic Fabric
● Cotton ● Linen
● Nylon ● Olefin
● Polyester
● Spandex

Fresh blood stains can usually be removed by a thorough laundering in cold water. If any stain remains, soak it in a solution of 1 quart warm water, ½ teaspoon dishwashing or liquid laundry detergent, and 1 tablespoon ammonia for 15 minutes. Tamp* or scrape,* blotting occasionally with an absorbent pad. Continue as long as any stain is being removed. Rinse well with water, making sure to remove all traces of the ammonia. If stain persists, presoak* in a solution

(continued)

*See Chapter 4 for specific technique instructions.

(continued from preceding page) of 1 quart warm water and 1 table-spoon **Axion** or **Biz,** enzyme pre-soaks. After 30 minutes, rinse well, then dry or launder.

- Acrylic Plastic
- Aluminum
- Asphalt ●Brass
- Bronze
- Ceramic Glass/Tile
- Chromium
- Copper ●Coral
- Cork ●Enamel
- Glass ●Gold ●Iron
- Ivory ●Jade
- Linoleum ●Opal
- Paint/Flat
- Paint/Gloss
- Pearls ●Pewter
- Platinum
- Plexiglas
- Polyurethane
- Porcelain
- Stainless Steel
- Tin ●Vinyl Clothing
- Vinyl Tile
- Vinyl Wallcovering
- Zinc

Wipe up stain with a sponge or cloth dipped in cool water or warm sudsy water. Dry with a clean cloth.

- Alabaster ●Marble

Wipe stain with a sponge dipped in cold water. If stain remains, mix a poultice of water, powdered deter-gent, and chlorine bleach. Apply it thickly to the stain and cover with a damp cloth to retard drying. When the stain has been bleached out, rinse thoroughly and dry.

- Bamboo ●Cane

Wash with a cloth or brush dipped in warm soapy water to which a few drops of ammonia have been added. Rinse with clear water and dry.

●**Bluestone** ●**Brick**
●**Concrete**
●**Flagstone**
●**Granite**
●**Limestone**
●**Masonry Tile**
●**Sandstone** ●**Slate**
●**Terrazzo**

Try wiping up the stain with a sponge dipped in cool water. If any stain remains, wash or brush* stain with a solution of washing soda or detergent in warm water. Rinse well and allow to dry.

●**Carpet/Synthetic**
●**Carpet/Wool**
●**Foam Rubber**

Squirt **Stain-X Carpet Stain Remover** on the stained area. Another way to remove blood is to mix 1 teaspoon of a mild, non-alkali detergent with ½ pint lukewarm water. Add a small amount to the stain and blot the liquid. Do not force the stain further into the fibers. Continue blotting until no more stain is removed. If stain remains, add 1 tablespoon ammonia to 1 cup water (do not use on wool), sponge stain, and blot liquid. Continue until no more stain is removed. Place an absorbent pad over the damp area and weight it down. When no more liquid is drawn out, remove the pad and allow it to air dry thoroughly.

●**Fur/Natural**
●**Fur/Synthetic**

Blot up excess. Wring a cloth in the suds of a mild detergent to which a few drops of ammonia have been added. Rub with the nap, taking care not to over-wet the pelt or backing. To rinse, dip a cloth in cool water, wring almost dry, and stroke with the nap. Air dry away from heat.

●**Grout**

Wipe the stain with a sponge dipped in cool water. If any remains, dip a wet toothbrush into a little baking soda or powdered cleanser, or apply **Afta Tile & Grout Cleaner,** and gently scrub the grout. Rinse thoroughly and dry.

See Chapter 4 for specific technique instructions.

●**Leather** ●**Suede**	Mix a solution of mild soap in luke-warm water. Swish to create a great volume of suds. Apply only the foam with a sponge and gently rub the stained area, taking care not to spread the stain. Wipe dry with a clean soft cloth. On leather only, fol-low with **The Tannery** or **Fiebing's Saddle Soap** to condition the leather.
●**Silver**	Wash silver in hot sudsy water. Rinse in hot water and wipe dry immediately with a soft cloth to prevent tarnish.
●**Wallpaper**	Blood can permanently stain wall-paper. Try dipping a cloth in cool water, wringing until damp, and gently sponging the area, taking care not to spread the stain. Overlap the strokes slightly to prevent streaking. Gently pat dry.
●**Wood**	Wipe the stain with a cloth dipped in cool water. Wipe dry immediately and polish or wax as usual.

Bluing   (*Follow procedures for* Fabric Softener.)

Blusher

●**Acetate** ●**Carpet/Synthetic** ●**Carpet/Wool** ●**Fiberglass** ●**Rayon** ●**Silk** ●**Triacetate** ●**Wool**	Brush* or blot up any excess, taking care not to spread the stain. Flush* with a dry-cleaning solvent—**Carbona No. 10 Special Spot Remover/Carbona Cleaning Fluid** or **Afta Cleaning Fluid.** Apply a Dry Spotter to the stain and cover with an absorbent pad dampened with the Dry Spotter. Check the stain every 5 minutes. Before changing pads, *(continued)*

*See Chapter 4 for specific technique instructions.

(continued from preceding page) press hard against the stain. Continue the alternate soaking and pressing until no more stain is being removed. Flush with one of the dry-cleaning solvents and allow to dry. If any stain remains, flush it with water and apply a Wet Spotter with a few drops of ammonia. (Do not use ammonia on silk or wool.) Cover with an absorbent pad dampened with the Wet Spotter. Let it stand as long as any stain is being removed. Change the pad as it picks up the stain. Keep the stain and pad moist. Flush well with water. Repeat if necessary; allow to dry.

●**Acrylic Fabric**
●**Cotton** ●**Linen**
●**Modacrylic** ●**Nylon**
●**Olefin** ●**Polyester**
●**Spandex**

Brush* or blot up any excess, taking care not to spread the stain. Flush* with a dry-cleaning solvent, either **Carbona No. 10 Special Spot Remover/Carbona Cleaning Fluid** or **Afta Cleaning Fluid.** Apply a Dry Spotter to the stain and cover with a cloth dampened with the Dry Spotter. Check the stain often, tamping* before changing the pad. Continue alternate soaking and tamping until no more stain is lifted. Flush with a dry-cleaning solvent and allow to dry. If any stain remains, try the same procedure of soaking and tamping using a Wet Spotter and a few drops of ammonia. When the stain is gone, be sure to flush the area with water to remove all traces of ammonia. Launder as soon as possible.

●**Acrylic Plastic**
●**Alabaster**
●**Asphalt** ●**Bamboo**
●**Cane**
●**Ceramic Glass/Tile**
●**Cork**
(continued)

Wipe any spills or brush* away any excess. With a cloth or sponge dipped in warm sudsy water, wash the surface. Rinse well with water and wipe dry with a clean cloth.

See Chapter 4 for specific technique instructions.

- **Enamel**
- **Glass** • **Gold**
- **Ivory** • **Jade**
- **Linoleum**
- **Marble**
- **Paint/Flat**
- **Paint/Gloss**
- **Plexiglas**
- **Polyurethane**
- **Stainless Steel**
- **Vinyl Clothing**
- **Vinyl Tile**
- **Vinyl Wallcovering**

(see base of preceding page)

- **Bluestone**
- **Masonry Tile**
- **Sandstone** • **Slate**
- **Terrazzo**

Remove excess. Mix a solution of washing soda or detergent (not soap) and water. Wash the stained area. Rinse well with clear water and allow to dry.

- **Leather** • **Suede**

Gently remove excess. Mix a solution of mild soap in lukewarm water. Swish to create a great volume of suds. Apply only the foam with a sponge. Wipe dry with a clean cloth. If a greasy or oily stain remains, powder it with an absorbent such as cornmeal. Give it plenty of time to work. Gently brush* or shake the absorbent from the surface. Repeat if necessary. On leather only, follow with **The Tannery** or **Fiebing's Saddle Soap** to condition the leather. On suede apply **Child Life Suede & Fabric Cleaner.**

- **Wood**

Mix dishwashing detergent in hot water and swish to make a great volume of suds. Dip a cloth in only the foam and apply to the stain. Rinse with clear water. Wipe dry immediately with a soft cloth and polish or wax as usual.

See Chapter 4 for specific technique instructions.

Butter

- **Acetate** - **Burlap**
- **Carpet/Synthetic**
- **Carpet/Wool**
- **Fiberglass**
- **Rayon** - **Rope**
- **Silk** - **Triacetate**
- **Wool**

Scrape* as much of the solid butter as you can without driving any of it further into the fibers. Apply an absorbent (cornmeal for light colors, fuller's earth for darks), but do not press it in. Give the absorbent plenty of time to work. Remove the absorbent and if needed, repeat the application. If any residue remains, sponge* the spot with **Afta Cleaning Fluid, Carbona No. 10 Special Spot Remover/ Carbona Cleaning Fluid,** or **K2r Spot-lifter** (tube).

- **Acrylic Fabric**
- **Cotton** - **Linen**
- **Modacrylic** - **Nylon**
- **Olefin** - **Polyester**
- **Spandex**

Scrape* any excess. Pretreat* with **Magic Pre-Wash** or **Shout Laundry Soil & Stain Remover,** blot the stained area, and launder as usual. If the stain remains, or if immediate laundering is impossible, place the fabric stainside down on an absorbent pad. Flush* with **Afta Cleaning Fluid** or **Carbona Cleaning Fluid** through the back of the stain and blot with a clean absorbent pad. Pretreat again and rinse well or launder.

- **Acrylic Plastic**
- **Alabaster**
- **Aluminum**
- **Asphalt** - **Bamboo**
- **Brass** - **Bronze**
- **Cane**
- **Ceramic Glass/Tile**
- **Chromium**
- **Copper** - **Cork**
- **Enamel** - **Glass**
- **Gold** - **Grout** - **Iron**
- **Linoleum** - **Marble**
- **Paint/Gloss**

Scrape* to remove as much excess as possible. Wipe with a clean sponge or cloth dipped in warm sudsy water. Rinse with clear water and wipe dry.

(continued)

See Chapter 4 for specific technique instructions.

- Pewter • Plexiglas
- Polyurethane
- Porcelain
- Stainless Steel
- Tin • Vinyl Clothing
- Vinyl Tile
- Vinyl Wallcovering
- Zinc

(see base of preceding page)

- Bluestone • Brick
- Concrete
- Flagstone
- Granite
- Limestone
- Masonry Tile
- Sandstone • Slate
- Terrazzo

Wipe up excess. Mix a solution of washing soda or detergent and water. Scrub any remaining stain. Rinse well and allow to dry.

- Felt

Scrape* to remove excess, without forcing any butter further into the fibers. Dust the stain with an absorbent—cornmeal (for light colors) or fuller's earth (for dark colors). Allow plenty of time for the grease to be absorbed. Gently brush* absorbent off in the direction of the nap. If any stain remains, reapply fresh absorbent. Allow absorbent to work, then gently brush off.

- Leather • Suede

Gently scrape* to remove excess. Rub the stain with a thick paste of fuller's earth and water. Let it dry and gently brush* off the powder. Repeat if necessary, then, for leather only, apply **The Tannery** or **Fiebing's Saddle Soap** to condition the leather.

- Paint/Flat
- Wallpaper

Scrape* to remove excess. Rub the stain with **Suede Stone.** Or, make a thick paste of fuller's earth (on dark surfaces) or cornmeal (on light sur-

(continued)

---

*See Chapter 4 for specific technique instructions.

(continued from preceding page) faces) and press the paste onto the stain with the palm of your hand. Allow to dry, then carefully brush* off with a clean cloth.

•Silver	Wash silver in hot soapy water. Rinse in hot water and wipe dry immediately with a clean soft cloth.
•Wood	Wipe up excess with a clean dry cloth. Dip a cloth into warm sudsy water and wipe away any greasy residue. Rinse well and polish or wax.

Candle Wax

•Acetate •Burlap •Fiberglass •Rayon •Rope •Silk •Triacetate •Wool/nonwashable	Freeze* to harden the wax. Carefully scrape* the excess, then place an absorbent pad under the stain and flush* with **Carbona No. 10 Special Spot Remover/Carbona Cleaning Fluid** or **Afta Cleaning Fluid.** Allow to dry. Repeat if necessary.
•Acrylic Fabric •Cotton •Linen •Modacrylic •Nylon •Olefin •Polyester •Spandex •Wool/washable	Scrape* to remove excess. Place the stained area between two pieces of white blotting paper and press with a warm iron. Change the paper as it absorbs the stain. This stain can easily spread, so use care while pressing. On colorfast fabrics, white cotton, or linen, try pouring boiling water through the stain. After using either method, allow to dry. If any trace remains, flush* it with **Afta Cleaning Fluid, Carbona Cleaning Fluid,** or **Brush Top Spot Remover,** dry-cleaning fluids. If any dye remains, sponge it with 1 part rubbing alcohol (do not use on acrylic or modacrylic fabric) mixed with 2 parts water. Rinse well with clear water and dry.

See Chapter 4 for specific technique instructions.

- Acrylic Plastic
- Alabaster
- Aluminum
- Bamboo
- Bluestone •Brass
- Bronze •Cane
- Ceramic Glass/Tile
- Concrete •Copper
- Enamel
- Flagstone •Glass
- Gold •Granite
- Grout •Iron
- Ivory •Jade
- Limestone
- Marble •Paint/Flat
- Paint/Gloss
- Pewter •Plexiglas
- Polyurethane
- Porcelain
- Sandstone •Slate
- Stainless Steel
- Terrazzo •Tin
- Vinyl Clothing

Freeze* to harden the wax, then gently scrape* the residue from the surface. Take care not to scratch the surface. This should be sufficient. Wipe with a sponge dipped in a solution of washing soda or detergent and water. Rinse well and wipe dry.

- Asphalt •Cork
- Linoleum
- Vinyl Tile

Freeze* to harden the wax. Gently scrape* it off with a metal spatula, taking care not to gouge the stained surface. Dip a corner of a clean cloth into rubbing alcohol and wipe stain. Wash and wipe dry. Polish or wax as usual.

- Carpet/Synthetic
- Carpet/Wool

Freeze* to harden the wax. Gently scrape* to remove excess from the surface. To prevent damage to the backing, add a small amount of **Afta Cleaning Fluid, Carbona No. 10 Special Spot Remover/Carbona Cleaning Fluid,** or **K2r Spot-lifter** (aerosol). Blot with an absorbent pad. Continue until no more stain is removed. If a dye remains, dilute 1

(continued)

See Chapter 4 for specific technique instructions.

(continued from preceding page) part rubbing alcohol with 2 parts water and apply it to the stain in small amounts, blotting well after each application. Allow to dry.

●**Felt**

Freeze* to harden the wax. Very carefully scrape* the residue, taking care not to shred the felt fibers. If any residue remains, try brushing gently with a stiff-bristled brush. In extreme cases, use a razor blade to gently scrape the excess. Use this as a last resort as it will damage some of the fibers.

●**Leather** ●**Suede**

Freeze* with ice cubes in a plastic bag to harden the wax. Gently scrape* the wax. If any stain remains, mix a thick paste of fuller's earth with water and apply it to the stain. Allow the paste to dry, then carefully brush* it off with a soft-bristled brush or toothbrush. Repeat if necessary. When the stain has been removed, on leather only, apply **The Tannery** or **Fiebing's Saddle Soap** to condition the leather.

●**Silver**

Freeze* to harden the wax. Carefully scrape* with a plastic spatula until no more wax can be removed. Wash the silver in hot soapy water. Rinse in hot water and wipe dry immediately to prevent tarnish.

●**Wood**

Freeze* to harden the wax. Gently scrape* it up to avoid gouging the wood. When all wax has been removed, buff the wood with a chamois cloth.

Candy/Chocolate
(*Follow procedures for* Chocolate/Cocoa.)

*See Chapter 4 for specific technique instructions.

Candy/Nonchocolate

- Acetate •Burlap
- Carpet/Synthetic
- Carpet/Wool
- Fiberglass •Rayon
- Rope •Silk
- Triacetate •Wool

Scrape* to remove as much of the excess as possible. Sponge* with warm water. Spray on **Amway Remove Fabric Spot Cleaner** or apply a Wet Spotter with a few drops of white vinegar added. Let it stand as long as any stain is being removed. Press down on the stain with a clean absorbent pad every 5 minutes. Keep the stain moist with the Wet Spotter and vinegar. When no more stain is being removed, flush* with water. If any stain remains, repeat the process, using rubbing alcohol instead of the Wet Spotter and vinegar. (Do not use the alcohol treatment on acetate or triacetate.) When the stain is removed, rinse well with water to remove all sugar.

On carpeting, blot the excess liquid with an absorbent pad. Then apply **Spot Shot Carpet Stain Remover** or **Stain-X Carpet Stain Remover**. Allow to dry.

- Acrylic Fabric
- Cotton •Linen
- Modacrylic •Nylon
- Olefin •Polyester
- Spandex

Usually, soaking or laundering in warm sudsy water will remove the stain. If the stain persists, spray on **Amway Remove Fabric Spot Cleaner** or resoak the fabric, adding a few drops of ammonia to the soaking solution. Let the fabric soak for 30 minutes and rinse thoroughly with water. Next, soak in a solution of 1 quart warm water and 1 tablespoon white vinegar for 1 hour (30 minutes for cotton and linen). Rinse well and dry. If stain persists, apply rubbing alcohol (do not use on acrylic or modacrylic) to the stain and tamp* gently. Keep the stain moist with alcohol and blot occasionally. Con-

(continued)

See Chapter 4 for specific technique instructions.

(continued from preceding page) tinue as long as any stain is being removed. Rinse well with water. Dry or launder as soon as possible.

●**Acrylic Plastic** ●**Aluminum** ●**Asphalt** ●**Bamboo** ●**Brass** ●**Bronze** ●**Cane** ●**Ceramic Glass/Tile** ●**Copper** ●**Cork** ●**Enamel** ●**Glass** ●**Gold** ●**Iron** ●**Ivory** ●**Linoleum** ●**Paint/Flat** ●**Paint/Gloss** ●**Pewter** ●**Plexiglas** ●**Polyurethane** ●**Porcelain** ●**Sandstone** ●**Stainless Steel** ●**Tin** ●**Vinyl Clothing** ●**Vinyl Tile** ●**Vinyl Wallcovering** ●**Zinc**	With a cloth dipped in warm sudsy water, wipe stain from the surface. Rinse thoroughly and wipe dry.
●**Bluestone** ●**Brick** ●**Concrete** ●**Flagstone** ●**Granite** ●**Limestone** ●**Masonry Tile** ●**Sandstone** ●**Slate** ●**Terrazzo**	Scrape* any excess you can from the surface, taking care not to gouge the softer stones. Wash or scrub any remainder with a solution of washing soda or detergent (never use soap—it leaves a scum impossible to remove) and water. Rinse well and dry.
●**Leather** ●**Suede**	Gently scrape* any excess from the hide. Mix a solution of mild soap in lukewarm water. Swish to create a great volume of suds. Apply only the foam with a sponge, stroking with the nap on suede. Wipe dry with a clean cloth. On leather only, follow with **The** *(continued)*

*See Chapter 4 for specific technique instructions.

(continued from preceding page) **Tannery** or **Fiebing's Saddle Soap** to condition the leather.

●**Silver**

Wash the silver in hot sudsy water. This should dissolve any candy residue. Rinse in hot water and wipe dry with a soft clean cloth to prevent tarnish.

●**Wood**

Wipe the stain with a cloth dipped in warm, mild sudsy water. Rinse with a clean damp cloth. Wipe dry and polish or wax as usual.

Carbon Paper/ Typewriter Ribbon

●**Acetate** ●**Burlap**
●**Carpet/Synthetic**
●**Carpet/Wool**
●**Cotton**
●**Fiberglass** ●**Linen**
●**Rope** ●**Silk**
●**Triacetate** ●**Wool**

Apply a Dry Spotter to the stain and cover it with an absorbent pad dampened with the Dry Spotter. Keep the stain and pad moist. Let it stand as long as any stain is being removed. Change the pad as it picks up the stain. When no more stain is being picked up, flush* with **Afta Cleaning Fluid,** or **Carbona Cleaning Fluid.** Scrape* or tamp* to help loosen the stain. When not working on the stain, keep it covered to minimize evaporation. Flush* the stain with the cleaning fluid. Allow to dry.

On carpets, blot any excess liquid, then apply **Spot Shot Carpet Stain Remover** or **Afta Carpet Stain Remover.** Work undiluted liquid detergent into the stain, then rinse. If stain persists, apply amyl acetate to the stain and cover with an absorbent pad dampened with amyl acetate. Keep moist for 15 minutes, blotting occasionally with a clean absorbent pad.

*See Chapter 4 for specific technique instructions.

- Acrylic Plastic
- Bamboo • Cane
- Glass • Linoleum
- Paint/Flat
- Paint/Gloss
- Plexiglas
- Polyurethane
- Vinyl Clothing

Wipe the stain with a cloth dipped in warm sudsy water to which a few drops of ammonia have been added. Rinse well and wipe dry.

Catsup

- Acetate • Burlap
- Carpet/Synthetic
- Carpet/Wool
- Fiberglass • Rayon
- Rope • Silk
- Triacetate • Wool

Gently scrape* any excess from fabric. Sponge* with **Carbona Cleaning Fluid** or treat silk by applying **K2r Spot-lifter** (tube). Apply a Dry Spotter to the stain and cover with an absorbent pad dampened with the Dry Spotter. Keep the stain and pad moist. Let it stand as long as any stain is being removed. Change the pad as it picks up the stain. When no more stain is being removed, flush* with Carbona Cleaning Fluid or reapply K2r Spot-lifter on silk. Allow to dry. If any stain remains, moisten it with a solution of ½ teaspoon **Axion,** an enzyme presoak product (do not use on silk and wool) and ½ cup warm water. Cover with a clean pad that has been dipped in the enzyme presoak solution and squeezed nearly dry. Let stand for 30 minutes, adding more solution as needed to keep the area warm and moist, but do not let the wet area spread. Flush* with water and allow to dry. On carpets, place a clean dry pad over the area and weight it down. When no more liquid is being absorbed, allow to air dry thoroughly.

- Acrylic Fabric
- Cotton • Linen

(continued)

Scrape* as much of the excess as possible with a spatula. Apply a Wet

(continued from preceding page)

- **Modacrylic** ● **Nylon**
- **Olefin** ● **Polyester**
- **Spandex**

Spotter and work into the fabric. Rinse thoroughly with water and launder. If laundering must wait, and there is any stain remaining, apply an enzyme presoak paste made from **Axion** or **Biz** and let it work awhile, keeping the paste moist. Thoroughly rinse area to remove all traces of enzyme presoak paste. Allow to dry and launder as soon as possible.

- **Acrylic Plastic**
- **Aluminum**
- **Asphalt**
- **Bamboo** ● **Bronze**
- **Cane**
- **Ceramic Glass/Tile**
- **Chromium**
- **Copper** ● **Cork**
- **Enamel** ● **Glass**
- **Gold** ● **Iron** ● **Ivory**
- **Linoleum**
- **Paint/Flat**
- **Paint/Gloss**
- **Pewter**
- **Plexiglas**
- **Polyurethane**
- **Porcelain Dishes**
- **Stainless Steel**
- **Tin** ● **Vinyl Clothing**
- **Vinyl Tile**
- **Vinyl Wallcovering**
- **Zinc**

Wipe up spills as soon as possible— the tomato in catsup can permanently stain many of these surfaces—with a cloth or sponge dipped in warm sudsy water. Rinse with clean water and wipe dry.

- **Alabaster**
- **Bluestone**
- **Concrete**
- **Flagstone**
- **Granite**
- **Limestone**
- **Marble**

Remove excess. Wipe with a cloth dipped in a solution of washing soda or detergent in warm water. If any stain remains, mix a poultice of water, mild bleach, and a powdered detergent and apply to the stained area. Cover with a damp cloth to re-

(continued)

(continued from preceding page)

•**Masonry Tile** •**Sandstone** •**Slate** •**Terrazzo**	tard evaporation. When stain is gone, rinse well and wipe dry.
•**Leather** •**Suede**	Mix a solution of mild soap in luke-warm water. Swish to create a great volume of suds. Apply only the foam with a sponge. Wipe dry with a clean cloth. On leather only, follow with **The Tannery** or **Fiebing's Saddle Soap** to condition the leather.
•**Silver**	Take care of silver as soon as possible, as tomato can pit the metal. Wash silver in hot soapy water. Rinse in hot water and wipe dry with a clean soft cloth.
•**Wallpaper**	Wipe immediately, as catsup often permanently stains wallpaper. Use a damp cloth or sponge, overlapping strokes to prevent streaks. Gently pat dry.
•**Wood**	Catsup spills usually occur on wood (tabletops, etc.) that has a treated surface, such as polyurethane sealer. Wiping these surfaces with a damp cloth is sufficient to remove the spill. Nontreated surfaces should be wiped immediately with a cloth dipped in warm sudsy water, rinsed with a clean damp cloth, wiped dry, and polished or waxed as usual.

Cement/Contact

•**Acetate** •**Acrylic Fabric** •**Burlap** •**Carpet/Synthetic** *(continued)*	Carefully scrape* any excess from fabric. Sponge* stain with **Afta Cleaning Fluid** or **Carbona No. 10 Special Spot Remover/Carbona**

*See Chapter 4 for specific technique instructions.

(continued from preceding page)

- **Carpet/Wool**
- **Cotton •Linen**
- **Nylon •Olefin**
- **Polyester •Rayon**
- **Silk •Spandex**
- **Triacetate •Wool**

Cleaning Fluid, dry-cleaning solvents. Apply a Dry Spotter and cover with an absorbent pad dampened with Dry Spotter. Let stand as long as any stain is being removed. Change pad as it picks up any stain, keeping stain and pad moist with Dry Spotter. Flush* with dry-cleaning solvent. If any stain remains, repeat the above process using amyl acetate (do not use this step on cotton and linen), and flush with one of the dry-cleaning solvents. If stain persists on cotton and linen only, try flushing it with a few drops of acetone, then rinse with one of the dry-cleaning solvents.

- **Acrylic Plastic**
- **Aluminum**
- **Ceramic Glass/Tile**
- **Cork •Glass**
- **Linoleum**
- **Paint/Flat**
- **Paint/Gloss**
- **Plexiglas**
- **Polyurethane**
- **Vinyl Clothing**
- **Vinyl Tile**
- **Vinyl Wallcovering**

Remove any matter before it has a chance to set. Try wiping with a cloth dipped in warm sudsy water to which a few drops of amyl acetate has been added. Rinse well and wipe dry. Cement can eventually damage the surface beyond repair, so work promptly.

Cement/Epoxy

- **All Surfaces**

This stain cannot be removed.

Cement/Household

- **Acetate**
- **Acrylic Fabric**
- **Burlap**
- **Carpet/Synthetic**

(continued)

Carefully scrape* excess from fabric. Sponge* stain with a dry-cleaning solvent, **Carbona No. 10 Special Spot Remover/Carbona Cleaning**

See Chapter 4 for specific technique instructions.

(continued from preceding page)

- ●Carpet/Wool
- ●Cotton ●Linen
- ●Modacrylic ●Nylon
- ●Olefin ●Polyester
- ●Rayon ●Silk
- ●Spandex
- ●Triacetate ●Wool

Fluid or **Afta Cleaning Fluid.** Apply a Dry Spotter and cover with an absorbent pad dampened with Dry Spotter. Let stand as long as any stain is being removed. Change pad as it picks up any stain, keeping stain and pad moist with Dry Spotter. Flush* with one of the dry-cleaning solvents. If any stain remains, repeat the above procedure using amyl acetate (do not use this step on cotton and linen), and flush with one of the dry-cleaning solvents. If stain persists on cotton and linen only, try flushing it with a few drops of acetone, then rinse with a Dry Spotter.

- ●Acrylic Plastic
- ●Aluminum
- ●Ceramic Glass/Tile
- ●Cork ●Glass
- ●Linoleum
- ●Paint/Flat
- ●Paint/Gloss
- ●Plexiglas
- ●Polyurethane
- ●Vinyl Clothing
- ●Vinyl Tile
- ●Vinyl Wallcovering

Before cement has a chance to set, wipe the stain up with a cloth dipped in warm sudsy water to which a few drops of amyl acetate has been added. Rinse well and wipe dry. Cement can eventually damage the surface beyond repair, so work promptly.

Cement/Rubber

- ●Acetate
- ●Acrylic Fabric
- ●Burlap
- ●Carpet/Synthetic
- ●Carpet/Wool
- ●Cotton
- ●Fiberglass
- ●Linen ●Modacrylic
- ●Nylon ●Olefin

Rub away as much excess as possible. If stain remains, place a clean, absorbent pad under the stain, if possible. Apply a dry-cleaning solvent, **Carbona No. 10 Special Spot Remover/Carbona Cleaning Fluid** or **Afta Cleaning Fluid,** and cover the stain with an absorbent pad dampened with the dry-cleaning solvent.

(continued)

See Chapter 4 for specific technique instructions.

(continued from preceding page)

●**Polyester** ●**Rayon**
●**Silk** ●**Spandex**
●**Triacetate** ●**Wool**

Change the pads as they pick up the stain. Keep stain and pads moist. Apply a Dry Spotter. Cover with a pad dampened with the Dry Spotter. Remove pad every 5 minutes. Press the pad hard into the stain—don't rub. Continue with the alternate soaking and pressing until all the stain has been removed. Flush* with dry-cleaning solvent and allow to dry.

●**Acrylic Plastic**
●**Aluminum**
●**Ceramic Glass/Tile**
●**Cork** ●**Glass**
●**Leather** ●**Linoleum**
●**Paint/Flat**
●**Paint/Gloss**
●**Plexiglas**
●**Stainless Steel**
●**Suede**
●**Vinyl Clothing**
●**Vinyl Tile**
●**Vinyl Wallcovering**
●**Wood**

Scrape* to remove liquid. Use a rubber cement pick-up, available at most art or stationery stores, to gently rub any remaining cement. This should remove any trace of the stain.

Cheese

●**Acetate** ●**Burlap**
●**Carpet/Synthetic**
●**Carpet/Wool**
●**Fiberglass** ●**Rayon**
●**Silk** ●**Triacetate**
●**Wool**

Scrape* to remove excess. Sponge* the stain with **Carbona No. 10 Special Spot Remover/Carbona Cleaning Fluid** or **Afta Cleaning Fluid,** dry-cleaning solvents. Apply a Dry Spotter to the stain and cover with an absorbent pad dampened with Dry Spotter. Let it stand as long as any stain is being removed. Change the pad as it picks up the stain. Keep the stain and pad moist with the Dry Spotter. Flush* with one of the dry-cleaning solvents. If any stain re-

(continued)

*See Chapter 4 for specific technique instructions.

(continued from preceding page) mains, moisten it with a solution of 1 teaspoon of **Axion** enzyme pre-soak—not for use on silk or wool—and 1 cup water. Cover with a clean pad that has been dipped in the solution and wrung almost dry. Let it stand for 30 minutes. Add more solution if needed to keep the area warm and moist, but do not allow the wet area to spread. When no more stain is being lifted, flush thoroughly with water and allow to dry.

•Acrylic Fabric
•Cotton •Linen
•Modacrylic •Nylon
•Olefin •Polyester
•Spandex

Scrape* to remove excess. Sponge* the area with a dry-cleaning solvent, either **Afta Cleaning Fluid, Carbona No. 10 Special Spot Remover/Carbona Cleaning Fluid,** or **K2r Spotlifter** (aerosol). Apply Dry Spotter to the stain and cover with an absorbent pad dampened with the Dry Spotter. Let it stand as long as any stain is being removed. Change the pad as it picks up the stain. Keep the stain and pad moist with the Dry Spotter. Flush* with one of the liquid dry-cleaning solvents. If any stain remains, apply a few drops of dish-washing detergent and a few drops of ammonia to the stain, then tamp* or scrape. Keep the stain moist with detergent and ammonia and blot occasionally with an absorbent pad. Flush well with water to remove all traces of ammonia. Allow to dry or launder as usual.

•Acrylic Plastic
•Alabaster
•Aluminum
•Asphalt •Brass
•Bronze
•Ceramic Glass/Tile
•Copper •Cork
(continued)

Scrape* to remove excess. Wipe the surface with a cloth or sponge dipped in warm sudsy water. Rinse well and wipe dry with a soft cloth.

See Chapter 4 for specific technique instructions.

●Enamel ●Glass   *(see base of preceding page)*
●Grout ●Iron
●Ivory ●Linoleum
●Marble
●Paint/Flat
●Paint/Gloss
●Pewter ●Plexiglas
●Polyurethane
●Porcelain
●Stainless Steel
●Tin ●Vinyl Clothing
●Vinyl Tile
●Vinyl Wallcovering
●Zinc

●Bamboo ●Cane   Scrape* as much excess as you can without gouging the fibers. Wipe with a cloth dipped in a solution of mild pure suds and water. Rinse thoroughly and allow to dry.

●Bluestone ●Brick   Scrape* to remove excess. Wash the
●Concrete   area with a solution of washing soda
●Flagstone   or a detergent (never use soap) and
●Granite   water. Use a cloth or gentle brush.
●Limestone   Rinse thoroughly with clear water
●Masonry Tile   and allow to dry.
●Sandstone ●Slate
●Terrazzo

●Leather ●Suede   Gently scrape* excess. Mix a solution of mild soap in lukewarm water. Swish to create a great volume of suds. Apply only the foam with a sponge. Wipe dry with a clean cloth. If a grease stain remains, powder the stain with an absorbent such as cornmeal. Give it plenty of time to work. Gently brush* it off. Repeat if necessary. On leather only, follow with **The Tannery** or **Fiebing's Saddle Soap** to condition the leather.

See Chapter 4 for specific technique instructions.

●**Silver**	Wash the silver as soon as possible in hot sudsy water. Rinse in hot water and dry immediately with a soft cloth to prevent tarnish.
●**Wallpaper**	Carefully remove excess. Make a paste of cornstarch and water. Apply it to the stain and allow it to dry. Brush* it off, repeating if necessary.
●**Wood**	Mix dishwashing detergent in hot water and swish to make a great volume of suds. Dip a cloth in only the foam and apply. Rinse with a clean cloth dipped in clear water and wrung until damp. Dry immediately. Polish or wax as soon as possible.

Cherry

●**Acetate**
●**Carpet/Synthetic**
●**Carpet/Wool**
●**Fiberglass** ●**Rayon**
●**Rope** ●**Triacetate**
●**Wool**

Spray on **Amway Remove Fabric Spot Cleaner.** If stain remains, sponge* with cool water. Then sponge the area with lemon juice (or rub the cut sides of a slice of lemon over the stain). Flush* with water. Blot as much excess liquid as possible and allow to dry. If stain still persists, apply a Wet Spotter. Cover with an absorbent pad moistened with Wet Spotter. Let stand as long as any stain is being removed. Change the pad as it picks up the stain. Keep the pad and stained area moist with Wet Spotter. Flush with water. If any trace of stain still appears, moisten the area with a solution of 1 cup warm water and 1 teaspoon **Axion,** an enzyme presoak product—do not use on silk or wool. Cover with a clean absorbent pad that has been dipped in the solution and wrung almost dry. Let it stand for 30 minutes. Add

(continued)

See Chapter 4 for specific technique instructions.

(continued from preceding page) enough solution to keep the stain and pad moist, but do not allow the wet area to spread. When no more stain is visible, flush thoroughly with water and allow to air dry.

●**Acrylic Fabric**
●**Modacrylic** ●**Nylon**
●**Olefin** ●**Polyester**
●**Spandex**

Spray on **Amway Remove Fabric Spot Cleaner.** If stain remains, sponge* with cool water immediately. Then sponge with lemon juice or rub a lemon slice over the stain. Flush* with water. Blot as much excess liquid as is possible and allow to dry. If any trace of stain still exists, presoak* in a solution of 1 quart warm water, ½ teaspoon liquid dishwashing or laundry detergent, and 1 tablespoon white vinegar for 15 minutes. Rinse with water and launder if possible. If not, soak in a solution of 1 quart water and 1 tablespoon **Axion,** an enzyme presoak product, for 30 minutes. Rinse well with water and launder as soon as possible.

●**Acrylic Plastic**
●**Aluminum**
●**Asphalt**
●**Bamboo** ●**Brass**
●**Bronze** ●**Cane**
●**Ceramic Glass/Tile**
●**Copper** ●**Enamel**
●**Glass** ●**Grout**
●**Iron**
●**Paint/Flat**
●**Paint/Gloss**
●**Plexiglas**
●**Polyurethane**
●**Porcelain Dishes**
●**Porcelain Fixtures**
●**Stainless Steel**
●**Vinyl Clothing**
●**Vinyl Wallcovering**

Wipe up any excess spill with a cloth or sponge dipped in warm sudsy water. Rinse well and wipe dry.

See Chapter 4 for specific technique instructions.

•Bluestone •Brick •Concrete •Flagstone •Granite •Masonry Tile •Slate •Terrazzo	Wipe up excess spill. Wash area with a solution of washing soda or detergent (not soap) and water. Use a soft cloth or soft-bristled brush. Rinse thoroughly with clear water and allow to dry.
•Cork •Linoleum •Vinyl Tile	Wipe up excess spill and wash the area with a solution of washing soda or detergent and water. Use a soft-bristled brush or cloth to scrub gently. Rinse thoroughly with clear water and allow to dry. If stain persists, wipe area with a cloth dampened in a solution of 1 tablespoon oxalic acid and 1 pint water. Rinse well and wipe dry. Repolish the surface if necessary.
•Cotton •Linen	Test fabric for colorfastness. If color doesn't change, stretch the stain over a bowl; fasten in place with a rubber band. Pour boiling water through the fabric from the height of 2 or 3 feet. Avoid splatters. This procedure must be done immediately. If stain persists, soak in a solution of 1 quart warm water and ½ teaspoon detergent for 15 minutes. Rinse with water. Sponge* area with rubbing alcohol and launder if possible. If not, presoak* in a solution of 1 quart warm water and 1 tablespoon **Axion** or **Biz** (enzyme presoak products) for 30 minutes. Rinse well and launder.
•Leather •Suede	Blot up any excess liquid. Mix a solution of mild soap in lukewarm water. Swish to create a great volume of suds. Apply only the foam with a sponge. Wipe with a clean dry cloth. On leather only, follow with **The Tannery** or **Fiebing's Saddle Soap** to condition the leather.

*See Chapter 4 for specific technique instructions.

●Marble	After wiping up any excess liquid, wipe surface with a cloth or sponge dipped in warm sudsy water. Rinse well and wipe dry. If any stain or discoloration remains, mix a poultice of water, powdered detergent, and chlorine bleach. Apply a thick paste to the stain and cover with a damp cloth to retard evaporation. When the stain has been bleached out, rinse thoroughly and dry.
●Silver	Wash silver as soon as possible in hot sudsy water. Rinse in hot water and dry immediately with a soft cloth to prevent tarnish.
●Wood	Mix dishwashing detergent in hot water and swish to make a great volume of suds. Dip a cloth in only the foam and apply to the stain. Rinse with a clean cloth dampened with clear water. If any stain remains, rub the area with a cloth dampened in a solution of 1 tablespoon oxalic acid to 1 pint water. Rinse well and wipe dry. Wax or polish as soon as possible.

Chewing Gum

●Acetate **●Acrylic Fabric** **●Burlap** **●Carpet/Synthetic** **●Carpet/Wool** **●Cotton** **●Fiberglass ●Linen** **●Modacrylic ●Nylon** **●Olefin ●Polyester** **●Rayon ●Silk** **●Spandex** **●Triacetate ●Wool**	Freeze* until gum gets hard. Carefully scrape* or rub the matter from the fabric. Sponge with a dry-cleaning solvent, **Carbona No. 10 Special Spot Remover/Carbona Cleaning Fluid** or **Afta Cleaning Fluid.** Apply a Dry Spotter to the stain and cover with an absorbent pad dampened with the Dry Spotter. Let it stand as long as any stain is being removed. Change the pad as it picks up the stain. Keep the stain and pad moist with the Dry Spotter. Flush* with one

(continued)

*See Chapter 4 for specific technique instructions.

(continued from preceding page) of the dry-cleaning solvents. If stain remains, reapply the Dry Spotter and cover. Check the stain every 5 minutes and press hard against the stain when you are checking. Continue the alternate soaking and pressing until all the stain has been removed. Flush with the dry-cleaning solvent. Dry.

- **Acrylic Plastic**
- **Aluminum**
- **Asphalt**
- **Paint/Flat**
- **Paint/Gloss**
- **Plexiglas**
- **Polyurethane**
- **Vinyl Clothing**

Freeze* until gum gets hard. Carefully scrape* or rub the substance from the surface. With a clean cloth dipped in warm sudsy water, wipe the surface until all traces of the gum have been removed. Rinse well and wipe dry.

- **Bamboo** • **Cane**

Freeze* until gum gets hard. Carefully scrape any excess. Wipe with a cloth dipped in a solution of warm sudsy water to which a few drops of ammonia have been added. Rinse well and allow to dry.

- **Felt**

Since felt is not woven, but rather fused together, take every precaution in removing any excess gum as chunks of the felt may come with it. Freeze* to harden the remainder and gently brush* with a sponge or fine-bristled brush (such as a toothbrush). This should remove any excess that remains on the surface. In extreme cases, very carefully rub a razor blade with the nap. This will remove any stubborn matter, but will also remove some of the felt fibers. If stain persists, make a paste of cornmeal and a small amount of water and apply it to the stain. Give it plenty of time to work. When it is dry, carefully brush it off with the nap.

See Chapter 4 for specific technique instructions.

•Fur/Natural
•Fur/Synthetic

Take care not to remove the fur when removing the gum. Freeze* to harden the remainder and gently rub it with a dry sponge or brush to remove the remaining gum. Very careful treatment with **Afta Spot Wipes,** disposable cloths, works well. Another effective treatment is to dampen a sponge or cloth in the suds of a mild detergent and wipe in the direction of the nap to remove any sugary residue. Take care not to over-wet the pelt or backing. Allow to air dry.

•Leather

Carefully scrape* excess gum. Mix a solution of mild soap in lukewarm water. Swish to create a great volume of suds. Apply only the foam with a sponge and scrub gently until matter is removed. Dry with a clean cloth. Follow with **The Tannery** or **Fiebing's Saddle Soap** to condition the leather.

•Linoleum
•Vinyl Tile
•Vinyl Wallcovering

Freeze* the gum to harden it. Use a dull tool such as a metal spatula to scrape* the brittle matter without gouging the surface. If there is any residue, try rubbing it with a cloth dipped in **Carbona No. 10 Special Spot Remover/Carbona Cleaning Fluid** or **Afta Cleaning Fluid.** Wipe gingerly, then rub with extra fine (number 000) steel wool. Wash the area and wax when dry.

•Suede

Very carefully scrape* to remove excess. Gently rub an artgum eraser over the remaining substance. If any stain remains, apply a treatment of **Child Life Suede & Fabric Cleaner.** If there is still some remaining, cautiously rub the spot with an emery board or extra fine (number 000)

(continued)

See Chapter 4 for specific technique instructions.

(continued from preceding page) sandpaper. In either case, you are removing a fine layer of the hide, so work slowly and carefully.

●**Wood**

Take special precautions in removing any excess so as not to remove any of the finish. Rub gently with a cloth dipped in the suds of hot soapy water. Rub only on the portion that is stained. Rinse by wiping with a cloth dipped in clear water. Wipe dry immediately and polish or wax as usual.

Chlorine

●**Acetate**
●**Acrylic Fabric**
●**Burlap** ●**Cotton**
●**Linen** ●**Modacrylic**
●**Nylon** ●**Olefin**
●**Polyester** ●**Rayon**
●**Silk** ●**Spandex**
●**Wool**

Immediately flush* the stain with a solution of 1 teaspoon sodium thiosulfate in 1 quart water. When stain has been neutralized, flush well with water to remove chemicals. If stain remains, mix ¼ teaspoon **Rit Color Remover** with ½ cup cool water. Sponge* the stain with the solution, and flush well with water. Chlorine stains are often permanent.

●**Acrylic Plastic**
●**Asphalt** ●**Cork**
●**Linoleum**
●**Masonry Tile**
●**Plexiglas**
●**Vinyl Tile**

As chlorine stains may bleach out surface color, treat immediately. Wipe up any excess spill, then sponge* surface with a cloth dipped in warm sudsy water. Rinse well and wipe dry.

●**Leather** ●**Suede**
●**Vinyl Clothing**
●**Vinyl Wallcovering**

Chlorine will immediately change the color of these materials on contact. There is no way to remove the stain.

Chocolate/Cocoa

●**Acetate** ●**Burlap**
●**Fiberglass** ●**Rayon**
●**Rope** ●**Silk**
(continued)

Blot up any excess, or scrape* any matter from the surface. Flush* the stain with club soda to prevent set-

See Chapter 4 for specific technique instructions.

(continued from preceding page)

●**Triacetate** ●**Wool**

ting. Sponge* the stain with a dry-cleaning solvent, either **Carbona No. 10 Special Spot Remover/Carbona Cleaning Fluid, K2r Spot-lifter** (tube), or **Afta Cleaning Fluid.** Then apply a Dry Spotter to the stain and cover with an absorbent pad dampened with the Dry Spotter. Keep the stain and pad moist with the Dry Spotter. Let it stand as long as any stain is being removed. Change the pad as it picks up the stain. Flush with one of the dry-cleaning solvents. If a stain remains, moisten it with a solution of 1 cup warm water and 1 teaspoon **Axion,** an enzyme presoak—but do not use on silk or wool. Cover with a clean pad that has been dipped in the solution and wrung almost dry. Let it stand at least 30 minutes. Add more solution if needed to keep the stain warm and moist, but do not allow the wet area to spread. When the stain is lifted, flush thoroughly with water and allow to dry.

●**Acrylic Fabric**
●**Cotton** ●**Linen**
●**Nylon** ●**Modacrylic**
●**Olefin** ●**Polyester**
●**Spandex**

Wipe up as much excess as possible without driving the stain further into the fibers. Flush* the stain with club soda. Sponge* the area with a dry-cleaning solvent, **Carbona Cleaning Fluid, K2r Spot-lifter** (aerosol), or **Afta Cleaning Fluid.** Apply a Dry Spotter to the stain and cover with an absorbent pad dampened with the Dry Spotter. Keep the stain moist with Dry Spotter. Let it stand as long as any stain is being lifted. Change the pad as it picks up the stain. Flush with one of the liquid dry-cleaning solvents. If any stain remains, apply a few drops of dishwashing detergent and a few drops of ammonia to the

(continued)

See Chapter 4 for specific technique instructions.

(continued from preceding page) stain, then tamp* or scrape.* Keep the stain moist with the detergent and ammonia and blot occasionally with an absorbent pad. Flush well with water to remove all traces of ammonia. Allow to dry or launder as usual.

- **Acrylic Plastic**
- **Aluminum**
- **Asphalt** ● **Bamboo**
- **Brass** ● **Bronze**
- **Cane**
- **Ceramic Glass/Tile**
- **Copper** ● **Cork**
- **Enamel** ● **Glass**
- **Gold** ● **Iron** ● **Ivory**
- **Jade** ● **Paint/Flat**
- **Paint/Gloss**
- **Pewter** ● **Plexiglas**
- **Polyurethane**
- **Porcelain**
- **Stainless Steel**
- **Tin** ● **Vinyl Clothing**
- **Vinyl Tile**
- **Vinyl Wallcovering**
- **Zinc**

Scrape* to remove excess. Wipe the surface with a cloth dipped in warm sudsy water. Rinse well and wipe dry.

- **Alabaster** ● **Marble**

Carefully scrape* excess. Wipe with a clean cloth dipped in a solution of washing soda or detergent and water. Rinse well and wipe dry. If any stain remains, mix a few drops of ammonia with 1 cup 3% hydrogen peroxide. Soak a white blotter with the solution and place it over the stain. Weight it down with a heavy object. Continue applying the solution until the oil has been drawn out and any remaining stain bleached out.

- **Bluestone** ● **Brick**
- **Concrete**

(continued)

Scrape* to remove excess, taking care not to gouge the surface. Wash

---

See Chapter 4 for specific technique instructions.

(continued from preceding page)

●**Flagstone**
●**Granite**
●**Limestone**
●**Masonry Tile**
●**Sandstone** ●**Slate**
●**Terrazzo**

with a solution of washing soda or detergent (never use soap) and water. Use a cloth or a gentle brush. Rinse thoroughly with clear water and allow to dry.

●**Carpet/Synthetic**
●**Carpet/Wool**

Blot up or scrape* as much of the excess as possible. To prevent setting stain, flush* with club soda. Try an application of **Spot Shot Carpet Stain Remover** or a concentrated solution of a non-alkali carpet shampoo. After drying and vacuuming, if stain remains, mix 1 tablespoon ammonia to 1 cup water and carefully drop small amounts onto the stain. (On wool carpets, test in an inconspicuous corner first, as ammonia can harm wool.) Blot with an absorbent pad. Flush* area rugs or sponge* carpeting with clear water. It is important to remove all traces of ammonia. Place a clean absorbent pad over the area and weight it down. When no more liquid is being absorbed, allow it to thoroughly air dry.

●**Felt** ●**Fur/Natural**
●**Fur/Synthetic**

Gently scrape* to remove excess. Mix a mild soap in hot water and swish to make a great volume of suds. Dip a cloth in only the foam and apply. Rinse by wiping with a clean cloth dampened with clear water. If a grease stain remains, powder the stain with an absorbent such as cornmeal. Give it plenty of time to work. Gently brush* it out. Take care not to force the absorbent further into the hairs. Repeat if necessary.

●**Grout**

Wipe excess with a cloth dipped in warm sudsy water. If any stain re-
(continued)

*See Chapter 4 for specific technique instructions.

(continued from preceding page) mains, dip a wet toothbrush into baking soda or powdered cleanser, or apply **Afta Tile & Grout Cleaner** and gently scrub the spot. Rinse well and wipe dry.

•Leather •Suede	Gently scrape* excess from the surface. Mix a solution of mild soap in lukewarm water. Swish to create a great volume of suds. Apply only the foam with a sponge. Wipe dry with a clean cloth. If a stain remains, powder it with an absorbent such as cornmeal. Give it plenty of time to work. Gently brush* it off. Repeat if necessary; on leather only, follow with **The Tannery** or **Fiebing's Saddle Soap** to condition the leather.
•Silver	Wash silver in hot sudsy water. Rinse thoroughly in hot water. Wipe dry immediately with a clean soft cloth to prevent tarnish.
•Wood	Mix dishwashing detergent in hot water and swish to make a great volume of suds. Dip a cloth in only the foam and apply. Rinse with a clean cloth dampened with clear water. Polish or wax as usual.

Coffee

•Acetate **•Fiberglass •Rayon** **•Triacetate**	Blot up with a clean cloth. Sponge* the stain with water. Apply **Amway Remove Fabric Spot Cleaner** or a Wet Spotter and a few drops of white vinegar. Cover with an absorbent pad dampened with the Wet Spotter. Keep the stain and pad moist with the Wet Spotter and vinegar. Let it stand as long as any stain is being removed. Change the pad as it picks up the stain. Flush* with water. Repeat

(continued)

*See Chapter 4 for specific technique instructions.

(continued from preceding page) until no more stain is removed. If a stain remains, moisten it with a solution of 1 teaspoon **Axion,** an enzyme presoak, and 1 cup warm water. Cover with a clean pad that has been dipped in the solution and wrung almost dry. Let it stand for at least 30 minutes. Add more solution if needed to keep the area warm and moist, but do not allow the wet area to spread. When the stain is removed, or no more is being lifted, flush thoroughly with water and allow to dry. (If coffee contained cream and any greasy stain remains, follow procedures for Cream.)

●**Acrylic Fabric**
●**Modacrylic** ●**Nylon**
●**Olefin** ●**Polyester**
●**Spandex**

Blot up any excess with a clean cloth. Presoak* the stain in a solution of 1 quart warm water, ½ teaspoon dishwashing detergent, and 1 tablespoon white vinegar for 15 minutes. Rinse with water. Sponge* the remaining stain with rubbing alcohol and launder if possible. If not, presoak it in a solution of 1 quart warm water and 1 tablespoon **Axion,** an enzyme presoak, for 30 minutes. Rinse well with water. Allow to dry, but launder as soon as possible. (If coffee contained cream and any greasy stain remains, follow procedures for Cream.)

●**Acrylic Plastic**
●**Aluminum**
●**Asphalt** ●**Bamboo**
●**Brass** ●**Bronze**
●**Cane**
●**Ceramic Glass/Tile**
●**Copper** ●**Cork**
●**Enamel** ●**Glass**
●**Gold** ●**Grout** ●**Iron**
●**Ivory** ●**Jade**
(continued)

Blot up any excess. Wipe the surface with a cloth or sponge dipped in warm sudsy water. Rinse well and wipe dry.

*See Chapter 4 for specific technique instructions.

- **Linoleum**   *(see base of preceding page)*
- **Paint/Flat**
- **Paint/Gloss**
- **Pewter** **Plexiglas**
- **Polyurethane**
- **Stainless Steel**
- **Tin** **Vinyl Clothing**
- **Vinyl Tile**
- **Vinyl Wallcovering**
- **Zinc**

- **Alabaster** **Marble**

Blot up any excess. Wipe the surface with a cloth dipped in a solution of washing soda or detergent and water. Rinse well and wipe dry. If a stain remains, mix a few drops of ammonia with 1 cup 3% hydrogen peroxide. Soak a white blotter with the solution and place it over the stain. Cover it with a piece of glass or other heavy object. Continue applying the solution until the oil has been drawn out and any remaining stain is bleached out.

- **Bluestone** **Brick**
- **Concrete**
- **Flagstone**
- **Granite**
- **Limestone**
- **Masonry Tile**
- **Sandstone** **Slate**
- **Terrazzo**

Mix a solution of washing soda or a detergent in water. Gently brush* stain away. Wash with clear water and allow to dry.

- **Burlap** **Silk**
- **Wool**

Blot up excess. Sponge* the stain with water. Apply **Amway Remove Fabric Spot Cleaner** or a Wet Spotter and a few drops of white vinegar. Cover with an absorbent pad dampened with the Wet Spotter. Let it stand as long as any stain is being lifted. Change the pad as it picks up the stain. Keep the stain and pad

(continued)

---

*See Chapter 4 for specific technique instructions.

(continued from preceding page) moist with the Wet Spotter and vinegar. Flush* with water. Repeat until no more stain is being removed. If any stain remains, apply rubbing alcohol to the stain and cover with an absorbent pad dampened with alcohol. Let it stand as long as it is picking up stain, changing the pad as it does. Keep the stain and pad moist with alcohol. Flush with water. For a stubborn or old stain, try moistening the stain with a solution of 1 teaspoon **Axion** (an enzyme presoak product) and 1 cup warm water—use only on burlap. Cover with a clean pad dipped in the solution and squeezed almost dry. Let it stand for at least 30 minutes. Add more solution as needed to keep the area warm and moist, but do not allow the wet area to spread. When the stain is lifted, flush thoroughly with water. (If the coffee contained cream and any greasy stain remains, follow procedures for Cream.)

●**Carpet/Synthetic**
●**Carpet/Wool**
●**Foam Rubber**

Blot up what you can. Apply **Stain-X Carpet Stain Remover, Spot Shot Carpet Stain Remover,** or **Afta Carpet Stain Remover.** Flush* the stain with a solution of 1 quart warm water, ½ teaspoon liquid laundry or dishwashing detergent, and 1 tablespoon white vinegar. Blot with a clean pad and rinse well with water. If the stain remains, try flushing it with a solution of 1 quart warm water and 1 tablespoon enzyme presoak—**Axion or Biz** (do not use on wool). Blot and flush alternately until no more stain is left. Sponge* the area well with water. Blot all excess liquid and place a clean pad over the area and weight it down. When no more is being absorbed, allow the area to thoroughly

(continued)

---

*See Chapter 4 for specific technique instructions.

(continued from preceding page) air dry. (If coffee contained cream and any greasy stain remains, follow procedures for Cream.)

●Cotton ●Linen

Blot up excess. Pretreat* with **Miracle White Laundry Soil & Stain Remover** or **Shout Laundry Soil & Stain Remover,** then launder immediately. If that is not possible, soak the stain in a solution of 1 quart warm water and ½ teaspoon dishwashing detergent for 15 minutes. Rinse well with water. Next, sponge* the stain with rubbing alcohol. Rinse and allow to dry. If the stain remains, presoak* it in a solution of warm water and **Axion** or **Biz,** enzyme presoak products, for 30 minutes. Rinse well with water and dry. Launder as soon as possible.

Another method that has worked is to stretch the stained area over a bowl and secure with a rubber band. Pour boiling water through the stain from a height of 2 to 3 feet. Stand back to avoid splatters. Although cotton and linen can stand boiling water, some of the finishes and colors used on the fabrics might be damaged by such harsh treatment. Be sure to test on an inconspicuous corner first. (If coffee contained cream and any greasy stain remains, follow procedures for Cream.)

●Felt ●Fur/Natural ●Fur/Synthetic

Blot up what you can without forcing the stain further into the fibers. Mix a mild soap in hot water and swish to make a great volume of suds. Dip a cloth in only the foam and apply. Rinse with a cloth dipped in clear water and wrung nearly dry. If an oily residue remains, powder the stain with an absorbent such as cornmeal.

(continued)

*See Chapter 4 for specific technique instructions.

(continued from preceding page) Don't push the powder into the fibers or pelt. Give it plenty of time to work. Gently brush* or shake it out. Repeat if necessary. Make sure the material is dry before applying powder. (If coffee contained cream and any greasy stain remains, follow procedures for Cream.)

●Leather ●Suede

Carefully blot up excess liquid. Mix a solution of mild soap in lukewarm water. Swish to create a great volume of suds. Apply only the foam with a sponge. Wipe dry with a clean dry cloth. If an oily stain remains, powder the stain with an absorbent such as cornmeal. Give it plenty of time to work. Gently brush* it off. Repeat if necessary. On leather only, follow with **The Tannery** or **Fiebing's Saddle Soap** to condition the leather (If coffee contained cream and any greasy stain remains, follow procedures for Cream.)

●Porcelain Dishes
●Porcelain Fixtures

Clean the stain by washing it in warm sudsy water or wiping it with a cloth dipped in warm sudsy water. Rinse well and wipe it dry. To remove old stain from the bottom of cups, dip a soft, damp cloth into baking soda and wipe any remaining stain. Rinse well and dry.

●Silver

Wash silver in hot soapy water. Rinse in hot water and wipe dry immediately with a soft cloth.

●Wood

Gently wipe the surface with a cloth dipped in the suds of a mild detergent and water. Rinse well with a clean cloth dampened with clear water. Polish or wax the wood as soon as possible.

*See Chapter 4 for specific technique instructions.

Cologne

- **Acetate**
- **Fiberglass** • **Rayon**
- **Silk** • **Triacetate**

Flush* the stain with water. Spray on **Amway Remove Fabric Spot Cleaner.** An alternate method is to flush, then add a few drops of glycerine. Rinse well with water. If some stain remains, cautiously try a diluted solution of white vinegar. Make sure you work the stain outward from the center to avoid leaving a ring. Flush with water to remove the vinegar and allow to dry.

- **Acrylic Fabric**
- **Burlap**
- **Carpet/Synthetic**
- **Carpet/Wool**
- **Cotton** • **Linen**
- **Modacrylic** • **Nylon**
- **Olefin** • **Polyester**
- **Rope** • **Spandex**
- **Wool**

Sponge* the stain with water. Spray on **Amway Remove Fabric Spot Cleaner.** If stain remains, apply a Wet Spotter and cover with an absorbent pad dampened with the Wet Spotter. Let it stand as long as any stain is being removed. Change the pad as it picks up the stain. Keep the stain and pad moist with the Wet Spotter. Flush* well with water. Repeat until no more stain is being lifted. If any stain remains, apply rubbing alcohol (do not use this on acrylic or modacrylic) to the stain and cover it with an absorbent pad dampened with alcohol. Let it stand as long as any stain is being lifted. Change the pad as it picks up the stain. Keep the stain and pad moist with alcohol. Flush well with water and allow to dry.

- **Acrylic Plastic**
- **Alabaster**
- **Asphalt**
- **Ceramic Glass/Tile**
- **Cork** • **Glass**
- **Gold** • **Ivory** • **Jade**
- **Linoleum** • **Marble**
- **Paint/Flat**

(continued)

Wash spill with a solution of warm sudsy water. Rinse well and wipe dry with a clean cloth.

*See Chapter 4 for specific technique instructions.

- **Paint/Gloss**   *(see base of preceding page)*
- **Plexiglas**
- **Polyurethane**
- **Stainless Steel**
- **Vinyl Clothing**
- **Vinyl Tile**
- **Vinyl Wallcovering**

- **Bluestone** • **Brick**
- **Concrete**
- **Flagstone**
- **Granite**
- **Limestone**
- **Masonry Tile**
- **Sandstone** • **Slate**
- **Terrazzo**

Wash stained area with a solution of washing soda or detergent and water. Use a cloth or gentle brush to scrub. Rinse thoroughly and allow to dry.

- **Leather** • **Suede**

Gently blot excess. Mix a solution of mild soap in lukewarm water. Swish to create a great volume of suds. Apply only the foam with a sponge. Wipe with a clean dry cloth. If an oily stain remains, powder the stain with an absorbent, such as cornmeal. Give it plenty of time to work. Gently brush* it out. Repeat if necessary. On leather only, follow with **The Tannery** or **Fiebing's Saddle Soap** to condition the leather.

- **Wallpaper**

Cologne often permanently stains paper, so treat the stain immediately. Carefully wipe with a sponge dipped in clear warm water and wrung out until damp. Strokes should be overlapped to prevent streaking. Gently pat dry with a clean cloth.

- **Wood**

Rub the stain with a little denatured alcohol, immediately if possible. Follow this with a liberal application of boiled linseed oil. If the stain persists, leave some oil on the surface for 24
(continued)

---

*See Chapter 4 for specific technique instructions.

(continued from preceding page) hours, then wipe with a clean soft cloth and polish or wax as usual.

Cosmetics

(See Blusher, Eye Pencil/Eyeliner/Eyeshadow, Face Powder, Lipstick, Liquid Foundation, Lotions/Body, Facial, Foot, Hair, Lotion/Hand, Lotion/Suntan, Mascara, Rouge.)

Cough Syrup

●Acetate
●Fiberglass ●Rayon
●Silk ●Triacetate
●Wool

Sponge* the area with water. Spray on **Amway Remove Fabric Spot Cleaner.** Then apply a Wet Spotter and a few drops of white vinegar. Cover with an absorbent pad dampened with the Wet Spotter. Let it stand as long as any stain is being removed. Change the pad as it picks up the stain. Keep stain and pad moist with the Wet Spotter and vinegar. Repeat until no more stain is removed. If any remains, soak in a solution of 1 quart warm water, ½ teaspoon liquid detergent, and 1 tablespoon white vinegar for 15 minutes. Rinse with water.

●Acrylic Fabric
●Spandex

Sponge* the area with water. Spray on **Amway Remove Fabric Spot Cleaner.** Then apply a Wet Spotter and a few drops white vinegar. Cover with an absorbent pad dampened with the Wet Spotter. Let it stand as long as any stain is being removed. Tamp* occasionally and change the pad as it picks up the stain. Flush* with water. If stain remains, soak in a solution of 1 quart warm water, ½ teaspoon liquid detergent, and 1 tablespoon white vinegar for 15 min-

(continued)

*See Chapter 4 for specific technique instructions.

(continued from preceding page) utes. Launder if possible. If not, soak in a solution of 1 quart warm water and 1 tablespoon **Axion** or **Biz** (enzyme presoak products) for 30 minutes. Rinse well with water and launder as soon as possible.

- Acrylic Plastic
- Alabaster
- Aluminum
- Asphalt •Bamboo
- Cane
- Ceramic Glass/Tile
- Cork •Glass
- Linoleum •Marble
- Paint/Flat
- Paint/Gloss
- Plexiglas
- Polyurethane
- Stainless Steel
- Vinyl Tile
- Vinyl Wallcovering

Wipe up any excess immediately as cough syrup contains not only alcohol, but food coloring that can permanently stain and damage the surface. Wipe surface with a cloth or sponge dipped in warm sudsy water. Rinse well and wipe dry.

- Bluestone
- Concrete
- Flagstone •Slate

Wipe up excess spill. Wash with a solution of washing soda or detergent (never use soap) and water. Use a cloth or gentle brush. Rinse thoroughly with clear water and allow to dry.

- Carpet/Synthetic
- Carpet/Wool
- Cotton •Linen
- Nylon •Olefin
- Polyester

Sponge* area with water. Apply a spot remover—**Amway Remove Fabric Spot Cleaner, Stain-X Carpet Stain Remover** or **Afta Carpet Stain Remover** for carpeting. Then apply a Wet Spotter and a few drops of white vinegar (do not use vinegar on cotton and linen). Cover with an absorbent pad dampened with the Wet Spotter. Let stand as long as stain is being removed. Change the pad as it picks up the stain. Keep stain and pad moist with the Wet

(continued)

*See Chapter 4 for specific technique instructions.

(continued from preceding page) Spotter and vinegar. Flush* with water. Repeat until no more stain is removed. If stain persists, then apply rubbing alcohol to the stain and cover with an absorbent pad dampened with alcohol. Let it stand as long as any stain is being removed. Change the pad as it picks up the stain. Keep stain and pad moist with alcohol. If stain still remains, presoak* in a solution of 1 quart warm water, ½ teaspoon liquid detergent, and 1 tablespoon white vinegar for 15 minutes, if possible. Rinse with water. Sponge with alcohol. Launder if possible. If not, presoak in a solution of 1 quart warm water and 1 tablespoon **Axion** or **Biz** (enzyme presoak products that are not for use on wool carpets) for 30 minutes. Rinse well with water. Launder as soon as possible. For carpets, thoroughly dampen the area with solution and cover with an absorbent pad moistened with the solution. Keep covered for 30 minutes. Using absorbent pads, remove as much moisture as possible. Allow the area to thoroughly air dry.

●**Grout**

Wipe excess immediately with a cloth dipped in warm sudsy water. If any stain remains, dip a wet toothbrush into powdered cleanser or apply **Afta Tile & Grout Cleaner** and gently scrub spot. Rinse well and wipe dry.

●**Leather** ●**Suede**

Gently remove any excess liquid. Mix a solution of mild soap in lukewarm water. Swish to create a great volume of suds. Apply only the foam with a sponge. Wipe with a clean dry cloth. If a grease stain remains, powder the stain with an absorbent such as cornmeal. Allow plenty of time to work,

(continued)

*See Chapter 4 for specific technique instructions.

(continued from preceding page) and then gently brush* stain off. Repeat if necessary. On leather only, follow with **The Tannery** or **Fiebing's Saddle Soap** to condition the leather.

Crayon

●Acetate ●Burlap
●Fiberglass ●Rayon
●Rope ●Silk
●Triacetate
●Wool/nonwashable

Gently scrape* to remove excess matter. Place an absorbent pad under the stain and flush* with a dry-cleaning solvent, either **Carbona No. 10 Special Spot Remover/Carbona Cleaning Fluid** or **Afta Cleaning Fluid.** Allow to dry. Repeat if necessary.

●Acrylic Fabric
●Cotton ●Linen
●Modacrylic ●Nylon
●Olefin ●Polyester
●Spandex
●Wool/washable

Scrape* to remove the excess. Place the stain between two pieces of white blotting paper and press with a warm iron. Change the papers as the stain is absorbed. This stain can easily spread, so use care while pressing. On colorfast white cotton or linen, try pouring boiling water through the stain. After using either method, allow fabric to dry. If any trace remains, flush* it with a dry-cleaning solvent, **Carbona Cleaning Fluid** or **Afta Cleaning Fluid.** If any dye remains, sponge* it with 1 part rubbing alcohol (do not use on acrylic or modacrylic) in 2 parts water. Rinse well with clear water and allow to dry.

●Acrylic Plastic
●Alabaster
●Aluminum
●Bamboo
●Bluestone ●Brass
●Brick ●Bronze
●Cane
●Ceramic Glass/Tile

Gently scrape* any excess crayon from the surface. Take care not to scratch the surface. This should be sufficient to remove the stain. Wipe with a sponge dipped in a solution of washing soda or detergent (not soap) and water. Rinse well and wipe dry.

   On flat or gloss paint, grout, or

(continued)

See Chapter 4 for specific technique instructions.

(continued from preceding page)

- **Concrete** - **Copper**
- **Enamel**
- **Flagstone** - **Glass**
- **Gold** - **Granite**
- **Grout** - **Iron**
- **Ivory** - **Jade**
- **Limestone**
- **Marble**
- **Paint/Flat**
- **Paint/Gloss**
- **Pewter** - **Plexiglas**
- **Polyurethane**
- **Porcelain**
- **Sandstone** - **Slate**
- **Stainless Steel**
- **Terrazzo** - **Tin**
- **Vinyl Clothing**
- **Vinyl Tile**

marble, rub **Crayerase,** a mildly abrasive bar, lightly over the crayon marks. Remove any shine left on flat paint by sponging* lightly with hot water.

- **Asphalt** - **Cork**
- **Linoleum**

On linoleum floors, **Crayerase,** a mildly abrasive bar, rubbed lightly on the surface, removes crayon marks. Polish or wax as usual. A treatment for all of these surfaces involves using a metal spatula to gently scrape* the surface; take care not to gouge it.

- **Carpet/Synthetic**
- **Carpet/Wool**

Gently scrape* what you can from the surface. Add a small amount (to prevent damaging the carpet's backing) of dry-cleaning solvent, either **Carbona No. 10 Special Spot Remover/ Carbona Cleaning Fluid** or **Afta Cleaning Fluid,** and blot with an absorbent pad. Continue until no more stain is removed. If a dye remains, dilute 1 part rubbing alcohol with 2 parts water and test on an inconspicuous place. If the carpet is colorfast, apply the solution to the
(continued)

---

*See Chapter 4 for specific technique instructions.

(continued from preceding page) stain in small amounts, blotting well after each application. Allow to dry.

●**Felt**

Very carefully scrape* the residue off, taking care not to pull out the fibers. If any residue remains, try brushing* gently with a stiff-bristled brush. In extreme cases, use a razor blade to gently scrape the excess. Use this as a last resort as it will remove some of the fibers.

●**Leather** ●**Suede**

With a dull knife or your fingernail, gently scrape* up the crayon. If any stain remains, mix a thick paste of fuller's earth and water and apply it to the stain. Carefully brush* it off when dry. Repeat if necessary. When the stain has been removed, on leather only, follow with **The Tannery** or **Fiebing's Saddle Soap** to condition the leather.

●**Silver**

Scrape* any excess material with your fingernail or nonmetal utensil until no more can be removed. Wash the silver in hot soapy water. Rinse in hot water and wipe dry.

●**Wallpaper**

Rub the crayon marks lightly with the edge of **Crayerase,** a mildly abrasive bar, rubbing in several directions if the wallpaper is textured. An alternate method is to spray **K2r Spotlifter** (aerosol) onto the stain. Or, lightly rub the stain with a dry, soap-filled steel wool pad. If stain persists, rub very gently with baking soda sprinkled on a damp cloth. Wipe away any residue with a damp cloth and dry.

●**Wood**

Rub the crayon marks with **Crayerase,** a mildly abrasive bar, then
(continued)

*See Chapter 4 for specific technique instructions.

(continued from preceding page) polish or wax the wood. Or, gently remove any material by scraping* with a dull knife or your fingernail. Polish any remains with a chamois cloth.

Cream

- Acetate •Burlap
- Carpet/Synthetic
- Carpet/Wool
- Fiberglass •Rayon
- Rope •Silk
- Triacetate
- Wool/nonwashable

Remove any excess immediately. Sponge* with dry-cleaning solvent, either **Carbona Cleaning Fluid, K2r Spot-lifter** (tube), or **Afta Cleaning Fluid.** Then apply Dry Spotter to the stain and cover with an absorbent pad dampened with Dry Spotter. Let it stand as long as any stain is being removed. Change the pad as it picks up the stain. Keep the pad and stain moist with Dry Spotter. Flush* with a dry-cleaning solvent. If any stain remains, moisten the area with a solution of 1 cup warm water and 1 teaspoon **Axion,** an enzyme presoak product—do not use on silk or wool. Cover with a clean pad that has been dipped in the solution and wrung almost dry. Let it stand for 30 minutes. Add more solution if needed to keep the area warm and damp, but do not allow the wet area to spread. When no more stain is being lifted, flush the area thoroughly with water and allow to dry.

- Acrylic Fabric
- Cotton •Linen
- Modacrylic •Nylon
- Olefin •Polyester
- Spandex
- Wool/washable

Immediately remove any excess matter. Sponge* the stain with a dry-cleaning solvent, **Carbona No. 10 Special Spot Remover/Carbona Cleaning Fluid, K2r Spot-Lifter** (aerosol), or **Afta Cleaning Fluid.** Apply a Dry Spotter and cover with an absorbent pad dampened with Dry Spotter. Let it stand as long as any
(continued)

*See Chapter 4 for specific technique instructions.

(continued from preceding page) stain is being removed. Change pad as it picks up the stain. Keep stain and pad moist with Dry Spotter. Flush* with one of the liquid dry-cleaning solvents. If any stain remains, apply a few drops of dish-washing detergent and a few drops of ammonia to the area, then tamp* or scrape.* Keep the stain moist with detergent and ammonia and blot occasionally with an absorbent pad. Flush well with water to remove all ammonia and allow to dry.

- Acrylic Plastic
- Aluminum
- Asphalt
- Bamboo ●Brass
- Bronze ●Cane
- Ceramic Glass/Tile
- Copper ●Cork
- Enamel ●Glass
- Gold ●Iron
- Ivory ●Linoleum
- Paint/Flat
- Paint/Gloss
- Pewter ●Platinum
- Plexiglas
- Polyurethane
- Porcelain Dishes
- Stainless Steel
- Tin ●Vinyl Clothing
- Vinyl Tile
- Vinyl Wallcovering
- Zinc

Wipe up any excess spill immediately. Wipe the surface with a cloth or sponge dipped in warm sudsy water. Rinse well and wipe dry.

- Alabaster ●Marble

Wipe up any excess spill. Mix a few drops of ammonia with 1 cup of rubbing alcohol. Soak a white blotter (about the size of the stain) in the solution and place it over the area. Cover it with a heavy object. Con-

(continued)

---

*See Chapter 4 for specific technique instructions.

(continued from preceding page) tinue applying the solution until the oil has been drawn out and any remaining stain has been bleached out. If any stain does persist, make a poultice from bleach, water, and powdered detergent. Apply it to the stain. Cover with a damp cloth to minimize drying. Remove when the stain has been bleached out.

- **Bluestone** • **Brick**
- **Concrete**
- **Flagstone**
- **Granite**
- **Limestone**
- **Masonry Tile**
- **Sandstone** • **Slate**
- **Terrazzo**

Remove any excess. Wash the stained area with a solution of washing soda or detergent (never use soap) and water. Use a cloth or gently brush.* Rinse the area thoroughly with clear water and allow to dry.

- **Fur/Natural**
- **Fur/Synthetic**

Wipe up any excess spill. Mix dishwashing detergent in hot water and swish to make a great volume of suds. Dip a cloth in only the foam and apply. Wipe again with a clean dry cloth. If a grease stain remains, powder the stain with an absorbent, allowing plenty of time for it to work. Gently brush* out the powder and rinse the area with a damp cloth. Allow fur to air dry.

- **Grout**

Wipe up the excess with a cloth dipped in warm sudsy water. If any stain remains, apply **Afta Tile & Grout Cleaner** or dip a wet toothbrush into powdered cleanser and gently scrub the spot. Rinse well and wipe dry with a clean cloth.

- **Leather**

Wipe up any excess cream from the surface. Mix a solution of mild soap in lukewarm water. Swish to create a great volume of suds. Apply only the
(continued)

---

*See Chapter 4 for specific technique instructions.

(continued from preceding page) foam with a sponge. Wipe with a clean dry cloth. If a grease stain remains, powder the stain with an absorbent such as cornmeal. Give it plenty of time to work. Gently brush* it out. Repeat if necessary. Follow with **The Tannery** or **Fiebing's Saddle Soap** to condition the leather. If after applying the absorbent and brushing it off, any stain persists, use **The Tannery** or other liquid leather cleaner. Rub it in with a clean soft cloth and allow to dry. Again, condition as usual.

●Silver

Remove any excess spill with a cloth. Wash as soon as possible in hot sudsy water. Rinse in hot water and dry immediately with a soft cloth.

●Suede

Blot up excess spill from surface of fabric. Mix a solution of mild soap in lukewarm water. Swish to create a great volume of suds. Apply only the foam with a sponge. Wipe with a clean dry cloth. If a grease stain remains, powder the area with an absorbent, allowing plenty of time to work. Gently brush* the stain out.

●Wallpaper

Carefully blot up the excess. With a cloth or sponge dipped in cool clear water and squeezed almost dry, wipe the stained area. Overlap strokes to prevent streaking. Gently pat the area dry.

●Wood

Mix dishwashing detergent in hot water and swish to make a great volume of suds. Dip a cloth in only the foam and apply. Rinse with a clean cloth dipped in clear water and squeezed almost dry. Polish or wax as soon as possible.

*See Chapter 4 for specific technique instructions.

Deodorant

- Acetate • Burlap
- Carpet/Synthetic
- Carpet/Wool
- Cotton
- Fiberglass • Linen
- Rayon • Silk
- Triacetate • Wool

Spray on **Amway Remove Fabric Spot Cleaner.** Another method is to apply rubbing alcohol to the stain and cover with an absorbent pad dampened with alcohol (dilute alcohol with 2 parts water for acetate, rayon, and triacetate; test silk for colorfastness before using alcohol). Keep both moist. Allow to stand as long as any stain is being removed. If the stain remains (and as a last resort), flush* with a solution of warm sudsy water with a little ammonia added (use special care on silk and wool). Rinse with clear water. Apply a solution of warm water with a little white vinegar added, taking special care with this solution on cotton and linen. Rinse again with clear water. Dry thoroughly. (If the color of the fabric has been changed, it may possibly be restored by sponging* lightly with a solution of 2 parts water and 1 part ammonia.) **Caution:** Never iron material with a deodorant stain. The combination of chemical and heat interaction will ruin most fabrics.

- Acrylic Fabric
- Modacrylic • Nylon
- Olefin • Polyester
- Spandex

Most deodorant stains can be removed by pretreating* with a liquid detergent or prespotter—either **Miracle White Laundry Soil & Stain Remover, Magic Pre-Wash,** or **Shout Laundry Soil & Stain Remover**—and laundering as usual. If the stain doesn't seem to be loosening with the pretreatment, rinse out the detergent and flush* with white vinegar. Rinse in clear water. If the stain remains, flush the area with denatured alcohol. Rinse with clear water and dry or launder as usual.

*See Chapter 4 for specific technique instructions.

- **Acrylic Plastic**
- **Aluminum**
- **Asphalt**
- **Bamboo** • **Brass**
- **Bronze** • **Cane**
- **Ceramic Glass/Tile**
- **Chromium** • **Cork**
- **Enamel** • **Glass**
- **Gold** • **Grout** • **Iron**
- **Linoleum** • **Marble**
- **Masonry Tile**
- **Paint/Flat**
- **Paint/Gloss**
- **Plexiglas**
- **Polyurethane**
- **Stainless Steel**
- **Tin** • **Vinyl Clothing**
- **Vinyl Tile**
- **Vinyl Wallcovering**

Wipe the area with a cloth dipped in warm sudsy water. Rinse well and wipe dry with a clean cloth.

- **Leather** • **Suede**

Mix a solution of mild soap in lukewarm water. Swish to create a great volume of suds. Apply only the foam with a sponge. Wipe dry with a clean cloth. On leather only, follow with **The Tannery** or **Fiebing's Saddle Soap** to condition the leather.

- **Wallpaper**

Carefully wipe the wallpaper with a sponge dampened with clear warm water. Do this immediately after staining the wallpaper, as deodorants can permanently stain the paper. Strokes should be overlapped to prevent streaking. Gently pat dry with a clean cloth.

- **Wood**

Wipe spills or deodorant-sprayed area as soon as possible with a sponge or soft cloth dipped in mild sudsy water. Wipe dry and apply wax or polish as needed.

Dye (except red and yellow)

- Acetate
- Carpet/Synthetic
- Fiberglass • Rayon
- Triacetate

Sponge* with water. Spray on **Amway Remove Fabric Spot Cleaner.** Then apply a Wet Spotter and a few drops of white vinegar. Use an absorbent pad dampened with Wet Spotter to blot occasionally. Keep the stain moist with Wet Spotter and vinegar. When no more stain can be blotted, flush* with water. If stain persists, apply more Wet Spotter and a few drops of ammonia. Cover the stain this time with an absorbent pad and allow it to remain as long as any stain is being lifted. Keep stain and pad moist with Wet Spotter and ammonia. Flush with water and allow to dry.

- Acrylic Fabric
- Modacrylic • Nylon
- Olefin • Polyester
- Spandex

Presoak* in a solution of 1 quart warm water, ½ teaspoon liquid dishwashing or laundry detergent, and 1 tablespoon white vinegar for 15 minutes. Rinse well and launder if possible. If not, presoak in solution of 1 quart warm water and 1 tablespoon **Axion** or **Biz** (enzyme presoak products) for 30 minutes. Rinse well and launder as soon as possible. If stain still remains, mix a solution of 1 tablespoon ammonia to 1 cup water. Be sure to test on a hidden seam first, then carefully, using an eyedropper, drop solution onto stain. Blot with an absorbent pad. Flush* with clear water. Place an absorbent pad over the stain and weight it down. When no more liquid is absorbed, allow it to thoroughly air dry.

- Acrylic Plastic
- Aluminum
- Bamboo • Cane

(continued)

Immediately wipe up the spill with a cloth or sponge dipped in warm sudsy water. Rinse well and wipe dry.

See Chapter 4 for specific technique instructions.

- **Ceramic Glass/Tile**   *(see base of preceding page)*
- **Glass** • **Paint/Flat**
- **Paint/Gloss**
- **Plexiglas**
- **Polyurethane**
- **Vinyl Clothing**
- **Vinyl Wallcovering**

- **Alabaster** • **Marble**

Immediately wipe up the spill with a cloth or sponge dipped in warm sudsy water. Rinse well and wipe dry. If a stain persists, soak an absorbent pad in rubbing alcohol, wring almost dry, and place over the stain. Wait 5 minutes and apply an absorbent pad soaked in ammonia and squeezed nearly dry. Alternate alcohol and ammonia pads until stain has been removed. Wipe surface with a cloth moistened with cool clear water and wipe dry with a clean cloth.

- **Asphalt** • **Cork**
- **Linoleum**
- **Vinyl Tile**

Wipe up any excess with a cloth or sponge dipped in warm sudsy water. Rinse well and wipe dry. If a stain persists, cover the stain with an absorbent pad soaked in rubbing alcohol. Let it remain in place for several minutes, then wipe the area with a cloth dampened with ammonia —do not use ammonia on linoleum or vinyl floor tile. Rinse well with a cloth dipped in warm sudsy water and re-wipe with a cloth dampened with clear water. Allow to dry and polish or wax the surface.

- **Bluestone** • **Brick**
- **Concrete**
- **Flagstone**
- **Granite**
- **Limestone**
- **Masonry Tile**

Wipe up the excess dye. Wash with a solution of washing soda or detergent (not soap) and water. Use a cloth or soft-bristled brush to help scrub. Rinse thoroughly with clear water and allow to dry.

(continued)

•Sandstone •Slate •Terrazzo	*(see base of preceding page)*

•Carpet/Wool •Silk •Wool	Sponge* with water, then apply a Wet Spotter and a few drops of white vinegar. Blot frequently as the stain is loosened. Keep the stain moist with Wet Spotter and vinegar. Flush* with water when no more stain is removed. If stain remains, apply rubbing alcohol to the stain and cover with an absorbent pad moistened with alcohol. Let it remain as long as stain is being removed. Change the pad as it picks up the stain. Keep the stain and pad moist with alcohol. Allow to air dry.

•Cotton •Linen	Soak in a solution of 1 quart warm water, ½ teaspoon dishwashing detergent, and 1 tablespoon ammonia for 30 minutes. Rinse with water. Apply rubbing alcohol and tamp* or scrape.* Keep the stain moist with alcohol and blot occasionally. Continue as long as stain is being removed. Flush* with water and allow to dry. Launder as soon as possible.

•Grout	Wipe up excess with a cloth dipped in warm sudsy water. If any stain persists, apply **Afta Tile & Grout Cleaner** or dip a wet toothbrush into baking soda or powdered cleanser. Gently scrub the spot. Rinse well and wipe dry.

•Leather •Suede	Dye will immediately change the color of these materials. Once contact has been made, there is no way to remove the stain.

•Wood	Mix dishwashing detergent in hot water and swish to make a great vol-

(continued)

See Chapter 4 for specific technique instructions.

(continued from preceding page) ume of suds. Dip a cloth in only the foam and apply. Rinse with a clean cloth moistened with clear water. Polish or wax as soon as possible.

Dye/Red

- **Acetate**
- **Carpet/Synthetic**
- **Carpet/Wool**
- **Fiberglass** • **Rayon**
- **Silk** • **Triacetate**
- **Wool**

Sponge* the area immediately with water to dilute the spill. Carefully use a spot remover, **Amway Remove Fabric Spot Cleaner.** Apply a Wet Spotter and a few drops of ammonia. (Use ammonia sparingly on silk and wool.) Cover with an absorbent pad dampened with the Wet Spotter. Let the pad remain as long as any stain is being removed. Change the pad as it picks up the stain. Keep both the stain and pad moist with Wet Spotter and ammonia. Flush* well with water and repeat if necessary. If, after allowing to dry, a stain still persists, mix a little **Rit Color Remover** according to package direction. After testing on an inconspicuous place, flush it through the stain to an absorbent pad. When dealing with carpet, sponge it on the stain and blot with an absorbent pad. Rinse well with water and allow to dry thoroughly.

- **Acrylic Fabric**
- **Cotton** • **Linen**
- **Modacrylic** • **Nylon**
- **Olefin** • **Polyester**
- **Spandex**

Soak the item in a solution of 1 quart warm water, ½ teaspoon liquid dishwashing or laundry detergent, and 1 tablespoon ammonia for 30 minutes. Rinse well. If stain persists, soak in a solution of 1 quart warm water and 1 tablespoon white vinegar for 1 hour. Use white vinegar with care on cotton and linen. Rinse well with water and allow to dry. If stain is set, try applying rubbing alcohol to the area and tamping.* As stain loosens, blot liquid and

(continued)

*See Chapter 4 for specific technique instructions.

(continued from preceding page) stain with absorbent pad. Keep both the stain and pad moist with alcohol and change pad as it picks up stain. Allow to dry. As a last resort for any remaining traces of stain, mix **Rit Color Remover** according to package direction and apply to stain. After testing on a hidden place, flush* the solution through the stain. Rinse well with clear water and allow to dry thoroughly.

- **Acrylic Plastic**
- **Aluminum**
- **Bamboo** **Cane**
- **Ceramic Glass/Tile**
- **Glass** **Paint/Flat**
- **Paint/Gloss**
- **Plexiglas**
- **Polyurethane**
- **Vinyl Clothing**
- **Vinyl Wallcovering**

Immediately wipe up the spill with a cloth or sponge dipped in warm sudsy water. Rinse well and wipe dry.

- **Alabaster** **Marble**

Immediately wipe up the spill with a cloth or sponge dipped in warm sudsy water. Rinse well and wipe dry. If a stain persists, soak an absorbent pad in rubbing alcohol, wring dry, and place over the stain. Wait 5 minutes and apply an absorbent pad soaked in ammonia and wrung out. Alternate the alcohol and ammonia pads until stain has been removed. Wipe surface with cloth dampened with clear water, then wipe dry with clean cloth.

- **Asphalt** **Cork**
- **Linoleum**
- **Vinyl Tile**

Wipe up any excess with a cloth or sponge dipped in warm sudsy water. Rinse well and wipe dry. If a stain remains, cover it with an absorbent pad soaked in rubbing alcohol. Let it remain in place for several minutes, then wipe the area with a cloth *(continued)*

See Chapter 4 for specific technique instructions.

(continued from preceding page) dampened with ammonia. Do not use ammonia on linoleum or vinyl floor tile. Rinse well with cloth dipped in warm sudsy water and rewipe with a cloth dipped in clear water and squeezed almost dry. Allow to dry.

●**Bluestone** ●**Brick** ●**Concrete** ●**Flagstone** ●**Granite** ●**Limestone** ●**Masonry Tile** ●**Sandstone** ●**Slate** ●**Terrazzo**	Wipe up excess dye. Wash with a solution of washing soda or detergent (not soap) and water. Use a cloth or soft-bristled brush to help scrub. Rinse thoroughly with clear water and allow to dry.
●**Grout**	Wipe up excess with a cloth dipped in warm sudsy water. If any stain persists, dip a wet toothbrush into a little baking soda or powdered cleanser, or apply **Afta Tile & Grout Cleaner** and gently scrub the stain. Rinse well with water and wipe dry.
●**Leather** ●**Suede**	Dye will immediately act on the color of the hide. Once contact has been made, there is no way to remove the color.
●**Wood**	Mix dishwashing detergent in hot water and swish to make a great volume of suds. Dip a cloth in only the foam and apply. Rinse with a clean cloth dipped in clear water and wrung out. Polish or wax as soon as possible.

Dye/Yellow

●**Acetate** ●**Carpet/Synthetic** ●**Carpet/Wool** *(continued)*	Sponge* the area with dry-cleaning solvent, either **Carbona No. 10 Special Spot Remover/Carbona**

*See Chapter 4 for specific technique instructions.

(continued from preceding page)

●Fiberglass ●Rayon ●Silk ●Triacetate ●Wool

Cleaning Fluid, K2r Spot-lifter (tube), or **Afta Cleaning Fluid.** Then apply a Dry Spotter and tamp* or scrape* to loosen the stain. Flush* with one of the liquid dry-cleaning solvents. If stain persists, apply amyl acetate and tamp again. Flush with the dry-cleaning solvent and allow to dry. If any trace still remains, sponge stain with water and apply a few drops of white vinegar. Tamp or scrape again. Apply a Wet Spotter and a few drops of ammonia, then tamp again. Allow to dry. Sponge with rubbing alcohol and pat with a pad dampened with alcohol—do not use alcohol on acetate, rayon, or triacetate. Allow to dry.

●Acrylic Fabric ●Cotton ●Linen ●Modacrylic ●Nylon ●Olefin ●Polyester ●Spandex

Cover the stain with a rubbing alcohol compress (dilute alcohol with 2 parts water for acrylic and modacrylic and pretest its effects). Let the compress remain for a few minutes, then wipe stain with a cloth dampened with ammonia. If stain persists, sponge* area with either **Carbona No. 10 Special Spot Remover/Carbona Cleaning Fluid, K2r Spot-lifter** (aerosol), or **Afta Cleaning Fluid.** Then apply a Dry Spotter. Tamp* or scrape* to loosen the stain. Flush* with one of the liquid dry-cleaning solvents. If stain persists, apply amyl acetate and tamp again. Flush with the dry-cleaning solvent. If stain still remains, sponge with water and apply a Wet Spotter and a few drops of white vinegar—do not use vinegar on cotton or linen. Tamp again, then apply a Wet Spotter and a few drops of ammonia. Flush with the dry-cleaning solvent and allow to dry.

See Chapter 4 for specific technique instructions.

•Acrylic Plastic •Aluminum •Bamboo •Cane •Ceramic Glass/Tile •Glass •Paint/Flat •Paint/Gloss •Plexiglas •Polyurethane •Vinyl Clothing •Vinyl Wallcovering	Immediately wipe up the spill with a cloth or sponge dipped in warm sudsy water. Rinse well and wipe dry.
•Alabaster •Marble	Immediately wipe up the spill with a cloth or sponge dipped in warm sudsy water. Rinse well and wipe dry. If a stain persists, soak an absorbent pad in rubbing alcohol and place it over the stain. Wait 5 minutes, then apply an absorbent pad soaked with ammonia. Alternate pads until stain has been removed. Rinse surface with cloth dampened with clear water. Wipe dry with clean cloth.
•Asphalt •Cork •Linoleum •Vinyl Tile	Wipe up any excess with a cloth or sponge dipped in warm sudsy water. Rinse well and wipe dry. If stain remains, cover with an absorbent pad soaked in rubbing alcohol. Let it remain in place for several minutes, then wipe the area with a cloth dampened with ammonia. Do not use ammonia on linoleum or vinyl floor tile. Rinse with cloth dipped in warm sudsy water and follow with cloth dampened with clear water. Allow to dry.
•Bluestone •Brick •Concrete •Flagstone •Granite •Limestone •Masonry Tile	Wipe up excess dye. Wash with a solution of washing soda or detergent (not soap) and water. Use a cloth or soft-bristled brush to help scrub. Rinse thoroughly with clear water and allow to dry.

(continued)

•Sandstone •Slate •Terrazzo	*(see base of preceding page)*
•Grout	Wipe up any excess spill with a cloth dipped in warm sudsy water. If any stain persists, dip a wet toothbrush into a little baking soda or powdered cleanser, or use **Afta Tile & Grout Cleaner.** Gently scrub the stain. Rinse thoroughly and wipe dry.
•Leather •Suede	Dye will immediately discolor these materials on contact. There is no way to remove this discoloration, as it is absorbed into the hide.
•Wood	Mix dishwashing detergent in hot water and swish to make a great volume of suds. Dip a cloth in only the foam and apply. Rise with a clean cloth dampened with clear water. Polish or wax as soon as possible.

Egg

•Acetate •Burlap •Carpet/Synthetic •Carpet/Wool •Fiberglass •Rayon •Rope •Silk •Triacetate •Wool	Remove the excess material, then sponge with a dry-cleaning solvent, either **Carbona No. 10 Special Spot Remover/Carbona Cleaning Fluid, K2r Spot-lifter** (tube), or **Afta Cleaning Fluid.** Then apply a Dry Spotter to the stain and cover with an absorbent pad dampened with Dry Spotter. Let it stand as long as any stain is being removed. Change the pad as it picks up the stain. Keep the pad and stain moist with the Dry Spotter. Flush* with one of the liquid dry-cleaning solvents. If any stain remains, moisten it with a solution of 1 cup warm water and 1 teaspoon **Axion,** an enzyme presoak product —do not use on silk or wool. Cover

(continued)

*See Chapter 4 for specific technique instructions.

(continued from preceding page) with a clean pad that has been dipped in the solution and wrung almost dry. Let it stand 30 minutes. Add more solution if needed to keep the area warm and moist, but do not allow the wet area to spread. When no more stain is being lifted, flush with water.

•Acrylic Fabric
•Cotton •Linen
•Modacrylic •Nylon
•Olefin •Polyester
•Spandex

Scrape* to remove the excess and sponge* the stain with a dry-cleaning solvent, **Carbona No. 10 Special Spot Remover/Carbona Cleaning Fluid, K2r Spot-Lifter** (aerosol), or **Afta Cleaning Fluid.** Then apply a Dry Spotter to the stain and cover with an absorbent pad dampened with Dry Spotter. Let it stand as long as any stain is being removed. Change the pad as it picks up the stain. Keep both stain and pad moist with Dry Spotter. Flush* with one of the liquid dry-cleaning solvents. If any stain persists, apply a few drops of dishwashing detergent and a few drops of ammonia to the stain, then tamp* or scrape. Keep the stain moist with the detergent and ammonia and blot occasionally with an absorbent pad. Flush well with water to remove all ammonia. Allow to dry. If stain still remains, moisten it with a solution of 1 cup warm water and 1 teaspoon **Axion** or **Biz** (enzyme presoak products). Cover with a clean pad that has been dipped in the solution and wrung almost dry. Let it stand 30 minutes. Add more solution if needed to keep the area warm and moist, but do not allow the wet area to spread. When no more stain is being lifted, thoroughly flush the area with water.

•Acrylic Plastic
•Alabaster

(continued)

Scrape* up any excess egg with a dull knife. Wipe the area with a cloth

---

See Chapter 4 for specific technique instructions.

(continued from preceding page)

- **Aluminum**
- **Asphalt** ● **Bamboo**
- **Brass** ● **Bronze**
- **Cane**
- **Ceramic Glass/Tile**
- **Copper** ● **Cork**
- **Enamel** ● **Glass**
- **Gold** ● **Iron** ● **Ivory**
- **Jade** ● **Linoleum**
- **Marble** ● **Paint/Flat**
- **Paint/Gloss**
- **Pewter** ● **Plexiglas**
- **Polyurethane**
- **Porcelain Dishes**
- **Porcelain Fixtures**
- **Stainless Steel**
- **Tin** ● **Vinyl Clothing**
- **Vinyl Tile**
- **Vinyl Wallcovering**

or sponge dipped in warm sudsy water. Rinse well and wipe dry.

- **Bluestone** ● **Brick**
- **Concrete**
- **Flagstone**
- **Granite**
- **Limestone**
- **Masonry Tile**
- **Sandstone**
- **Slate**
- **Terrazzo**

Wipe up the excess. Wash with a solution of washing soda or detergent (never soap) and water. Use a cloth or soft-bristled brush. Rinse thoroughly with clear water and allow to air dry.

- **Felt** ● **Fur/Natural**
- **Fur/Synthetic**

Very gently scrape* the excess material from the surface. Mix dishwashing detergent in hot water and swish to make a great volume of suds. Dip a cloth in only the foam and apply. Wipe with a clean dry cloth. If a grease stain remains, powder the area with an absorbent such as cornmeal. Give it plenty of time to work, then gently brush* it out. Repeat if

(continued)

---

*See Chapter 4 for specific technique instructions.

(continued from preceding page) necessary. Using a damp cloth, gently remove any remaining powder.

•Grout

Wipe up the excess with a cloth dipped in warm sudsy water. If any stain remains, apply **Afta Tile & Grout Cleaner** or dip a wet toothbrush into a little powdered cleanser and gently scrub the spot. Rinse well with clear water and wipe dry.

•Leather •Suede

Very gently scrape* the excess egg. Mix a solution of mild soap in lukewarm water. Swish to create a great volume of suds. Apply only the foam with a sponge. Dry with a clean cloth. If a grease stain remains, powder the area with an absorbent such as cornmeal, allowing enough time for it to work. Gently brush* it off and repeat if necessary. On leather only, follow with **The Tannery** or **Fiebing's Saddle Soap** to condition the leather.

•Silver

Remove any excess spill. Wash as soon as possible in hot sudsy water. Rinse in hot water and dry immediately with a soft cloth to prevent tarnish.

•Wallpaper

Carefully wipe up the excess. With a cloth or sponge moistened with cool clear water, wipe the area. Overlap strokes to prevent streaking. Gently pat dry.

•Wood

Mix dishwashing detergent in hot water and swish to make a great volume of suds. Dip a cloth in only the foam and wipe off egg residue. Rinse with a clean cloth moistened with clear water. Polish or wax as soon as possible.

*See Chapter 4 for specific technique instructions.

Eyeliner/Eye Pencil/ Eyeshadow

- Acetate
- Carpet/Synthetic
- Carpet/Wool
- Fiberglass • Rayon
- Silk • Triacetate
- Wool

Brush* or blot up any excess, taking care not to spread the stain. Flush* with a dry-cleaning solvent, either **Carbona No. 10 Special Spot Remover/Carbona Cleaning Fluid** or **Afta Cleaning Fluid.** Apply a Dry Spotter to the stain and cover with an absorbent pad dampened with the Dry Spotter. Check the stain every 5 minutes. Before changing pads, press hard against the stain. Continue the alternate soaking and pressing until no more stain is being removed. Flush with one of the dry-cleaning solvents and allow to dry. If any stain remains, flush it with water and apply a Wet Spotter with a few drops of ammonia. (Do not use ammonia on silk or wool.) Cover with an absorbent pad dampened with the Wet Spotter. Let it stand as long as any stain is being removed. Change the pad as it picks up the stain. Keep the stain and pad moist. Flush well with water. Repeat if necessary; allow to dry.

- Acrylic Fabric
- Cotton • Linen
- Modacrylic • Nylon
- Olefin • Polyester
- Spandex

Brush* or blot away any excess, taking care not to spread the stain. Flush* with a dry-cleaning solvent, either **Carbona No. 10 Special Spot Remover/Carbona Cleaning Fluid** or **Afta Cleaning Fluid.** Apply a Dry Spotter to the stain and cover with a cloth dampened with the Dry Spotter. Check the stain often, tamping* before changing the pad. Continue alternate soaking and tamping until no more stain is lifted. Flush with one of the dry-cleaning solvents and
(continued)

*See Chapter 4 for specific technique instructions.

(continued from preceding page) allow to dry. If any stain remains, try the same procedure of soaking and tamping, using a Wet Spotter and a few drops of ammonia. When the stain is gone, be sure to flush the area with water to remove all traces of ammonia. Launder as soon as possible.

- **Acrylic Plastic**
- **Alabaster**
- **Asphalt** • **Bamboo**
- **Cane**
- **Ceramic Glass/Tile**
- **Cork** • **Enamel**
- **Glass** • **Gold**
- **Ivory** • **Jade**
- **Linoleum** • **Marble**
- **Paint/Flat**
- **Paint/Gloss**
- **Plexiglas**
- **Polyurethane**
- **Stainless Steel**
- **Vinyl Clothing**
- **Vinyl Tile**
- **Vinyl Wallcovering**

Wipe any spills or brush* away any excess. With a cloth or sponge dipped in warm sudsy water, wash the surface. Rinse well with water and wipe dry with a clean cloth.

- **Bluestone**
- **Limestone**
- **Masonry Tile**
- **Sandstone** • **Slate**
- **Terrazzo**

Wipe up excess. Mix a solution of washing soda or detergent (not soap) and water. Wash the stained area. Rinse well with clear water and allow to dry.

- **Leather** • **Suede**

Gently remove excess. Mix a solution of mild soap in lukewarm water. Swish to create a great volume of suds. Apply only the foam with a sponge. Wipe dry with a clean cloth. If a greasy or oily stain remains, powder it with an absorbent such as cornmeal. Give it plenty of time to work. Gently brush* or shake the absorbent from the surface. Repeat if necessary. On leather only, follow with **The**

(continued)

---

*See Chapter 4 for specific technique instructions.

(continued from preceding page) **Tannery** or **Fiebing's Saddle Soap** to condition the leather.

●**Wood**	Mix dishwashing detergent in hot water and swish to make a great volume of suds. Dip a cloth in only the foam and apply to the stain. Rinse with clear water. Wipe dry immediately with a soft cloth and polish or wax as usual.

Fabric Softener

●**Acetate** ●**Carpet/Synthetic** ●**Carpet/Wool** ●**Fiberglass** ●**Rayon** ●**Silk** ●**Triacetate** ●**Wool**	Dampen the stain with water and rub gently with bar soap (do not use a dedorant-type soap). Or, rub the area with liquid laundry detergent or **Shout Laundry Soil & Stain Remover.** Rinse thoroughly with clear water, then blot the excess liquid and allow to dry.
●**Acrylic Fabric** ●**Cotton** ●**Linen** ●**Modacrylic** ●**Nylon** ●**Olefin** ●**Polyester** ●**Spandex**	Dampen the area with water and gently rub with bar soap (do not use a deodorant-type soap). Or, rub the area with liquid laundry detergent or **Shout Laundry Soil & Stain Remover.** Rinse thoroughly. Blot the excess liquid and launder as soon as possible.
●**Acrylic Plastic** ●**Aluminum** ●**Asphalt** ●**Ceramic Glass/Tile** ●**Cork** ●**Glass** ●**Linoleum** ●**Paint/Flat** ●**Paint/Gloss** ●**Plexiglas** ●**Polyurethane** ●**Porcelain Dishes**	Wipe up any excess spill immediately, as the chemicals can injure the surface. Wipe the area with a cloth or sponge dipped in warm sudsy water. Rinse well and wipe dry.

(continued)

- **Porcelain Fixtures**   *(see base of preceding page)*
- **Vinyl Clothing**
- **Vinyl Tile**
- **Vinyl Wallcovering**

Face Powder

- **Acetate**
- **Carpet/Synthetic**
- **Carpet/Wool**
- **Fiberglass** •**Rayon**
- **Silk** •**Triacetate**
- **Wool**

Brush* or blot up any excess, taking care not to spread the stain. Flush* with a dry-cleaning solvent—**Carbona No. 10 Special Spot Remover/Carbona Cleaning Fluid** or **Afta Cleaning Fluid.** Apply a Dry Spotter to the stain and cover with an absorbent pad dampened with the Dry Spotter. Check the stain every 5 minutes. Before changing pads, press hard against the stain. Continue the alternate soaking and pressing until no more stain is being removed. Flush* with one of the dry-cleaning solvents and allow to dry. If any stain remains, flush it with water and apply a Wet Spotter with a few drops of ammonia. (Do not use ammonia on silk or wool.) Cover with an absorbent pad dampened with the Wet Spotter. Let it stand as long as any stain is being removed. Change the pad as it picks up the stain. Keep the stain and pad moist. Flush well with water. Repeat if necessary; allow to dry.

- **Acrylic Fabric**
- **Cotton** •**Linen**
- **Modacrylic** •**Nylon**
- **Olefin** •**Polyester**
- **Spandex**

Brush* or blot away any excess, taking care not to spread the stain. Flush* with a dry-cleaning solvent, either **Carbona No. 10 Special Spot Remover/Carbona Cleaning Fluid** or **Afta Cleaning Fluid.** Apply a Dry Spotter to the stain and cover with a cloth dampened with the Dry Spotter. Check the stain often, tamping* be-

(continued)

See Chapter 4 for specific technique instructions.

(continued from preceding page) fore changing the pad. Continue alternate soaking and tamping until no more stain is lifted. Flush with a dry-cleaning solvent and allow to dry. If any stain remains, try the same procedure of soaking and tamping using a Wet Spotter and a few drops of ammonia. When the stain is gone, be sure to flush the area with water to remove all traces of ammonia. Launder as soon as possible.

- **Acrylic Plastic**
- **Alabaster**
- **Asphalt** • **Bamboo**
- **Cane**
- **Ceramic Glass/Tile**
- **Cork** • **Enamel**
- **Glass** • **Gold**
- **Ivory** • **Jade**
- **Linoleum** • **Marble**
- **Paint/Flat**
- **Paint/Gloss**
- **Plexiglas**
- **Polyurethane**
- **Stainless Steel**
- **Vinyl Clothing**
- **Vinyl Tile**
- **Vinyl Wallcovering**

Wipe any spills or brush* away any excess. With a cloth or sponge dipped in warm sudsy water, wash the surface. Rinse well with water and wipe dry with a clean cloth.

- **Bluestone**
- **Masonry Tile**
- **Sandstone** • **Slate**
- **Terrazzo**

Remove excess. Mix a solution of washing soda or detergent (not soap) and water. Wash the stained area. Rinse well with clear water and allow to dry.

- **Leather** • **Suede**

Gently remove excess. Mix a solution of mild soap in lukewarm water. Swish to create a great volume of suds. Apply only the foam with a sponge. Wipe dry with a clean cloth. If a greasy or oily stain remains, powder it with an absorbent such as corn-

(continued)

---

*See Chapter 4 for specific technique instructions.

(continued from preceding page) meal. Give it plenty of time to work. Gently brush* or shake the absorbent from the surface. Repeat if necessary. On leather only, follow with **The Tannery** or **Fiebing's Saddle Soap** to condition the leather.

●**Wood**

Mix dishwashing detergent in hot water and swish to make a great volume of suds. Dip a cloth in only the foam and apply. Rinse with clean water. Wipe dry immediately with a soft cloth and polish or wax as usual.

Fingernail Polish

●**Acetate**
●**Fiberglass** ●**Rayon**
●**Silk** ●**Triacetate**
●**Wool**

Immediately scrape* any excess with a dull knife or spatula. Apply a Dry Spotter to the stain and cover with an absorbent pad dampened with Dry Spotter. Let it stand as long as any stain is being removed. Keep the pad and stain moist. Flush* with a dry-cleaning solvent, either **Carbona No. 10 Special Spot Remover/Carbona Cleaning Fluid** or **Afta Cleaning Fluid.** Allow to dry.

●**Acrylic Fabric**
●**Burlap** ●**Cotton**
●**Linen** ●**Modacrylic**
●**Nylon** ●**Olefin**
●**Polyester** ●**Rope**
●**Spandex**

Scrape* the excess. Test acetone on an inconspicuous place. If fiber color doesn't change, flush* acetone through the stain to an absorbent pad. When no more stain is being removed, change pads and flush well with dry-cleaning solvent, **Carbona No. 10 Special Spot Remover/Carbona Cleaning Fluid.** Allow to dry thoroughly.

●**Acrylic Plastic**
●**Asphalt** ●**Cork**
●**Linoleum**
●**Plexiglas**
(continued)

Fingernail polish contains chemicals that can quickly ruin the surface. Immediately scrape* up any excess spill. Dab the area with a cloth dipped

See Chapter 4 for specific technique instructions.

(continued from preceding page)

●**Polyurethane**
●**Vinyl Clothing**
●**Vinyl Tile**
●**Vinyl Wallcovering**

in amyl acetate and rinse, but this stain may be permanent.

●**Alabaster** ●**Marble**

Wipe up the excess immediately. Wipe the area with a cloth dampened with acetone. Rinse with a damp cloth and wipe dry. If any stain remains, make a poultice of water, 3% hydrogen peroxide, and a mild powder detergent. Apply the poultice to the stain and cover with a damp cloth. When the stain has been bleached out, rinse thoroughly and dry.

●**Aluminum** ●**Iron**
●**Stainless Steel**
●**Tin**

Wipe excess immediately. Since these surfaces aren't porous, there shouldn't be a stain, only a mild discoloration. To remove this discoloration, wash with a steel wool soap pad, rinse thoroughly, and dry.

●**Bamboo** ●**Cane**

Remove the excess and wipe the area with a cloth dipped in mild pure soapsuds to which a little ammonia has been added. If any stain remains, dip the edge of a clean cloth in acetone and gently dab at the stain—be careful not to force the stain into the plant fibers. If not treated immediately, this could be a permanent stain.

●**Bluestone** ●**Brick**
●**Concrete**
●**Flagstone**
●**Granite**
●**Limestone**
●**Masonry Tile**
●**Sandstone** ●**Slate**
●**Terrazzo**

Remove the excess as soon as possible. With a cloth dipped in acetone, dab at the remaining stain until no more is picked up. Wash the area using a soft-bristled brush with a solution of washing soda or detergent and water. Rinse with clear water and allow to dry.

•Carpet/Synthetic **•Carpet/Wool**	Scrape* as much of the excess as you can without forcing it into the pile. Apply amyl acetate to the stain and cover with an absorbent pad dampened with amyl acetate. Keep moist and let stand for about 15 minutes, blotting occasionally. Scrape to help loosen the stain. Flush* carefully with a dry-cleaning solvent, either **Afta Cleaning Fluid** or **Carbona No. 10 Special Spot Remover/Carbona Cleaning Fluid.** Allow to thoroughly dry.
•Ceramic Glass/Tile **•Enamel •Glass** **•Gold** **•Platinum** **•Porcelain** **•Rhinestones** **•Silver**	Wipe up excess polish as soon as possible. Wash with a cloth dipped in a solution of washing soda, water, and a few drops of ammonia. Rinse well and wipe dry. Hardened polish can sometimes be carefully scraped* away with a razor blade on ceramic tile, enamel, and glass.
•Grout	With a sponge, blot up as much polish as possible. Apply **Afta Tile & Grout Cleaner** or dip a wet toothbrush into a little powdered cleanser and scrub gently. Rinse well with clear water and wipe dry.
•Jade •Opal **•Pearls (except** **simulated)**	Blot up excess polish. Fingernail polish may permanently damage natural and cultured pearls and mother-of-pearl. A cotton swab moistened with oily fingernail polish remover (not acetone-based polish remover) and gently dabbed on the stain may be effective. After stained setting has been moistened, blot up stain with a dry cotton swab.
•Leather •Suede	Carefully scrape* excess with a dull knife or spatula. Mix a solution of mild soap in lukewarm water. Swish to

(continued)

*See Chapter 4 for specific technique instructions.

(continued from preceding page) create a great volume of suds. Apply only the foam with a sponge, but avoid spreading the stain. Dry with a clean cloth. If the polish has hardened, try gently rubbing an artgum eraser across it. As a last resort, cautiously file the area with an emery board or a piece of very fine (grade 6/0–8/0) sandpaper. As a thin layer of hide is removed, work carefully.

●**Paint/Flat**
●**Paint/Gloss**

Wipe away the excess, being careful not to spread the polish. Wipe the stain with a cloth dipped in ⅓ quart warm sudsy water to which 1 teaspoon borax has been added. Rinse with clear water and dry thoroughly.

Floor Wax

●**Acetate**
●**Carpet/Synthetic**
●**Carpet/Wool**
●**Rayon** ●**Silk**
●**Triacetate**
●**Wool**

Sponge* the area with a dry-cleaning solvent, either **Carbona No. 10 Special Spot Remover/Carbona Cleaning Fluid** or **K2r Spot-lifter** (tube). Then apply a Dry Spotter to the stain and cover with an absorbent pad dampened with Dry Spotter. Let it stand as long as any stain is being picked up. Change the pad as it removes the stain. Keep both the stained area and the pad moist with Dry Spotter. Flush* with a dry-cleaning solvent and allow to dry. If any stain remains, sponge with water and apply a few drops of ammonia (take care when using ammonia on silk and wool). Cover with an absorbent pad dampened with Wet Spotter. Let stand as long as any stain is being removed. Change the pad as it picks up the stain. Keep stain and pad moist with Wet Spotter and ammonia. Flush with water. Repeat until no more stain is removed.

See Chapter 4 for specific technique instructions.

- **Acrylic Fabric**
- **Cotton** • **Linen**
- **Modacrylic** • **Nylon**
- **Olefin** • **Polyester**
- **Spandex**

Remove any excess wax, then sponge* the area with a dry-cleaning solvent—**Carbona No. 10 Special Spot Remover/Carbona Cleaning Fluid** or **K2r Spot-lifter** (aerosol). Apply a Dry Spotter to the stain and cover with an absorbent pad dampened with the Dry Spotter. Let it stand as long as any stain is being removed. To help remove stubborn wax, tamp* the area, adding Dry Spotter as needed to keep it moist. Flush* the area with one of the liquid dry-cleaning solvents and allow to dry. If a stain persists, sponge it with water and apply a few drops of ammonia along with a Wet Spotter. Cover the area with an absorbent pad and let it remain as long as any stain is being removed. Change the pad as it picks up the stain. Keep the stain and pad moist with Wet Spotter and ammonia. Tamping again will help break up the stain. Flush with water. Repeat if necessary.

- **Acrylic Plastic**
- **Alabaster**
- **Asphalt** • **Bamboo**
- **Cane**
- **Ceramic Glass/Tile**
- **Cork** • **Paint/Flat**
- **Paint/Gloss**
- **Plexiglas**
- **Polyurethane**
- **Porcelain Dishes**
- **Porcelain Fixtures**
- **Vinyl Clothing**
- **Vinyl Wallcovering**

Remove any excess wax. Wipe the surface with a cloth or sponge dipped in warm sudsy water to which a few drops of ammonia have been added. Rinse well and wipe dry with a clean cloth.

- **Leather** • **Suede**

Blot up any excess wax. Apply **The Tannery** on leather or **Child Life Suede & Fabric Cleaner** on suede.

(continued)

See Chapter 4 for specific technique instructions.

(continued from preceding page) Rub it in with a soft cloth and allow it to dry. Next, if any waxy residue remains, test a dry-cleaning solvent, **Carbona No. 10 Special Spot Remover/Carbona Cleaning Fluid,** on an inconspicuous place; then if no color change occurs, gingerly apply. Allow to dry. On leather only, follow with **The Tannery** or **Fiebing's Saddle Soap** to condition the leather.

●**Wood**

Gently wipe up the excess with a cloth dipped in the suds of a mild detergent and water to which a small amount of ammonia has been added. Rinse well with a clean cloth moistened with the solution. Polish or wax as soon as possible.

Flowers *(Follow procedures for Grass.)*

Food Coloring *(See Dye, Dye/Red, Dye/Yellow.)*

Fruits *(See Apple, Berries, Cherry, Grape, Orange, Prune.)*

Furniture Polish

●**Acetate**
●**Fiberglass** ●**Rayon**
●**Silk** ●**Triacetate**
●**Wool**

Blot up the excess. Sponge* with a dry-cleaning solvent, either **Carbona No. 10 Special Spot Remover/Carbona Cleaning Fluid** or **Afta Cleaning Fluid.** Or, spray on **Amway Remove Fabric Spot Cleaner.** Apply a Dry Spotter and cover with an absorbent pad dampened with Dry Spotter. Check the stain every 5 minutes and change pads as they absorb the *(continued)*

*See Chapter 4 for specific technique instructions.

(continued from preceding page) stain. Press hard against the stain as you check it. Continue the alternate soaking and pressing until all the stain has been removed. Flush* with one of the dry-cleaning solvents and allow to dry. If any stain remains, sponge the stain with water and apply a Wet Spotter and a few drops of white vinegar. Cover with an absorbent pad dampened with the Wet Spotter. Let stand as long as any stain is being removed. Change the pad as it picks up the stain. Keep the stain and pad moist with Wet Spotter and vinegar. Flush with water and repeat until no more stain is visible. Flush with water and allow to dry.

●**Acrylic Fabric**
●**Cotton** ●**Linen**
●**Modacrylic** ●**Nylon**
●**Olefin** ●**Polyester**
●**Spandex**

Blot up the excess polish. Apply a Dry Spotter and cover with an absorbent pad dampened with Dry Spotter. Tamp* the stain, then press the pad into the stained area to absorb any loosened material. Continue tamping and pressing until the stain has been removed. Flush* with a dry-cleaning solvent, either **Carbona No. 10 Special Spot Remover/Carbona Cleaning Fluid** or **Afta Cleaning Fluid,** and allow to dry. If any stain remains, spray on **Amway Remove Fabric Spot Cleaner** or sponge* the area with water, then apply Wet Spotter and a few drops of white vinegar (do not use vinegar on cotton or linen).Tamp the area and blot up the material with a dry, clean absorbent pad. Keep the stain moist with Wet Spotter and vinegar. When no more stain is visible, flush well with water and allow to dry.

●**Aluminum**
●**Asphalt**
(continued)

Wipe up excess spill with a cloth or sponge dipped in warm sudsy water.

See Chapter 4 for specific technique instructions.

(continued from preceding page)

●Cork ●Glass
●Linoleum
●Porcelain Dishes
●Stainless Steel
●Vinyl Clothing
●Vinyl Tile
●Vinyl Wallcovering

Rinse well and wipe dry. If a waxy residue still exists, wipe again with cloth dipped in warm sudsy water to which a few drops of ammonia have been added. Rinse again and wipe dry with clean cloth.

●Bluestone ●Brick
●Concrete
●Flagstone

Wipe up the excess. Wash with a solution of washing soda or detergent (never soap) and water. Use a soft-bristled brush or soft cloth to scrub the area. Rinse thoroughly with clear water and allow to dry.

●Carpet/Synthetic
●Carpet/Wool

Scrape* to remove excess, then apply **Spot Shot Carpet Stain Remover** or **Stain-X Carpet Stain Remover.** Or, powder the stained area with an absorbent such as cornmeal. Let it stand, then brush* it out. If a stain still remains, spray on a foam rug shampoo or apply a Dry Spotter. Cover with an absorbent pad dampened with Dry Spotter. Check the stain every 5 minutes, changing pads as the stain is absorbed, and press hard against the stain. Continue to alternate applying Dry Spotter and pressing until all the stain has been removed. Gently sponge the area with a dry-cleaning solvent, either **Carbona No. 10 Special Spot Remover/Carbona Cleaning Fluid** or **Afta Cleaning Fluid.** Allow to dry. If a stain persists, sponge with water and apply a Wet Spotter and a few drops of white vinegar. Cover with an absorbent pad dampened with Wet Spotter. Let the pad remain as long as any stain is being removed. As the pad picks up the stain, change it. Keep the pad and stain moist with

(continued)

See Chapter 4 for specific technique instructions.

(continued from preceding page) Wet Spotter and vinegar, but avoid soaking the carpet. Sponge* with water and blot up excess liquid. Repeat until no more stain is removed and air dry.

●**Leather** ●**Suede**	Mix a solution of mild soap in luke-warm water. Swish to create a great volume of suds. Apply only the foam with a sponge. Wipe with a clean dry cloth. If a greasy or waxy stain remains, powder the area with an absorbent, such as fuller's earth or cornmeal, allowing plenty of time for it to work. Gently brush* the absorbent off. Repeat if necessary. On leather only, follow with **The Tannery** or **Fiebing's Saddle Soap** to condition the leather.
●**Silver**	Wash the item as soon as possible in hot sudsy water. Rinse in hot water and dry immediately with a soft cloth to prevent tarnish.

Gelatin

●**Acetate** ●**Carpet/Synthetic** ●**Carpet/Wool** ●**Fiberglass** ●**Rayon** ●**Silk** ●**Triacetate** ●**Wool**	Scrape* to remove excess. Make a poultice, or paste, with **Axion,** an enzyme presoak product—do not use on silk or wool. Let it stand on the stain for 15 minutes. Rinse thoroughly with water. For carpets, blot the excess water and allow to air dry. Be certain that all sugar has been removed. If any discoloration remains, treat it as a dye. (*See* Dye.)
●**Acrylic Fabric** ●**Cotton** ●**Linen** ●**Modacrylic** ●**Nylon** ●**Olefin** ●**Polyester** ●**Spandex**	Remove any excess material. Presoak* in **Shout Laundry Soil & Stain Remover** or **Magic Pre-Wash** as directed and launder as soon as possible.

See Chapter 4 for specific technique instructions.

- Acrylic Plastic
- Aluminum
- Asphalt •Bamboo
- Brass •Bronze
- Cane
- Ceramic Glass/Tile
- Copper •Cork
- Glass •Iron
- Linoleum
- Marble
- Paint/Flat
- Paint/Gloss
- Plexiglas
- Polyurethane
- Porcelain Dishes
- Porcelain Fixtures
- Stainless Steel
- Tin •Vinyl Clothing
- Vinyl Tile
- Vinyl Wallcovering

Remove any excess immediately, before it sets. Wipe the surface with a cloth dipped in warm sudsy water. Rinse well and wipe dry.

- Bluestone •Brick
- Concrete •Slate
- Terrazzo

Carefully remove any excess gelatin. Wash with a solution of washing soda or detergent (not soap) and water, using a cloth or soft-bristled brush. Rinse thoroughly with clear water and allow to dry.

- Felt •Leather
- Suede

Gently scrape* to remove excess. Mix a solution of mild soap in luke-warm water. Swish to create a great volume of suds. Apply only the foam with a sponge. Wipe with a clean dry cloth. If a sticky feeling persists, wipe again and dry. On leather only, follow with **The Tannery** or **Fiebing's Saddle Soap** to condition the leather.

- Silver

Wash item as soon as possible in hot sudsy water. Rinse in hot water and dry immediately with a soft cloth to prevent tarnish.

---

*See Chapter 4 for specific technique instructions.

•Wood

Gently wipe any excess gelatin. Mix dishwashing detergent in hot water and swish to make a great volume of suds. Dip a cloth in only the foam and apply to the stain. Rinse with a clean cloth dipped and wrung out in clear water. Polish or wax as may be needed.

Glue

•Acetate
•Fiberglass •Rayon
•Silk •Triacetate
•Wool

Immediately sponge* the area with water. Spray on **Amway Remove Fabric Spot Cleaner.** Then apply a Wet Spotter and a few drops of white vinegar. Cover with an absorbent pad dampened with Wet Spotter. Let it stand as long as any stain is being picked up. Change the pad as it removes the stain. Keep both the stain and pad moist with Wet Spotter and vinegar. Flush* with water and repeat until no more stain is removed. For a lingering stain, moisten the area with a solution of 1 cup warm water and 1 teaspoon **Axion,** an enzyme presoak product—do not use on silk or wool. Cover with a clean pad that has been dipped in the solution and wrung dry. Let it stand 30 minutes. Keep the area and pad moist and warm, but do not let the wet area spread. When no more stain is removed, flush thoroughly with water and allow to dry.

•Acrylic Fabric
•Cotton •Linen
•Modacrylic •Olefin
•Polyester •Rayon
•Spandex

Soak in a solution of 1 quart warm water, ½ teaspoon liquid dishwashing or laundry detergent, and 1 tablespoon white vinegar. (Omit vinegar when treating cotton and linen.) Let soak for 15 minutes and rinse well with water. Sponge cotton or linen only with rubbing alcohol. Launder if

(continued)

See Chapter 4 for specific technique instructions.

(continued from preceding page) possible. If not, presoak* in a solution of 1 quart warm water and 1 tablespoon **Axion** or **Biz** (enzyme presoak products) for 30 minutes. Rinse well and launder as soon as possible.

•**Acrylic Plastic** •**Aluminum** •**Asphalt** •**Ceramic Glass/Tile** •**Cork** •**Glass** •**Linoleum** •**Paint/Flat** •**Paint/Gloss** •**Plexiglas** •**Polyurethane** •**Porcelain Dishes** •**Vinyl Clothing** •**Vinyl Tile** •**Vinyl Wallcovering**	Remove as much glue as possible with a dull knife or spatula. Wipe surface with a cloth or sponge dipped in warm sudsy water. Rinse well and wipe dry.
•**Bluestone** •**Brick** •**Concrete** •**Flagstone** •**Granite** •**Limestone** •**Slate** •**Terrazzo**	Carefully scrape* to remove any excess material. Wash with a solution of washing soda or detergent (not soap) and water. Use a cloth or soft-bristled brush to scrub. Rinse thoroughly with clear water and allow to air dry.
•**Grout**	Wipe up excess with a cloth dipped in warm sudsy water. To remove any dried material, apply **Afta Tile & Grout Cleaner** or dip a wet toothbrush into a little powdered cleanser and gently scrub the stain. Rinse well and wipe dry with a clean cloth.
•**Leather** •**Suede**	Very gently scrape* to remove any excess material. Mix a solution of mild soap in lukewarm water. Swish to create a great volume of suds. Apply only the foam with a sponge. Wipe with a clean dry cloth. Repeat if *(continued)*

**See Chapter 4 for specific technique instructions.*

(continued from preceding page) necessary to remove any sticky traces. If suede needs conditioning, apply **Child Life Suede & Fabric Cleaner.** On leather, follow with **The Tannery** or **Fiebing's Saddle Soap** to condition the leather.

●**Wallpaper**

Gently rub the glue with an artgum eraser. Use small, gentle strokes so you won't tear the paper. When the glue has been removed, wipe the area with a cloth dampened with clear water to remove any eraser particles.

●**Wood**

Mix dishwashing detergent in hot water and swish to make a great volume of suds. Dip a cloth or sponge in only the foam and apply. Rinse with a clean cloth dampened with clear water. Polish or wax as soon as possible.

Grape

●**Acetate**
●**Carpet/Synthetic**
●**Carpet/Wool**
●**Fiberglass** ●**Rayon**
●**Rope** ●**Triacetate**
●**Wool**

Spray on **Amway Remove Fabric Spot Cleaner.** If stain remains, sponge* with cool water. Then sponge the area with lemon juice (or rub the cut sides of a slice of lemon over the stain). Flush* with water. Blot as much excess liquid as possible and allow to dry. If stain still persists, apply a Wet Spotter. Cover with an absorbent pad moistened with Wet Spotter. Let stand as long as any stain is being removed. Change the pad as it picks up the stain. Keep the pad and stained area moist with Wet Spotter. Flush with water. If any trace of stain still appears, moisten the area with a solution of 1 cup warm water and 1 teaspoon **Axion,** an enzyme presoak product—do not use
(continued)

*See Chapter 4 for specific technique instructions.

(continued from preceding page) on silk or wool. Cover with clean absorbent pad that has been dipped in the solution and wrung almost dry. Let it stand for 30 minutes. Add enough solution to keep the stain and pad moist, but do not allow the wet area to spread. When no more stain is visible, flush thoroughly with water and allow to air dry.

- **Acrylic Fabric**
- **Modacrylic •Nylon**
- **Olefin •Polyester**
- **Spandex**

Spray on **Amway Remove Fabric Spot Cleaner.** If stain remains, sponge* with cool water immediately. Then sponge with lemon juice or rub a lemon slice over the stain. Flush* with water. Blot as much excess liquid as possible and allow to dry. If any trace of stain still exists, presoak* in a solution of 1 quart warm water, ½ teaspoon liquid dishwashing or laundry detergent, and 1 tablespoon white vinegar for 15 minutes. Rinse with water and launder if possible. If not, soak in a solution of 1 quart water and 1 tablespoon **Axion,** an enzyme presoak product, for 30 minutes. Rinse well with water and launder as soon as possible.

- **Acrylic Plastic**
- **Aluminum**
- **Asphalt •Bamboo**
- **Brass •Bronze**
- **Cane**
- **Ceramic Glass/Tile**
- **Copper •Enamel**
- **Glass •Grout**
- **Iron •Paint/Flat**
- **Paint/Gloss**
- **Plexiglas**
- **Polyurethane**
- **Porcelain Dishes**
- **Porcelain Fixtures**

Wipe up any excess spill with a cloth or sponge dipped in warm sudsy water. Rinse well and wipe dry.

(continued)

See Chapter 4 for specific technique instructions.

●**Stainless Steel** ●**Vinyl Clothing** ●**Vinyl Wallcovering**	*(see base of preceding page)*

●**Bluestone** ●**Brick** ●**Concrete** ●**Flagstone** ●**Granite** ●**Masonry Tile** ●**Slate** ●**Terrazzo**	Wipe up excess spill. Wash area with a solution of washing soda or detergent (not soap) and water. Use a soft cloth or soft-bristled brush. Rinse thoroughly with clear water and allow to dry.

●**Cork** ●**Linoleum** ●**Vinyl Tile**	Wipe up excess spill and wash the area with a solution of washing soda or detergent and water. Use a soft-bristled brush or cloth to scrub gently. Rinse thoroughly with clear water and allow to dry. If stain persists, wipe area with a cloth dampened in a solution of 1 tablespoon oxalic acid and 1 pint water. Rinse well and wipe dry. Repolish the surface if necessary.

●**Cotton** ●**Linen**	Test fabric for colorfastness. If color doesn't change, stretch the stain over a bowl; fasten in place with a rubber band. Pour boiling water through the fabric from the height of 2 or 3 feet. Avoid splatters. This procedure must be done immediately. If stain persists, soak in a solution of 1 quart warm water and ½ teaspoon detergent for 15 minutes. Rinse with water. Sponge area with rubbing alcohol and launder if possible. If not, presoak* in a solution of 1 quart warm water and 1 tablespoon **Axion** or **Biz** (enzyme presoak products) for 30 minutes. Rinse well and launder.

●**Leather** ●**Suede**	Blot up any excess liquid. Mix a solution of mild soap in lukewarm water. Swish to create a great volume of suds. Apply only the foam with a *(continued)*

See Chapter 4 for specific technique instructions.

(continued from preceding page) sponge. Wipe with a clean dry cloth. On leather only, follow with **The Tannery** or **Fiebing's Saddle Soap** to condition the leather.

●**Marble**

After wiping up any excess liquid, wipe surface with a cloth or sponge dipped in warm sudsy water. Rinse well and wipe dry. If any stain or discoloration remains, mix a poultice of water, powdered detergent, and chlorine bleach. Apply a thick paste to the stain and cover with a damp cloth to retard evaporation. When the stain has been bleached out, rinse thoroughly and dry.

●**Silver**

Wash silver as soon as possible in hot sudsy water. Rinse in hot water and dry immediately with a soft cloth to prevent tarnish.

●**Wood**

Mix dishwashing detergent in hot water and swish to make a great volume of suds. Dip a cloth in only the foam and apply to the grape stain. Rinse with a clean cloth dampened with clear water. If a stain remains, rub the area with a cloth dampened in a solution of 1 tablespoon oxalic acid to 1 pint water. Rinse well and wipe dry. Wax or polish as soon as possible.

Graphite *(Follow procedures for* Pencil Lead.)

Grass

●**Acetate**
●**Carpet/Synthetic**
●**Carpet/Wool**

(continued)

Sponge* the area with a dry-cleaning solvent—**Carbona No. 10 Special Spot Remover/Carbona Cleaning**

See Chapter 4 for specific technique instructions.

(continued from preceding page)

●Rayon ●Silk
●Triacetate
●Wool

Fluid or **Afta Cleaning Fluid.** Apply a Dry Spotter to the stain and cover with an absorbent pad dampened with the Dry Spotter. Let it stand as long as any stain is being removed. Change the pad as it picks up the stain. Keep both the stain and pad moist with Dry Spotter. Flush* with one of the dry-cleaning solvents and allow to dry thoroughly. When working on carpets, be sure to blot up the excess liquid during the procedure and before drying.

●Acrylic Fabric
●Cotton ●Linen
●Modacrylic ●Nylon
●Olefin ●Polyester
●Spandex

Work liquid dishwashing or laundry detergent into the stain and rinse well with water. If any stain remains, presoak* in **Axion** or **Biz** (enzyme presoak products). Rinse thoroughly and launder as soon as possible. If any stain still remains, test for color-fastness in an inconspicuous place, then use a mild sodium perborate bleach or 3% hydrogen peroxide. Thoroughly rinse with clear water, then launder as usual.

●Acrylic Plastic
●Aluminum
●Ceramic Glass/Tile
●Cork ●Linoleum
●Vinyl Clothing
●Vinyl Tile
●Vinyl Wallcovering

Remove any stains by wiping with a cloth dipped in warm sudsy water. Rinse well and wipe dry with a clean cloth.

●Bluestone ●Brick
●Concrete
●Flagstone
●Granite
●Limestone
●Masonry Tile
●Slate ●Terrazzo

Wash stain with a solution of washing soda or detergent (not soap) and water. Use a cloth or soft-bristled brush to gently scrub the stain. Rinse thoroughly with clear water and allow to dry.

See Chapter 4 for specific technique instructions.

●**Leather** ●**Suede**

Mix a solution of mild soap in luke-warm water. Swish to create a great volume of suds. Apply only the foam with a sponge. Wipe with a dry clean cloth. If an oily stain remains, powder the area with an absorbent, such as cornmeal. Allow plenty of time for the absorbent to work, then brush* off the stain and powder. Repeat if necessary. On leather only, follow with **The Tannery** or **Fiebing's Saddle Soap.**

Gravy

●**Acetate**
●**Fiberglass** ●**Rayon**
●**Silk** ●**Triacetate**
●**Wool**

Gently scrape* any excess spill. Sponge* the area with a dry-cleaning solvent, either **Carbona No. 10 Special Spot Remover/Carbona Cleaning Fluid, K2r Spot-lifter** (tube), or **Afta Cleaning Fluid.** Apply a Dry Spotter to the stain and cover with an absorbent pad dampened with Dry Spotter. Let it stand as long as any stain is being removed. Change the pad as it begins to pick up the stain. Keep both the stain and pad moist with Dry Spotter. Flush* with one of the liquid dry-cleaning solvents. If any stain persists, moisten the stain with a solution of 1 cup warm water and 1 teaspoon **Axion,** an enzyme presoak product —do not use on silk or wool. Cover with a clean pad that has been dipped in the solution and wrung dry. Let it remain for 30 minutes. Add enough solution to keep the area warm and moist, but do not let the stained area spread. When no more stain is being lifted, flush thoroughly with water and let dry.

●**Acrylic Fabric**
●**Cotton** ●**Linen**
(continued)

Gently scrape* any excess spill. Sponge* the area with a dry-cleaning

See Chapter 4 for specific technique instructions.

(continued from preceding page)

- Modacrylic • Nylon
- Olefin • Polyester
- Spandex

solvent, either **Carbona No. 10 Special Spot Remover/Carbona Cleaning Fluid, K2r Spot-lifter** (aerosol), or **Afta Cleaning Fluid.** Then apply a Dry Spotter to the stain and cover it with an absorbent pad dampened with Dry Spotter. Let it stand as long as any stain is being removed. Change the pad as it picks up the stain. Flush* the area with one of the liquid dry-cleaning solvents and allow to dry. If any stain persists, apply a few drops of dishwashing detergent and a few drops of ammonia to the stain, then gently tamp* or scrape to loosen the material. Keep the stain moist with detergent and ammonia and blot occasionally with an absorbent pad. Flush with water to remove all traces of ammonia. Allow to dry. If the stain still remains, moisten the stain with a solution of 1 cup warm water and 1 teaspoon **Axion** or **Biz** (enzyme presoak products). Cover with a clean pad that has been dipped in the solution and wrung almost dry. Let it stand for 30 minutes. Add enough solution to keep the stained area warm and moist. When no more stain is being lifted, flush thoroughly with water and allow to dry.

- **Acrylic Plastic**
- **Aluminum**
- **Asphalt** • **Bamboo**
- **Cane**
- **Ceramic Glass/Tile**
- **Cork** • **Glass**
- **Linoleum**
- **Paint/Flat**
- **Paint/Gloss**

(continued)

Scrape* to remove excess gravy. Wash the surface with a cloth dipped into warm sudsy water. Rinse well and wipe dry.

See Chapter 4 for specific technique instructions.

- **Pewter** ●**Plexiglas**
- **Polyurethane**
- **Porcelain Dishes**
- **Stainless Steel**
- **Vinyl Clothing**
- **Vinyl Tile**
- **Vinyl Wallcovering**

(see base of preceding page)

- **Alabaster** ●**Marble**

Scrape* to remove excess gravy. Wash the surface with a cloth dipped into warm sudsy water. Rinse well and wipe dry. If any stain remains, mix a poultice of water, detergent, and bleach. Apply the paste to the surface, cover with a damp cloth to retard evaporation, and let it stand. When the stain has been bleached out, rinse well with clear water and wipe dry.

- **Bluestone** ●**Brick**
- **Concrete**
- **Flagstone**
- **Granite**
- **Masonry Tile**
- **Sandstone** ●**Slate**
- **Terrazzo**

Wipe up excess spill. Wash with a solution of washing soda or detergent (not soap) and water. Use a cloth or soft-bristled brush to gently scrub the surface. Rinse thoroughly with clear water and allow to dry.

- **Carpet/Synthetic**
- **Carpet/Wool**

Scrape* to remove as much of the spill as possible. Apply **Stain-X Carpet Stain Remover** or **Spot Shot Carpet Stain Remover.** Then apply an absorbent, such as cornmeal. Allow plenty of time for it to absorb the gravy. Gently brush* it out of the pile. If a stain still exists, carefully sponge* the area with a dry-cleaning solvent, either **Carbona No. 10 Special Spot Remover/Carbona Cleaning Fluid** or **Afta Cleaning Fluid.** Apply a Dry Spotter to the stain and cover with an absorbent pad dampened with Dry Spotter. Let it
(continued)

---

*See Chapter 4 for specific technique instructions.

(continued from preceding page) stand as long as any stain is being removed. Change the pad as it picks up the stain and remember to keep both the pad and stain moist with Dry Spotter. Sponge with one of the dry-cleaning solvents and let dry. If any trace of the stain still remains, moisten the area with a solution of 1 cup warm water and 1 teaspoon **Axion** or **Biz** (enzyme presoak products), but do not use on wool carpets. Cover with a clean pad that has been dipped into the solution and wrung almost dry. Let it stand for 30 minutes. Add enough solution to keep the stained area warm and moist. When no more stain is being lifted, sponge with clear water, let dry, and vacuum.

●Felt

Gently scrape* to remove any excess gravy. Mix dishwashing detergent in hot water and swish to make a great volume of suds. Dip a cloth in only the foam and wipe the stain. Wipe the area with a clean dry cloth. If a grease stain remains, powder the area with an absorbent, such as cornmeal. Allowing plenty of time for it to work, brush* it out of the felt when finished. Repeat if necessary.

●Leather ●Suede

Gently scrape* away the excess gravy. Mix a solution of mild soap in lukewarm water. Swish to create a great volume of suds. Apply only the foam with a sponge. Wipe with a clean dry cloth. If a grease stain remains, powder the area with an absorbent, such as cornmeal. Give it plenty of time to work. Gently brush* off the powder. Repeat if necessary. On leather only, follow with **The Tannery** or **Fiebing's Saddle Soap** to condition the leather.

*See Chapter 4 for specific technique instructions.

●**Silver**	Wash as soon as possible in hot sudsy water. Rinse in hot water and dry immediately with a soft cloth to prevent tarnish.
●**Wood**	Mix dishwashing detergent in hot water and swish to make a great volume of suds. Dip a cloth in only the foam and gently wipe the spill. Rinse with a clean cloth moistened with clear water. Polish or wax when dry.

Grease/Automotive, Cooking

●**Acetate**
●**Carpet/Synthetic**
●**Carpet/Wool**
●**Rayon** ●**Silk**
●**Triacetate**
●**Wool**

Blot up as much excess as possible and apply an absorbent, such as cornmeal. After letting the absorbent work, brush* it out of the fabric. If a stain remains, sponge* with a dry-cleaning solvent, either **Carbona No. 10 Special Spot Remover/Carbona Cleaning Fluid, K2r Spotlifter** (tube), or **Afta Cleaning Fluid.** Then apply a Dry Spotter to the area. Cover the stain with an absorbent pad dampened with Dry Spotter. Let it remain in place as long as any stain is being lifted. Change the pad as it picks up the stain. Keep both the stain and pad moist with Dry Spotter. Flush* with one of the dry-cleaning solvents. If a stain still persists, sponge stain with water and apply a Wet Spotter with a few drops of white vinegar. Cover the area with an absorbent pad moistened with Wet Spotter. Let it stand as long as any stain is being removed. Change the pad as it picks up the stain. Keep both the stain and pad moist with Wet Spotter and vinegar. Flush the area with water and repeat above procedure until no more stain is removed. Allow to dry.

*See Chapter 4 for specific technique instructions.

- **Acrylic Fabric**
- **Cotton • Linen**
- **Modacrylic**
- **Olefin • Polyester**
- **Spandex**

Blot up the excess grease as soon as possible. Apply an absorbent and let it soak up the spill. After brushing* out the powder, sponge* the area with a dry-cleaning solvent, either **Carbona No. 10 Special Spot Remover/ Carbona Cleaning Fluid, K2r Spotlifter** (aerosol), or **Afta Cleaning Fluid.** Then apply a Dry Spotter to any remaining stain. Cover the stain with an absorbent pad dampened with Dry Spotter and let it remain in place until no more stain is lifted. Change the pad as it picks up the stain. To help loosen the stain, occasionally tamp* the area, blotting up any loosened material. Flush* with one of the liquid dry-cleaning solvents. If any trace of stain remains, sponge stain with water and apply a Wet Spotter and a few drops of ammonia. Tamp the stain again, blotting with an absorbent pad to remove any loosened material. Flush the area with water and repeat until no more stain is removed. Allow to dry.

- **Acrylic Plastic**
- **Aluminum**
- **Asphalt • Bamboo**
- **Cane**
- **Ceramic Glass/Tile**
- **Cork • Glass**
- **Linoleum**
- **Paint/Flat**
- **Paint/Gloss**
- **Pewter • Plexiglas**
- **Polyurethane**
- **Porcelain Dishes**
- **Stainless Steel**
- **Vinyl Clothing**
- **Vinyl Tile**
- **Vinyl Wallcovering**

Blot up any excess grease. Wipe the surface with a cloth or sponge dipped in warm sudsy water. Rinse well and wipe dry.

*See Chapter 4 for specific technique instructions.

●Bluestone ●Brick
●Concrete
●Flagstone
●Granite
●Limestone
●Masonry Tile
●Sandstone ●Slate
●Terrazzo

Pour a strong solution of washing soda and boiling water onto the surface. Cover the stain with a paste made of fuller's earth and hot water. Leave overnight. Rinse with clear water. Repeat if necessary.

●Leather

Rub the stain with a thick paste of fuller's earth and water. Allow paste to dry, then brush* off the powder. Repeat if necessary. Follow with **The Tannery** or **Fiebing's Saddle Soap** to condition the leather.

●Marble

Wipe up any excess, then wipe surface with a cloth or sponge dipped in warm sudsy water. Rinse well and wipe dry with a clean cloth. If any residue remains, mix a poultice with water, detergent, and bleach. Apply the poultice to the stain and cover with a dampened cloth to retard evaporation. After the stain has been bleached out, rinse the area thoroughly with water and allow to dry.

●Silver

Immediately wash in hot sudsy water. Rinse thoroughly in hot water and dry with a soft clean cloth to prevent tarnish.

●Suede

Dip a clean cloth into ground cornmeal and rub in a circular motion into the stain. Gently brush* out all the powder with a wire brush. Repeat if necessary. If stain persists, pretest lemon juice in an inconspicuous place, then brush stain with the juice and wire brush. Hold in the steam of a boiling kettle for a few minutes. Brush with a wire brush.

---

*See Chapter 4 for specific technique instructions.

●**Wallpaper**

Make a paste of cornstarch and water. Apply it to the stain and allow to dry. Brush* off the powder and repeat if necessary. If the stain persists, make a paste of fuller's earth and trichloroethane. Apply and allow to dry. Brush it off.

●**Wood**

Mix dishwashing detergent in hot water and swish to make a great volume of suds. Dip a cloth in only the foam and gently wipe. Rinse with a clean cloth moistened with clear water. Polish or wax as soon as possible.

Hair Dyes (*See* Dye, Dye/Red, Dye/Yellow.)

Hair Spray

●**Acetate**
●**Acrylic Fabric**
●**Carpet/Synthetic**
●**Carpet/Wool**
●**Cotton**
●**Fiberglass** ●**Linen**
●**Modacrylic** ●**Nylon**
●**Olefin** ●**Polyester**
●**Rayon** ●**Silk**
●**Spandex**
●**Triacetate**
●**Wool**

Wipe up any excess spray. Sponge* the stain with a dry-cleaning solvent, either **Carbona No. 10 Special Spot Remover/Carbona Cleaning Fluid** or **Afta Cleaning Fluid.** For silk, apply **K2r Spot-lifter** (tube). Apply a Dry Spotter to the area and cover with an absorbent pad dampened with Dry Spotter. Let the cover stay in place as long as any stain is being removed. Change the pad as it picks up the stain. Keep both the pad and stained area moist with Dry Spotter. On stronger fabrics, tamp* any dried spray to help loosen it. Flush* the area with one of the liquid dry-cleaning solvents (or reapply K2r Spot-lifter on silk). If any stain remains, sponge the stain with water and apply a Wet Spotter and a few drops of ammonia. (Do not use ammonia on silk or wool.) Cover the stain with an

(continued)

*See Chapter 4 for specific technique instructions.

(continued from preceding page) absorbent pad moistened with Wet Spotter. Keep the pad in place as long as any stain is being removed. Change the pad as it picks up the stain. Keep both the stain and pad moist with Dry Spotter and ammonia mixture. Flush with water when stain has disappeared.

●**Acrylic Plastic**
●**Alabaster**
●**Aluminum**
●**Bamboo** ●**Cane**
●**Ceramic Glass/Tile**
●**Cork** ●**Glass**
●**Grout** ●**Linoleum**
●**Marble** ●**Paint/Flat**
●**Paint/Gloss**
●**Plexiglas**
●**Polyurethane**
●**Porcelain Fixtures**
●**Vinyl Clothing**
●**Vinyl Tile**
●**Vinyl Wallcovering**

Wipe up the excess with a cloth or sponge dipped in warm sudsy water. Rinse well and wipe dry.

●**Leather** ●**Suede**

Carefully test the effects of a dry-cleaning solvent in an inconspicuous place. Using a clean cloth, carefully dab a small amount of dry-cleaning solvent, **Carbona No. 10 Special Spot Remover/Carbona Cleaning Fluid,** on the stain. Allow it to air dry and then condition as usual.

●**Wallpaper**

Carefully wipe up any excess spray. With a cloth or sponge dampened with cool clear water, wipe the stained area. Be sure to overlap strokes to prevent streaking. Use a soft dry cloth to gently pat dry.

●**Wood**

Mix dishwashing detergent in hot water and swish to make a great vol-
(continued)

(continued from preceding page) ume of suds. Dip a cloth in only the foam and apply. Rinse with a clean cloth moistened with clear water. Polish or wax as soon as possible.

Heel Marks

• **Asphalt**
• **Linoleum**
• **Vinyl Tile**

Rub **Crayerase,** a nontoxic dry-chemical cleaning bar, on the heel marks. Polish or wax floor as usual. Or, try an all-purpose spray cleaner, following label directions. If any marks persist, use superfine (number 0000) steel wool dipped in a liquid wax and rub gently in a circular motion. Wipe with a damp cloth, dry with a clean cloth, and apply a coat of floor wax or polish.

• **Paint/Flat**
• **Paint/Gloss**

Rub **Crayerase,** a nontoxic, dry-chemical cleaning bar, on the marks. On flat paint, a shiny mark may be left; sponge* the shiny spot with a cloth moistened with hot water. Or, wipe the scuff marks from painted furniture legs with a cloth dipped in warm soapy water. If marks remain on the furniture, use a light application of liquid wax. Rub well and remove excess.

• **Wood**

On woodwork, rub **Crayerase,** a nontoxic dry-chemical cleaning bar, on the marks. On other wood, mix dishwashing detergent in hot water and swish to make a great volume of suds. Dip a cloth in only the foam and apply to the heel marks. Rinse with a clean cloth moistened with clear water. If any marks remain, use superfine (number 0000) steel wool and gently remove the stain with small circular motions. **Caution:** The

(continued)

*See Chapter 4 for specific technique instructions.

(continued from preceding page) steel wool actually will remove a light portion of the wood's finish, so be gentle. Polish or wax as soon as possible to reseal the exposed wood.

Ice Cream/Chocolate
(Follow procedures for Chocolate/cocoa.)

Ice Cream/Nonchocolate

- **Acetate** • **Burlap**
- **Carpet/Synthetic**
- **Carpet/Wool**
- **Fiberglass** • **Rayon**
- **Rope** • **Silk**
- **Triacetate**
- **Wool/nonwashable**

Scrape* to remove any excess immediately. Sponge* the area with a dry-cleaning solvent, either **Carbona No. 10 Special Spot Remover/Carbona Cleaning Fluid** or **Afta Cleaning Fluid.** Apply a Dry Spotter to the stain and cover with an absorbent pad moistened with Dry Spotter. Let it stand as long as any stain is being removed. Change the pad as it picks up the stain. Keep the pad and stain moist with Dry Spotter. Flush* with one of the dry-cleaning solvents. If any stain remains, moisten the area with a solution of 1 cup warm water and 1 teaspoon **Axion**, an enzyme presoak product—do not use on silk or wool. Cover with a clean pad that has been dipped in the solution and wrung almost dry. Let it stand for 30 minutes. Add enough solution to keep the area warm and moist, but do not allow the wet area to spread. When no more stain is being lifted, flush the area with water and allow to dry.

- **Acrylic Fabric**
- **Cotton** • **Linen**
- **Modacrylic** • **Nylon**
- **Olefin** • **Polyester**

(continued)

Immediately scrape* to remove any excess ice cream. Sponge the area with a dry-cleaning solvent, either **Carbona No. 10 Special Spot Remover/Carbona Cleaning Fluid,**

See Chapter 4 for specific technique instructions.

(continued from preceding page)

- **Spandex**
- **Wool/washable**

K2r Spot-lifter (aerosol), or **Afta Cleaning Fluid.** Then apply Dry Spotter and cover with an absorbent pad moisted with Dry Spotter. Let it stand as long as any stain is being removed. Change the pad as it picks up the stain and keep the stain and pad moist with Dry Spotter. Flush* with one of the liquid dry-cleaning solvents. If any stain remains, apply a few drops of liquid dishwashing or laundry detergent and a few drops of ammonia to the area. Tamp* or scrape to loosen the stain. Keep the stain moist with detergent and ammonia solution. Blot occasionally with an absorbent pad. Flush well with water to remove all ammonia and allow to dry.

- **Acrylic Plastic**
- **Aluminum**
- **Asphalt** •**Bamboo**
- **Brass** •**Bronze**
- **Cane**
- **Ceramic Glass/Tile**
- **Copper** •**Cork**
- **Enamel** •**Glass**
- **Gold** •**Iron** •**Ivory**
- **Linoleum**
- **Paint/Flat**
- **Paint/Gloss**
- **Pewter** •**Plexiglas**
- **Polyurethane**
- **Porcelain Dishes**
- **Porcelain Fixtures**
- **Stainless Steel**
- **Tin** •**Vinyl Clothing**
- **Vinyl Tile**
- **Vinyl Wallcovering**
- **Zinc**

Wipe up any excess ice cream immediately. Wipe the surface with a cloth or sponge dipped in warm sudsy water. Rinse well and wipe dry with a clean cloth.

See Chapter 4 for specific technique instructions.

•Alabaster •Marble

Wipe up any excess spill. Mix a few drops of ammonia with 1 cup rubbing alcohol. Soak a white blotter (about the size of the stain) in the solution and place it over the area. Weight it down with a piece of glass or other heavy object. Continue applying the solution until the grease is drawn out and any remaining stain has been bleached out. If any stain persists, make a poultice from bleach, water, and powdered detergent. Apply it to the stain. Cover with a damp cloth to retard evaporation. Remove when the stain has been bleached out.

•Bluestone •Brick
•Concrete
•Flagstone
•Granite
•Limestone
•Masonry Tile
•Sandstone •Slate
•Terrazzo

Wipe up any excess material. Wash the stained area with a solution of washing soda or detergent (never soap) and water. Use a soft-bristled brush or cloth to help scrub. Rinse the area thoroughly with clear water and allow to dry.

•Fur/Natural
•Fur/Synthetic

Wipe up any excess spill. Then wipe the surface with a cloth dipped in the suds of a mild detergent and water. Wipe again with a clean dry cloth. If a grease stain persists, powder the area with an absorbent, such as cornmeal, allowing plenty of time for it to work. Gently brush* out the powder and sponge* the area with a damp cloth. Allow the fur to air dry.

•Grout

Wipe up any excess spill with a cloth dipped in warm sudsy water. If any stain remains, apply **Afta Tile & Grout Cleaner** or dip a wet toothbrush into a little powdered cleanser or baking soda and gently scrub the stain. Rinse well with water and wipe dry with a clean cloth.

*See Chapter 4 for specific technique instructions.

●**Leather**

Gently scrape* any excess ice cream from the leather. Mix a solution of mild soap in lukewarm water. Swish to create a great volume of suds. Apply only the foam with a sponge. Wipe with a clean dry cloth. If a grease stain remains, powder the area with an absorbent, such as cornmeal. Give it plenty of time to work. Gently brush* the stain off the leather. If after trying the cornmeal absorbent any trace still remains, try a leather cleaner, **The Tannery.** Rub it in with a clean soft cloth and allow to dry. After either method, condition the leather with The Tannery or **Fiebing's Saddle Soap.**

●**Silver**

Remove any excess spill with a cloth. Wash as soon as possible in hot sudsy water. Rinse in hot water and dry immediately with a soft cloth to prevent tarnish.

●**Suede**

Very gently scrape* to remove the excess ice cream from the suede. Wipe the stain with a cloth dipped in the suds of a mild detergent and water. Wipe with a clean dry cloth. If a grease stain remains, powder the area with an absorbent, allowing plenty of time for it to work. Gently brush* the absorbent off.

●**Wallpaper**

Carefully remove the excess spill. With a cloth or sponge moistened with cool clear water, wipe the stained area. Overlap strokes to prevent streaking. Gently pat the area dry with an absorbent pad.

●**Wood**

Wipe up any excess. Mix dishwashing detergent in hot water and swish to make a great volume of

(continued)

*See Chapter 4 for specific technique instructions.

(continued from preceding page) suds. Dip a cloth in only the foam and apply to the stain. Rinse with a clean cloth moistened with clear water. Polish or wax as soon as possible.

Ink/Ballpoint, Stamp Pad (except red)

- ●Acetate ●Burlap
- ●Carpet/Synthetic
- ●Carpet/Wool
- ●Fiberglass ●Rayon
- ●Silk ●Triacetate
- ●Wool

Sponge* the stain with water. Try a light spray of hair spray to loosen the stain, then apply a Wet Spotter and a few drops of white vinegar. Let stand for 30 minutes, blotting every 5 minutes with a clean absorbent pad. Spray on **Amway Remove Fabric Spot Cleaner.** Add Wet Spotter and vinegar as needed to keep the stain moist. Flush* with water. If the stain persists, apply rubbing alcohol to the stain and cover with an absorbent pad moistened with alcohol. Let it stand as long as any stain is being removed. Change the pad as it picks up the stain. Flush with alcohol. (Do not use alcohol on acetate, rayon, or triacetate.) If stain traces remain, sponge area with water and apply a Wet Spotter and a few drops of ammonia. Let stand for 30 minutes, blotting every 5 minutes. Add enough Wet Spotter and ammonia (do not use ammonia on silk or wool) to keep the stain moist. Flush with water and allow to dry.

- ●Acrylic Fabric
- ●Cotton ●Linen
- ●Modacrylic ●Nylon
- ●Olefin ●Polyester
- ●Spandex

Try a light spray of hair spray to loosen the stain. Soak in a solution of 1 quart warm water, ½ teaspoon dishwashing detergent, and 1 tablespoon white vinegar for 30 minutes—use care when using vinegar on cotton and linen. Rinse with water and *(continued)*

*See Chapter 4 for specific technique instructions.

(continued from preceding page) allow to dry. If stain persists, apply rubbing alcohol to the stain and cover with an absorbent pad moistened with alcohol (use alcohol sparingly on acrylic and modacrylic). Let stand as long as any stain is being removed. Change pad as it picks up the stain. Keep both the stain and pad moist with alcohol. Flush* with alcohol and allow to dry. If any trace of stain remains, soak in a solution of 1 quart warm water, ½ teaspoon dishwashing detergent, and 1 tablespoon ammonia for 30 minutes. Rinse thoroughly with water and allow to dry.

●**Acrylic Plastic** ●**Ceramic Glass/Tile** ●**Cork** ●**Glass** ●**Plexiglas** ●**Polyurethane** ●**Porcelain Dishes** ●**Porcelain Fixtures** ●**Vinyl Clothing** ●**Vinyl Wallcovering**	Apply an all-purpose spray cleaner, following label directions. If any trace of stain remains, cover area with a compress sprinkled with ammonia. Rinse well and wash with a cloth dipped in warm sudsy water. Rinse again and allow to dry.
●**Alabaster** ●**Marble**	Wipe the surface with a cloth or sponge dipped in warm sudsy water. Rinse well and wipe dry. If any trace of stain persists, apply an absorbent pad dampened with rubbing alcohol. After several minutes, replace the pad with one moistened with ammonia. Continue alternating alcohol and ammonia treatment until stain is removed. Rinse well and wipe dry.
●**Asphalt** ●**Bluestone** ●**Brick** ●**Concrete** ●**Flagstone** ●**Sandstone** ●**Slate** ●**Terrazzo**	Wash with a solution of washing soda or detergent (not soap) and water. Use a cloth or soft-bristled brush to help scrub. Rinse thoroughly with clear water and allow to dry.

*See Chapter 4 for specific technique instructions.

●**Bamboo** ●**Cane** ●**Paint/Flat** ●**Paint/Gloss**	Wipe with a cloth dipped in a solution of mild pure soap and water to which a few drops of ammonia have been added. Rinse well and dry thoroughly.
●**Grout**	Wipe stain with a cloth dipped in warm sudsy water. If a stain remains, apply **Afta Tile & Grout Cleaner** or dip a wet toothbrush into a litle baking soda or powdered cleanser and gently scrub. Rinse well and wipe dry.
●**Leather** ●**Suede**	On leather, apply a cleaner, **The Tannery.** On suede, apply **Child Life Suede & Fabric Cleaner.** Rub it in with a clean soft cloth and let it dry. If any stain still remains, try gingerly applying a dry-cleaning solvent, **Carbona No. 10 Special Spot Remover/Carbona Cleaning Fluid.** Dab it on with a clean cloth, after testing on a hidden seam. Allow to air dry. On leather only, follow with The Tannery or **Fiebing's Saddle Soap** to condition the leather. **Caution:** There is no guaranteed way to remove this stain from these materials.
●**Linoleum** ●**Vinyl Tile**	First, apply an all-purpose spray cleaner according to package directions. If any stain remains, cover the area with a compress made with rubbing alcohol. Rinse with clear water. If stain persists, rub the area with superfine (number 0000) steel wool dipped in liquid floor wax. Wash the area with soapy water, dry, then wax as usual.
●**Wallpaper**	Try removing any ink with a soft eraser. Work in small movements to avoid tearing the paper. If the stain persists, wipe the area with a cloth or sponge moistened with cool clear

(continued)

(continued from preceding page) water. Overlap the strokes to avoid streaking. Use a clean cloth to gently pat dry.

●**Wood**

Mix dishwashing detergent in hot water and swish to make a great volume of suds. Dip a cloth in only the foam and gently wipe the stain. Rinse with a clean cloth moistened with clear water. If a stain remains, rub the area with superfine (number 0000) steel wool dipped in liquid wax. Rub lightly, because steel wool will remove a fine layer of the surface. Polish or wax as soon as possible.

Ink/Ballpoint, Stamp Pad (Red)

●**Acetate**
●**Carpet/Synthetic**
●**Carpet/Wool**
●**Fiberglass** ●**Rayon**
●**Silk** ●**Triacetate**
●**Wool**

Sponge* the area immediately with water to dilute the ink. Spraying on **Amway Remove Fabric Spot Cleaner** may help to remove the ink. Apply a Wet Spotter and a few drops of ammonia. (Use ammonia with care on silk and wool.) Cover with an absorbent pad dampened with the Wet Spotter. Let the pad remain as long as any stain is being removed. Change the pad as it picks up the stain. Flush* well with water and repeat if necessary. If after drying, a stain persists, mix **Rit Color Remover** according to package directions. After testing on a hidden seam, flush it through the stain to an absorbent pad beneath. When dealing with carpeting, sponge the color remover on the stain and blot with an absorbent pad. Rinse well with water and allow to dry thoroughly.

●**Acrylic Fabric**
●**Cotton** ●**Linen**
(continued)

Soak the item in a solution of 1 quart warm water, ½ teaspoon dishwash-

*See Chapter 4 for specific technique instructions.

(continued from preceding page)

- **Modacrylic** • **Nylon**
- **Olefin** • **Polyester**
- **Spandex**

ing detergent, and 1 tablespoon ammonia for 30 minutes. Rinse well. If stain remains, soak in a solution of 1 quart warm water and 1 tablespoon white vinegar for 1 hour. (Take care when using vinegar on cotton and linen.) Rinse well and allow to dry. If stain has set, apply rubbing alcohol to the area (dilute with 2 parts water for acrylic or modacrylic) and tamp.* As stain loosens, blot liquid and stain with an absorbent pad. Keep both the stain and pad moist with alcohol and change pad as it picks up the stain. Allow to dry. As a last resort for any remaining stain, pretest **Rit Color Remover** in an inconspicuous place, then apply to the stain. Flush* the solution through the stain and into an absorbent pad beneath. Rinse well with clear water and allow to dry.

- **Acrylic Plastic**
- **Aluminum**
- **Bamboo** • **Cane**
- **Ceramic Glass/Tile**
- **Glass** • **Paint/Flat**
- **Paint/Gloss**
- **Plexiglas**
- **Polyurethane**
- **Vinyl Clothing**
- **Vinyl Wallcovering**

Immediately wipe up the spill with a cloth or sponge dipped in warm sudsy water. Rinse well and wipe dry.

- **Alabaster** • **Marble**

Immediately wipe up the spill with a cloth or sponge dipped in warm sudsy water. Rinse well and wipe dry. If a stain remains, soak an absorbent pad in rubbing alcohol, wring almost dry, and place over the stain. Wait 5 minutes and apply an absorbent pad soaked with ammonia and squeezed until damp. Alternate pads until stain

(continued)

See Chapter 4 for specific technique instructions.

(continued from preceding page) has been removed. Wipe surface with cloth moistened with clear water and wipe dry with a clean cloth.

•Asphalt •Cork •Linoleum •Vinyl Tile	Wipe up any excess ink with a cloth or sponge dipped in warm sudsy water. Rinse well and wipe dry. If a stain remains, cover the stain with an absorbent pad soaked in rubbing alcohol. Let it remain in place for several minutes, then wipe the area with a cloth dampened with ammonia. (Do not use ammonia on linoleum or vinyl floor tile.) Rinse well with a cloth dipped in warm sudsy water. Wipe with a cloth moistened with clear water and allow to dry.
•Bluestone •Brick •Concrete •Flagstone •Granite •Masonry Tile •Sandstone •Slate •Terrazzo	Wipe up the excess. Wash with a solution of washing soda or detergent (not soap) and water. Use a cloth or soft-bristled brush to help scrub. Rinse thoroughly with clear water and allow to dry.
•Grout	Wipe up excess with a cloth dipped in warm sudsy water. If any stain remains, apply **Afta Tile & Grout Cleaner** or dip a wet toothbrush into baking soda or powdered cleanser and gently scrub the stain. Rinse well with water and wipe dry.
•Leather •Suede	Ink spilled on these materials will act immediately on the hide. Once contact has been made, it is impossible to remove.
•Wood	Mix dishwashing detergent in hot water and swish to make a great volume of suds. Dip a cloth in only the foam and gently wipe up the ink. *(continued)*

(continued from preceding page) Rinse with a clean cloth moistened with clear water. Polish or wax as soon as possible.

Ink/Felt Tip, India

●**Acetate** ●**Burlap**
●**Fiberglass** ●**Rayon**
●**Rope** ●**Silk**
●**Triacetate**
●**Wool**

Sponge* the area with a dry-cleaning solvent, either **Carbona No. 10 Special Spot Remover/Carbona Cleaning Fluid, K2r Spot-lifter** (tube), or **Afta Cleaning Fluid,** then apply a Dry Spotter to the stain. Cover with an absorbent pad moistened with Dry Spotter. Be sure to keep the stain from bleeding. Change the pad as it picks up the stain. Keep the stain and pad moist with Dry Spotter. Flush* with one of the liquid dry-cleaning solvents. If stain persists, sponge with water and apply a Wet Spotter and a few drops of ammonia. (Do not use ammonia on silk or wool.) Cover the stain with an absorbent pad moistened with Wet Spotter. Change the pad as it picks up the stain. Keep both the pad and stain moist with Wet Spotter and white vinegar. Flush with water and repeat as necessary. Allow to dry. Note: Permanent inks are almost impossible to remove.

●**Acrylic Fabric**
●**Cotton** ●**Linen**
●**Modacrylic**

Sponge* the area with a dry-cleaning solvent, either **Carbona No. 10 Special Spot Remover/Carbona Cleaning Fluid, K2r Spot-lifter** (aerosol), or **Afta Cleaning Fluid.** If stain remains, mix a paste of powdered detergent, water, and a few drops of ammonia. Apply to the stain. Place an absorbent pad under the stain. When no more stain is being removed, flush* thoroughly with

(continued)

*See Chapter 4 for specific technique instructions.

(continued from preceding page) water and launder. Note: Permanent inks are almost impossible to remove.

•Acrylic Plastic •Aluminum •Asphalt •Bamboo •Cane •Ceramic Glass/Tile •Enamel •Glass •Paint/Flat •Paint/Gloss •Plexiglas •Polyurethane •Porcelain Dishes •Porcelain Fixtures •Stainless Steel •Vinyl Clothing •Vinyl Wallcovering	Wipe the surface with a cloth or sponge dipped in warm sudsy water to which a few drops of ammonia have been added. Rinse well with clear water and wipe dry. Note: Permanent inks are almost impossible to remove.
•Alabaster •Marble	Wipe surface with a cloth or sponge dipped in warm sudsy water to which a few drops of ammonia have been added. Rinse well and wipe dry. If stain persists, apply a cloth soaked in rubbing alcohol; allow it to stand for 15 minutes. Next, apply a cloth soaked with ammonia for 15 minutes. Alternate alcohol and ammonia applications until stain is removed. Rinse thoroughly and wipe dry.
•Bluestone •Brick •Concrete •Flagstone •Granite •Limestone •Masonry Tile •Sandstone •Slate •Terrazzo	Wash stain with a solution of washing soda or detergent (never soap) and water. Use a cloth or soft-bristled brush to help scrub. Rinse thoroughly with clear water and allow to dry.
•Carpet/Synthetic •Carpet/Wool	Blot as much stain as possible without forcing it deeper into the pile.

(continued)

(continued from preceding page) Sponge* the stain with a concentrated solution of carpet spotter, either **Stain-X Carpet Stain Remover** or **Afta Carpet Stain Remover. Caution:** Never rub ink stains on carpet. Continue to sponge the area, rinsing the sponge as it picks up the stain. Repeat until no more stain is removed. If the stain persists, have the rug professionally cleaned. Repeated applications of a liquid all-purpose cleaner solution also will help remove the ink. Note: Permanent inks are almost impossible to remove.

●**Cork** ●**Linoleum** ●**Vinyl Tile**

Cover the stain with a compress made with rubbing alcohol. Let the compress remain in place for 5 minutes. Wipe the area with a cloth dampened with ammonia. Do not use ammonia on linoleum or vinyl tile. Rinse well with water and allow to dry. Note: Permanent inks are almost impossible to remove.

●**Felt** ●**Fur/Natural** ●**Fur/Synthetic** ●**Leather** ●**Suede**

Due to the nature of the material involved, this stain cannot be removed by a nonprofessional.

●**Grout**

Wipe stain with cloth dipped in warm sudsy water. If stain remains, apply **Afta Tile & Grout Cleaner** or dip a wet toothbrush into a little baking soda or powdered cleanser. Gently scrub the spot. Rinse and wipe dry.

●**Nylon** ●**Olefin** ●**Polyester** ●**Spandex**

Sponge* stain with detergent solution immediately. Then apply either **Carbona No. 10 Special Spot Remover/Carbona Cleaning Fluid, K2r Spot-lifter** (aerosol), or **Afta Cleaning Fluid.** Sprinkle lemon juice

(continued)

*See Chapter 4 for specific technique instructions.

(continued from preceding page) and salt over the stain and leave for 1 hour. Rinse well, repeat if necessary, and launder as soon as possible.

●**Wallpaper**

Try erasing light marks with an art-gum eraser or **Suede Stone,** an abrasive cleaner. Remember not to push hard. If stain remains, rub area lightly with a dry steel wool soap pad. If the stain persists, rub very gently with baking soda sprinkled on a damp cloth. Then wipe the area with a cloth or sponge moistened in cool clear water. Overlap strokes to prevent streaking. Use a clean pad to gently pat dry.

●**Wood**

Dilute oxalic acid in warm water and apply with an artist's brush to the stained area. **Caution:** Oxalic acid is poisonous, so wear rubber gloves when applying it. On painted surfaces, wipe with a cloth moistened with detergent suds. For unpainted or stripped surfaces, after applying the oxalic acid, neutralize the area with white vinegar and rinse with rubbing alcohol. Allow to dry. Note: Permanent inks are almost impossible to remove.

Insecticide

●**Acetate**
●**Carpet/Synthetic**
●**Carpet/Wool**
●**Fiberglass** ●**Rayon**
●**Silk** ●**Triacetate**
●**Wool**

Sponge* the area with a dry-cleaning solvent, either **Carbona No. 10 Special Spot Remover/Carbona Cleaning Fluid, K2r Spot-lifter** (tube), or **Afta Cleaning Fluid.** Then apply a Dry Spotter to the stain and cover with an absorbent pad moistened with Dry Spotter. Let it stand as long as any stain is being removed. Change the pad as it picks up the stain. Keep the stain and pad moist

(continued)

*See Chapter 4 for specific technique instructions.

(continued from preceding page) with Dry Spotter. Flush* with one of the liquid dry-cleaning solvents. If any stain persists, sponge it with water and apply Wet Spotter and a few drops of ammonia. Cover with a pad dampened with Wet Spotter. Let stand as long as any stain is being removed. Change the pad as it picks up the stain. Keep the stain and pad moist with Wet Spotter and ammonia —do not use ammonia on silk or wool. Flush with water and allow to dry.

- **Acrylic Fabric**
- **Cotton** • **Linen**
- **Nylon** • **Olefin**
- **Polyester**
- **Spandex**

Sponge* the area with a dry-cleaning solvent, either **Carbona No. 10 Special Spot Remover/Carbona Cleaning Fluid, K2r Spot-lifter** (aerosol), or **Afta Dry Cleaning Fluid.** Apply a Dry Spotter to the stain and cover with an absorbent pad moistened with Dry Spotter. Let it stand as long as any stain is being removed. Change the pad as it picks up the stain. Keep the stain and pad moist with Dry Spotter. Flush* with one of the liquid dry-cleaning solvents. If any stain remains, sponge it with water and apply a Wet Spotter and a few drops of ammonia. Cover with a pad dampened with Wet Spotter. Let stand as long as any stain is being removed. Change the pad as it picks up the stain. Keep the stain and pad moist with Wet Spotter and ammonia. Flush with water and allow to dry.

- **Acrylic Plastic**
- **Aluminum**
- **Bamboo** • **Cane**
- **Cork** • **Glass**
- **Linoleum**
- **Paint/Flat**

(continued)

Wipe surface with a cloth or sponge dipped in warm sudsy water to which a few drops of ammonia have been added. Rinse well and wipe dry.

*See Chapter 4 for specific technique instructions.

- **Paint/Gloss**
- **Plexiglas**
- **Polyurethane**
- **Porcelain Dishes**
- **Porcelain Fixtures**
- **Stainless Steel**
- **Vinyl Clothing**
- **Vinyl Tile**
- **Vinyl Wallcovering**

(see base of preceding page)

- **Asphalt**
- **Bluestone** • **Brick**
- **Concrete**
- **Flagstone**
- **Granite**
- **Masonry Tile**
- **Sandstone**
- **Slate**
- **Terrazzo**

Wash stain with a solution of washing soda or detergent (never soap) and water. Use a cloth or soft-bristled brush. Rinse thoroughly with clear water and allow to dry.

- **Leather** • **Suede**

Mix a solution of mild soap in lukewarm water. Swish to create a great volume of suds. Apply only the foam with a sponge or cloth. Wipe with a clean dry cloth. If a grease stain remains, powder the area with an absorbent such as cornmeal. Give it plenty of time to work, then gently brush* it off. Repeat if necessary. On leather only, follow with **The Tannery** or **Fiebing's Saddle Soap** to condition the leather.

- **Wallpaper**

Wipe the area with a cloth or sponge moistened with cool clear water. Overlap the strokes to prevent streaking. With a clean cloth, gently pat area dry.

- **Wood**

Mix dishwashing detergent in hot water and swish to make a great volume of suds. Dip a cloth in only the foam and apply to the stain. Rinse
(continued)

See Chapter 4 for specific technique instructions.

(continued from preceding page) with a clean cloth moistened with clear water. Polish or wax as soon as possible.

Iodine

- ●Acetate
- ●Acrylic Fabric
- ●Carpet/Synthetic
- ●Carpet/Wool
- ●Cotton
- ●Fiberglass ●Linen
- ●Modacrylic ●Nylon
- ●Olefin
- ●Polyester
- ●Rayon ●Silk
- ●Spandex
- ●Triacetate
- ●Wool

Since iodine is a dye, it must be treated immediately to prevent a permanent stain. Sponge* the area thoroughly with water. Add 1 teaspoon sodium thiosulfate (available at drug stores) to ½ cup warm water and stir until crystals are completely dissolved. Test the fabric with the solution; if color doesn't change, wet the stain with this solution, blotting with an absorbent pad. Flush* well with clear water and repeat if necessary.

- ●Acrylic Plastic
- ●Ceramic Glass/Tile
- ●Glass ●Paint/Flat
- ●Paint/Gloss
- ●Plexiglas
- ●Polyurethane
- ●Porcelain Fixtures
- ●Vinyl Clothing
- ●Vinyl Wallcovering

Wipe the stain with a cloth or sponge dipped in warm sudsy water to which a few drops of ammonia have been added. Rinse well and wipe dry.

- ●Alabaster ●Marble

Mix a few drops of ammonia with a cup of 3% hydrogen peroxide. Soak a white blotter (about the size of the stain) with the solution and place it over the stain. Weight it down with a piece of glass or other heavy object. Continue applying the solution until the stain has been bleached out. For tougher stains, make a bleach poultice from powdered detergent, bleach, and water. Apply this paste to the stain and cover with a damp pad

(continued)

---

*See Chapter 4 for specific technique instructions.

(continued from preceding page) to retard evaporation. Leave over-night. Then remove the dried paste, rinse the area with clear water, and dry.

•Asphalt •Cork •Linoleum	Rub the stain with a cloth dampened in a solution of ammonia and water. If any stain remains, saturate the cloth in the solution and place it over the stain until it is either removed or no more stain is being lifted. Wash the area and wax as usual.
•Bluestone •Brick •Concrete •Flagstone •Granite •Masonry Tile •Slate •Terrazzo	Wash with a solution of washing soda or detergent (not soap) and water. Use a cloth or soft-bristled brush to help scrub. Rinse thoroughly with clear water and allow to dry.
•Grout	Wipe the area with a cloth dipped in warm sudsy water. If any stain remains, apply **Afta Tile & Grout Cleaner** or dip a wet toothbrush into baking soda or powdered cleanser and gently scrub the spot. Rinse well and wipe dry.
•Leather •Suede	Because iodine contains a dye, it affects the hide of these materials on contact. Therefore it cannot be removed.
•Wood	Mix dishwashing detergent in hot water and swish to make a great volume of suds. Dip a cloth in only the foam and apply to the iodine stain. Rinse with a clean cloth moistened with clear water. Polish or wax as soon as possible.

Iron *(Follow procedures for Rust.)*

Jam/Jelly
(See Apple, Berries, Cherry, Grape, Orange, Prune.)

Juice
(See Apple, Berries, Cherry, Grape, Orange, Prune, Tomato.)

Ketchup   *(See* Catsup.)

Lacquer

●**Acetate** ●**Fiberglass ●Rayon** ●**Silk ●Triacetate** ●**Wool**	Scrape* to remove excess. Apply a Dry Spotter to the stain and cover with an absorbent pad moistened with Dry Spotter. Let it stand as long as any stain is being removed. Keep the pad and stain moist. Flush* with a dry-cleaning solvent, **Carbona No. 10 Special Spot Remover/Carbona Cleaning Fluid,** and allow to dry.
●**Acrylic Fabric** ●**Burlap ●Cotton** ●**Linen ●Modacrylic** ●**Nylon ●Olefin** ●**Polyester ●Rope** ●**Spandex**	Scrape* to remove any excess lacquer immediately. Flush* acetone through the stain to an absorbent pad underneath. When no more stain is being removed, change pads and flush well with a dry-cleaning solvent, either **Carbona No. 10 Special Spot Remover/Carbona Cleaning Fluid** or **Afta Cleaning Fluid.** Allow to dry thoroughly.
●**Acrylic Plastic** ●**Asphalt ●Cork** ●**Linoleum** ●**Plexiglas** ●**Polyurethane** ●**Vinyl Clothing**	Lacquer can quickly damage or ruin these surfaces, so act immediately. Scrape* to remove any excess with a dull knife. Dab the area with a cloth dipped in amyl acetate. Rinse. Note: This stain may be permanent.

(continued)

*See Chapter 4 for specific technique instructions.

●**Vinyl Tile** ●**Vinyl Wallcovering**	*(see base of preceding page)*
●**Alabaster** ●**Marble**	Wipe up the excess immediately. Wipe the area with a cloth dampened with acetone. Rinse with a damp cloth and wipe dry. If any stain remains, make a poultice of water, 3% hydrogen peroxide, and a mild powder detergent. Apply the poultice to the stain and cover with a damp cloth to retard evaporation. When the stain has been bleached out, rinse thoroughly with water and wipe dry.
●**Aluminum** ●**Iron** ●**Stainless Steel** ●**Tin**	Wipe excess immediately. To remove any discoloration, wash with a steel wool soap pad. Rinse thoroughly and wipe dry.
●**Bamboo** ●**Cane**	Remove the excess and wipe the area with a cloth dipped in mild pure soapsuds to which a little ammonia has been added. If any stain remains, try dipping the edge of a clean cloth into acetone and gently dab at the stain—be careful not to force any staining material into the surface. Note: If not treated immediately, this could become a permanent stain.
●**Bluestone** ●**Brick** ●**Concrete** ●**Flagstone** ●**Granite** ●**Limestone** ●**Masonry Tile** ●**Sandstone** ●**Slate** ●**Terrazzo**	Remove the excess as soon as possible. With a cloth dipped in acetone, dab at the remaining stain until no more is picked up. Wash the area with a soft-bristled brush, using a solution of washing soda or detergent (not soap) and water. Rinse with clear water and allow to dry.
●**Carpet/Synthetic** ●**Carpet/Wool**	Scrape* as much of the excess as you can without forcing the lacquer

(continued)

See Chapter 4 for specific technique instructions.

(continued from preceding page) deeper into the fiber. Apply amyl acetate to the stain and cover with an absorbent pad dampened with amyl acetate. Keep moist and let stand for about 15 minutes, blotting occasionally. Scrape to help loosen the stain. Carefully apply **Carbona Spray Spot Remover** and allow to thoroughly dry.

•Ceramic Glass/Tile
•Enamel •Glass
•Porcelain Fixtures

Wipe up excess lacquer as soon as possible. Wash with a cloth dipped in a solution of washing soda, water, and a few drops of ammonia. Rinse well and wipe dry. Hardened lacquer can sometimes be carefully scraped* with a razor blade on all surfaces except porcelain.

•Grout

Wipe up as much excess as possible. Apply **Afta Tile & Grout Cleaner** or dip a wet toothbrush into a little baking soda or powdered cleanser and scrub gently. Rinse well with clear water and wipe dry.

•Leather •Suede

Carefully scrape* to remove excess lacquer. Mix a solution of mild soap in lukewarm water. Swish to create a great volume of suds. Apply only the foam with a sponge. Dry with a clean cloth. If the lacquer has hardened, gently rub it with an emery board or a piece of fine sandpaper. As a thin layer of the hide will also be removed, work slowly and lightly.

•Paint/Flat
•Paint/Gloss

Wipe away the excess, being careful not to spread the lacquer. Wipe the stain with a cloth dipped in 1 pint warm water mixed with 1 tablespoon borax. Rinse with clear water and dry thoroughly.

---

*See Chapter 4 for specific technique instructions.

Lipstick

- **Acetate**
- **Carpet/Synthetic**
- **Carpet/Wool**
- **Fiberglass**
- **Modacrylic**
- **Rayon** ●**Silk**
- **Triacetate** ●**Wool**

Sponge* the area with a dry-cleaning solvent, either **Carbona No. 10 Special Spot Remover/Carbona Cleaning Fluid, K2r Spot-lifter** (tube), or **Afta Cleaning Fluid.** Then apply a Dry Spotter and blot immediately with an absorbent pad. Continue sponging and blotting until no more stain is removed. If stain begins to spread, flush* immediately with one of the liquid dry-cleaning solvents. Let all the solvent evaporate, then sponge the area with water. Apply Wet Spotter and a few drops of ammonia (do not use ammonia on silk or wool). Blot frequently with an absorbent pad. Flush with water to remove all ammonia. Apply Wet Spotter and a few drops of white vinegar. Blot frequently with an absorbent pad. Flush with water and allow to dry.

- **Acrylic Fabric**
- **Cotton** ●**Linen**
- **Nylon** ●**Olefin**
- **Polyester**
- **Spandex**

Pretreat* with **Shout Laundry Soil & Stain Remover** or **Magic Pre-Wash** as directed and rinse in warm water. If color remains, presoak* in 1 quart warm water and 1 tablespoon **Axion** or **Biz** (enzyme presoaks) for 1 hour. Launder immediately, if possible. If not, rinse well and dry thoroughly. If any stain remains, apply a dry-cleaning solvent—either **Carbona No. 10 Special Spot Remover/Carbona Cleaning Fluid, K2r Spot-lifter** (aerosol), or **Afta Cleaning Fluid**— and Dry Spotter. Blot immediately with an absorbent pad. If stain begins to spread, flush* immediately with one of the liquid dry-cleaning solvents. Let all the solvent evaporate. If stain still remains, sponge* with

(continued)

*See Chapter 4 for specific technique instructions.

(continued from preceding page) water and apply a Wet Spotter with a few drops of ammonia. Tamp* and blot frequently with an absorbent pad. Flush well with water. Allow to dry. Launder as soon as possible.

●Acrylic Plastic ●Ceramic Glass/Tile ●Glass ●Paint/Flat ●Paint/Gloss ●Plexiglas ●Polyurethane ●Porcelain Dishes ●Porcelain Fixtures ●Stainless Steel ●Vinyl Clothing ●Vinyl Wallcovering	Wipe stain with a cloth dipped in warm sudsy water. Rinse well and wipe dry. If stain remains, add a few drops of ammonia to warm sudsy water and wipe. Rinse well, then dry with a clean cloth.
●Alabaster ●Marble	Mix a few drops of ammonia in 1 cup rubbing alcohol. Soak a white blotter with the solution and place it over the stain. Weight it down with a piece of glass or other heavy object. Continue applying the solution until the grease is drawn out and any remaining stain is bleached out. If any color remains, make a poultice of bleach, powdered detergent, and water. Apply to the stain and cover with a damp cloth to retard drying. Leave until stain has been bleached out.
●Asphalt ●Cork ●Linoleum ●Vinyl Tile	Mix a solution of warm sudsy water and a few drops of ammonia. Dip a plastic scouring pad (do not use steel wool) into the solution and rub gently. Rinse well and wipe dry.
●Fur/Natural ●Fur/Synthetic ●Leather ●Suede	Gently scrape* to remove excess lipstick. Wipe stain with a cloth dipped in the suds of a mild detergent and water. Wipe with a clean dry cloth. If a grease stain remains, powder the *(continued)*

See Chapter 4 for specific technique instructions.

(continued from preceding page) stain with an absorbent such as cornmeal. Give it plenty of time to work. Gently brush* it out. Repeat if necessary. As a last resort, dip a cloth in either **Carbona No. 10 Special Spot Remover/Carbona Cleaning Fluid** or **Afta Cleaning Fluid** and dab gently at stain. Do not rub. On leather only, follow with **The Tannery** or **Fiebing's Saddle Soap** to condition the leather.

Liquid Foundation

- **Acetate**
- **Carpet/Synthetic**
- **Carpet/Wool**
- **Fiberglass** ●**Rayon**
- **Silk** ●**Triacetate**
- **Wool**

Brush* or blot up any excess, taking care not to spread the stain. Flush* with a dry-cleaning solvent, either **Carbona No. 10 Special Spot Remover/Carbona Cleaning Fluid, K2r Spot-lifter** (tube), or **Afta Cleaning Fluid.** Apply a Dry Spotter to the stain and cover with an absorbent pad dampened with the Dry Spotter. Check the stain every 5 minutes. Before changing pads, press hard against the stain. Continue the alternate soaking and pressing until no more stain is being removed. Flush with one of the liquid dry-cleaning solvents and allow to dry. If any stain remains, flush it with water and apply a Wet Spotter with a few drops of ammonia. (Do not use ammonia on silk or wool.) Cover with an absorbent pad dampened with the Wet Spotter. Let it stand as long as any stain is being removed. Change the pad as it picks up the stain. Keep the stain and pad moist. Flush well with water. Repeat if necessary; allow to dry.

- **Acrylic Fabric**
- **Cotton** ●**Linen**
- **Modacrylic** ●**Nylon**

(continued)

Brush* or blot up any excess, taking care not to spread the stain. Flush* with a dry-cleaning solvent, either

See Chapter 4 for specific technique instructions.

(continued from preceding page)

●Olefin ●Polyester
●Spandex

Carbona No. 10 Special Spot Remover/Carbona Cleaning Fluid or **Afta Cleaning Fluid.** Apply a Dry Spotter to the stain and cover with a cloth dampened with the Dry Spotter. Check the stain often, tamping* before changing the pad. Continue alternate soaking and tamping until no more stain is lifted. Flush with a dry-cleaning solvent and allow to dry. If any stain remains, try the same procedure of soaking and tamping using a Wet Spotter and a few drops of ammonia. When the stain is gone, be sure to flush the area with water to remove all traces of ammonia. Launder as soon as possible.

●**Acrylic Plastic**
●**Alabaster**
●**Asphalt** ●**Bamboo**
●**Cane**
●**Ceramic Glass/Tile**
●**Cork** ●**Enamel**
●**Glass** ●**Gold**
●**Ivory** ●**Jade**
●**Linoleum** ●**Marble**
●**Paint/Flat**
●**Paint/Gloss**
●**Plexiglas**
●**Polyurethane**
●**Stainless Steel**
●**Vinyl Clothing**
●**Vinyl Tile**
●**Vinyl Wallcovering**

Wipe any spills or brush* away any excess. With a cloth or sponge dipped in warm sudsy water, wash the surface. Rinse well with water and wipe dry with a clean cloth.

●**Bluestone**
●**Masonry Tile**
●**Sandstone** ●**Slate**
●**Terrazzo**

Remove excess. Mix a solution of washing soda or detergent (not soap) and water. Wash the stained area. Rinse well with clear water and allow to dry.

---

*See Chapter 4 for specific technique instructions.

•Leather •Suede	Gently remove excess. Mix a solution of mild soap in lukewarm water. Swish to create a great volume of suds. Apply only the foam with a sponge. Wipe dry with a clean cloth. If a greasy or oily stain remains, powder it with an absorbent such as cornmeal. Give it plenty of time to work. Gently brush* or shake the absorbent from the surface. Repeat if necessary. On leather only, follow with **The Tannery** or **Fiebing's Saddle Soap** to condition the leather.
•Wood	Mix dishwashing detergent in hot water and swish to make a great volume of suds. Dip a cloth in only the foam and apply to the stain. Rinse with clear water. Wipe dry immediately with a soft cloth and polish or wax as usual.

Lotions/Body, Facial, Foot, Hair

•Acetate •Carpet/Synthetic •Carpet/Wool •Fiberglass •Rayon •Silk •Triacetate •Wool	Blot up any excess lotion, taking care not to spread the stain. Flush* with a dry-cleaning solvent, either **Carbona No. 10 Special Spot Remover/ Carbona Cleaning Fluid, K2r Spotlifter** (tube), or **Afta Cleaning Fluid** and apply a Dry Spotter to the stain. Cover with an absorbent pad dampened with Dry Spotter. Check the stain every 5 minutes. Before changing pads, press hard against the stain. Continue the alternate soaking and pressing until no more stain is being removed. Flush with one of the liquid dry-cleaning solvents and allow to dry. If any stain remains, flush with water and apply a

(continued)

See Chapter 4 for specific technique instructions.

(continued from preceding page) Wet Spotter with a few drops of ammonia added. (Do not use ammonia on silk or wool.) Cover with an absorbent pad moistened with Wet Spotter. Let it stand as long as any stain is being removed. Change the pad as it picks up the stain. Keep the stain and pad moist with Wet Spotter. Flush well with water and allow to dry. Repeat if necessary.

●**Acrylic Fabric**
●**Cotton** ●**Linen**
●**Modacrylic** ●**Nylon**
●**Olefin** ●**Polyester**
●**Spandex**

Blot as much excess as possible. Flush* stain with dry-cleaning solvent, either **Carbona No. 10 Special Spot Remover/Carbona Cleaning Fluid, K2r Spot-lifter** (aerosol), or **Afta Cleaning Fluid** and apply a Dry Spotter. Cover with an absorbent pad dampened with Dry Spotter. Check the stain often, tamping before changing the pad. Continue alternate soaking and tamping until no more stain is removed. Flush with one of the liquid dry-cleaning solvents and allow to dry. If any stain remains, try the same soaking/tamping procedure, using a Wet Spotter and a few drops of ammonia. After stain has been removed, flush area with water to remove all traces of ammonia. Launder as soon as possible.

●**Acrylic Plastic**
●**Alabaster**
●**Asphalt** ●**Bamboo**
●**Cane**
●**Ceramic Glass/Tile**
●**Cork** ●**Enamel**
●**Glass** ●**Gold**
●**Ivory** ●**Jade**
●**Linoleum** ●**Marble**
●**Paint/Flat**
●**Paint/Gloss**

Wipe any spills immediately with a cloth dipped in warm sudsy water. Rinse well with water and wipe dry with a clean cloth.

(continued)

*See Chapter 4 for specific technique instructions.

- **Platinum**   *(see base of preceding page)*
- **Plexiglas**
- **Polyurethane**
- **Stainless Steel**
- **Vinyl Clothing**
- **Vinyl Tile**
- **Vinyl Wallcovering**

• **Bluestone** • **Brick** • **Masonry Tile** • **Sandstone** • **Slate** • **Terrazzo**	Remove excess spill. Mix a solution of washing soda or detergent (not soap) and water. Wash the stained area using a cloth or soft-bristled brush. Rinse well with clear water and allow to dry.
• **Leather** • **Suede**	Very gently scrape* to remove any excess. Mix a solution of mild soap in lukewarm water. Swish to create a great volume of suds. Apply only the foam with a sponge. Wipe dry with a clean cloth. If a greasy or oily residue remains, powder it with an absorbent such as cornmeal. Allow plenty of time for it to work. Then gently brush* the powder off. Repeat the powdering procedure if necessary. On leather only, follow with **The Tannery** or **Fiebing's Saddle Soap** to condition the leather.
• **Wood**	Mix dishwashing detergent in hot water and swish to make a great volume of suds. Dip a cloth in only the foam and apply. Rinse with clear water. Wipe dry with a soft cloth and polish or wax as usual.

Lotion/Hand

• **Acetate** • **Carpet/Synthetic** • **Carpet/Wool**	Sponge* the area with a dry-cleaning solvent, either **Carbona No. 10 Special Spot Remover/Carbona**

(continued)

See Chapter 4 for specific technique instructions.

(continued from preceding page)

●**Fiberglass** ●**Rayon**
●**Silk** ●**Triacetate**
●**Wool**

Cleaning Fluid, K2r Spot-lifter (tube), or **Afta Cleaning Fluid.** Apply a Dry Spotter to the stain and cover with an absorbent pad dampened with Dry Spotter. Let pad remain as long as any stain is being picked up. Change the pad as it picks up the stain. Keep both the stain and pad moist with Dry Spotter. To help loosen stubborn stains on stronger fabrics, tamp* or scrape* the area. Flush* with one of the liquid dry-cleaning solvents. Repeat if necessary. If stain persists, sponge with water and apply a Wet Spotter and a few drops of ammonia. (Do not use ammonia on silk or wool.) Keep the stain moist and occasionally blot with an absorbent pad. Again, if the fabric is sturdy, tamp or scrape to help loosen the stain. Flush with water and allow to dry.

●**Acrylic Fabric**
●**Cotton** ●**Linen**
●**Modacrylic** ●**Nylon**
●**Olefin** ●**Polyester**
●**Spandex**

Gently scrape* to remove any excess lotion. Moisten the spot with water and apply a solution of 1 cup warm water and 1 tablespoon **Axion** or **Biz** (enzyme presoak products). Wait for 30 minutes, then flush* area with water. If possible launder immediately. If not, allow fabric to air dry.

●**Acrylic Plastic**
●**Aluminum**
●**Asphalt**
●**Ceramic Glass/Tile**
●**Chromium**
●**Copper** ●**Cork**
●**Glass** ●**Gold**
●**Ivory** ●**Jade**
●**Linoleum**
●**Paint/Flat**

Wipe up any excess with a cloth or sponge dipped in warm sudsy water. Rinse well with water and wipe dry.

(continued)

---

*See Chapter 4 for specific technique instructions.

- **Paint/Gloss**   *(see base of preceding page)*
- **Pearls**
- **Platinum**
- **Plexiglas**
- **Polyurethane**
- **Porcelain Fixtures**
- **Silver**
- **Stainless Steel**
- **Tin** •**Vinyl Clothing**
- **Vinyl Tile**
- **Vinyl Wallcovering**
- **Zinc**

•**Bluestone** •**Brick** •**Concrete**	Wipe up any excess. Wash with a solution of washing soda or detergent (not soap) and water. Use a cloth or soft-bristled brush to help scrub. Rinse thoroughly with clear water and allow to dry.
•**Leather** •**Suede**	Mix a solution of mild soap in luke-warm water. Swish to create a great volume of suds. Apply only the foam with a sponge. Wipe with a clean dry cloth. If any sticky trace remains, test a dry-cleaning solvent, **Carbona No. 10 Special Spot Remover/Carbona Cleaning Fluid,** on an inconspicuous place. Then dab the solvent on the spot with a soft cloth. Allow the area to thoroughly dry. On leather only, follow with **The Tannery** or **Fiebing's Saddle Soap** to condition the leather.
•**Wood**	Mix dishwashing detergent in hot water and swish to make a great volume of suds. Dip a cloth in only the foam and apply. Rinse with a clean cloth moistened with clear water. Polish or wax as soon as possible.

Lotion/Suntan

- Acetate
- Carpet/Synthetic
- Carpet/Wool
- Fiberglass ● Rayon
- Silk ● Triacetate
- Wool

Scrape* to remove as much excess as you can. Sponge* the area with a dry-cleaning solvent, either **Carbona No. 10 Special Spot Remover/Carbona Cleaning Fluid** or **Afta Cleaning Fluid.** Apply a Dry Spotter to the stain and cover it with an absorbent pad dampened with the Dry Spotter. Let the pad remain as long as it picks up any stain. Keep both the pad and stain wet with the Dry Spotter. Flush* the area with the dry-cleaning solvent. If stain persists, sponge with water and apply a Wet Spotter and a few drops of ammonia. Do not use the ammonia on silk or wool. Keep the stain moist and occasionally blot with an absorbent pad. Flush with water and make sure all traces of the ammonia are out of the fabric. Allow to dry.

- Acrylic Fabric
- Cotton ● Linen
- Modacrylic ● Nylon
- Olefin ● Polyester
- Spandex

Gently scrape* to remove excess lotion. Moisten the spot with water and apply a mixture of 1 tablespoon **Axion** or **Biz** (enzyme presoaks) and 1 cup warm water. Let the stain soak for 30 minutes. Flush* the area with water. If possible, launder immediately. If not, allow the fabric to air dry.

- Acrylic Plastic
- Aluminum
- Asphalt
- Ceramic Glass/Tile
- Copper ● Cork
- Glass ● Gold
- Ivory ● Jade
- Linoleum
- Paint/Flat
- Paint/Gloss

Wipe up any excess with a cloth or sponge dipped in warm sudsy water to which a few drops of ammonia have been added. Rinse well to remove all ammonia and wipe dry.

(continued)

*See Chapter 4 for specific technique instructions.

●Platinum   *(see base of preceding page)*
●Plexiglas
●Polyurethane
●Porcelain ●Silver
●Stainless Steel
●Vinyl Clothing
●Vinyl Tile
●Vinyl Wallcovering

●Bluestone ●Brick ●Concrete ●Flagstone ●Granite ●Limestone ●Slate ●Terrazzo	Wipe up any excess. Wash with a solution of washing soda or detergent (never soap) and water. Use a sponge or soft-bristled brush. Rinse thoroughly and allow to dry.
●Leather ●Suede	Mix a solution of mild soap in luke-warm water. Swish to create a great volume of suds. Apply only the foam with a sponge. Wipe dry with a clean cloth. If any sticky traces remain, test **Carbona No. 10 Special Spot Remover/Carbona Cleaning Fluid** on an inconspicuous place. If safe to use, gently dab the solvent onto the spot with a clean cloth. Allow the area to dry thoroughly. On leather only, follow with **The Tannery** or **Fiebing's Saddle Soap** to condition the leather.
●Wood	Wipe up any excess, then wash the spot with a cloth dipped in warm sudsy water. Rinse with a damp clean cloth and wipe dry. Polish or wax the wood as soon as possible.

Makeup
(*See* Blusher, Eye Pencil/Eyeliner/Eyeshadow, Face Powder, Lipstick, Liquid Foundation, Lotions/Body, Facial, Foot Hair, Lotion/Hand, Lotion/Suntan, Mascara, Rouge.)

Margarine (*Follow procedures for* Butter.)

Mascara

(*Follow procedures for* Eyeliner/Eye Pencil/Eyeshadow.)

Mayonnaise

- **Acetate** • **Burlap**
- **Carpet/Synthetic**
- **Carpet/Wool**
- **Fiberglass** • **Rayon**
- **Rope** • **Silk**
- **Triacetate**
- **Wool**

Gently scrape* to remove any excess. Sponge* the area with a dry-cleaning solvent, either **Carbona No. 10 Special Spot Remover/Carbona Cleaning Fluid** or **Afta Cleaning Fluid.** Apply a Dry Spotter to the stain and cover with an absorbent pad moistened with Dry Spotter. Let it stand as long as any stain is removed. Change the pad as it picks up the stain. Keep the stain and pad moist with Dry Spotter. When no more stain is removed, flush* with the dry-cleaning solvent. Allow to dry. If any stain persists, moisten it with a solution of ½ teaspoon **Axion** enzyme presoak and ½ cup warm water —do not use on silk or wool. Cover with a clean pad that has been dipped into the solution and wrung almost dry. Let it stand for 30 minutes; add enough solution to keep the area warm and moist but avoid letting the wet area spread. Flush area with water and allow to dry. On carpets, place a clean dry pad over the area and weight it down. When no more liquid is being absorbed, allow the area to thoroughly air dry.

- **Acrylic Fabric**
- **Cotton** • **Linen**
- **Modacrylic** • **Nylon**

(continued)

Scrape* to remove as much excess as possible. Apply a Wet Spotter and work it into the fabric. Rinse thor-

*See Chapter 4 for specific technique instructions.

(continued from preceding page)

● Olefin ● Polyester
● Spandex

oughly with water and launder. If laundering must wait and there is any trace of stain remaining, try applying a paste made with water and **Axion** or **Biz** (enzyme presoak products). Let the paste work awhile and keep it moist. Thoroughly rinse the area to remove all traces of the enzymes. Allow to dry and launder as soon as possible.

● Acrylic Plastic
● Aluminum
● Asphalt ● Bamboo
● Bronze ● Cane
● Ceramic Glass/Tile
● Chromium
● Copper ● Cork
● Enamel ● Glass
● Gold ● Iron ● Ivory
● Linoleum
● Paint/Flat
● Paint/Gloss
● Pewter ● Plexiglas
● Polyurethane
● Porcelain Dishes
● Porcelain Fixtures
● Stainless Steel
● Tin ● Vinyl Clothing
● Vinyl Tile
● Vinyl Wallcovering
● Zinc

Wipe up spill as soon as possible with a cloth or sponge dipped in warm sudsy water. Rinse with clear water and allow to dry.

● Alabaster
● Bluestone
● Concrete
● Flagstone
● Granite
● Limestone
● Marble
● Masonry Tile

Remove excess spill. Wipe with a cloth dipped in a solution of washing soda or detergent (not soap) and warm water. If any stain remains, mix a poultice of water, mild bleach, and a powdered detergent and apply to the stain. Cover with a damp cloth to retard evaporation. When stain is gone, rinse well with water and wipe dry.

(continued)

●Sandstone ●Slate ●Terrazzo	*(see base of preceding page)*
●Leather ●Suede	Mix a solution of mild soap in luke-warm water. Swish to create a great volume of suds. Apply only the foam with a sponge. Wipe dry with a clean cloth. On leather only, follow with **The Tannery** or **Fiebing's Saddle Soap** to condition the leather.
●Silver	Remove mayonnaise from silver by washing it in hot soapy water. Rinse in hot water and wipe dry with a soft cloth to prevent tarnish.
●Wallpaper	Wipe immediately with a damp cloth or sponge moistened with cool clear water. Overlap strokes to avoid streaking. Use a clean dry cloth to gently pat dry.
●Wood	Wipe surface with a cloth dipped in warm sudsy water. Rinse with clean damp cloth, wipe dry, and polish or wax as usual.

Mercurochrome/Merthiolate

●Acetate ●Fiberglass ●Rayon ●Silk ●Triacetate ●Wool	Sponge* area immediately with water to dilute the spill. Spray on **Amway Remove Fabric Spot Cleaner.** Then apply a Wet Spotter and a few drops of ammonia (use care with ammonia on silk and wool). Cover with an absorbent pad dampened with Wet Spotter. Let the pad remain in place as long as any stain is being removed, changing it as it picks up the stain. Keep both the stain and pad moist with Wet Spotter and ammonia. Flush* well with water and repeat if necessary. If, after drying, a stain

(continued)

See Chapter 4 for specific technique instructions.

(continued from preceding page) persists, mix a little **Rit Color Remover** according to package directions. After testing on an inconspicuous place, flush the color remover through the stain to an absorbent pad beneath. Rinse well with water and allow to dry.

- **Acrylic Fabric**
- **Cotton** ●**Linen**
- **Modacrylic** ●**Nylon**
- **Olefin** ●**Polyester**
- **Spandex**

Spray on **Amway Remove Fabric Spot Cleaner.** Then soak the item in a solution of 1 quart warm water, ½ teaspoon dishwashing detergent, and 1 tablespoon ammonia for 30 minutes. Rinse well with water. If stain persists, soak in a solution of 1 quart warm water and 1 tablespoon white vinegar. Use vinegar with care on cotton and linen. Rinse well with water and allow to dry. If stain has set, apply rubbing alcohol to the area and tamp.* As stain loosens, blot liquid and stain with an absorbent pad. Keep both the stain and pad moist with alcohol and change pad as it picks up stain. Allow to dry. As a last resort, mix **Rit Color Remover** according to package directions and test its action on a hidden place. If color of fabric doesn't change, flush color remover through the stain. Flush well with clear water and allow to dry thoroughly.

- **Acrylic Plastic**
- **Aluminum**
- **Bamboo** ●**Cane**
- **Ceramic Glass/Tile**
- **Glass** ●**Paint/Flat**
- **Paint/Gloss**
- **Plexiglas**
- **Polyurethane**
- **Vinyl Clothing**
- **Vinyl Wallcovering**

Immediately wipe up spill with a cloth or sponge dipped in warm sudsy water. Rinse well and wipe dry.

*See Chapter 4 for specific technique instructions.

•Alabaster •Marble	Immediately wipe up the spill with a cloth dipped in warm sudsy water. Rinse well and wipe dry. If a stain remains, soak an absorbent pad in rubbing alcohol, wring almost dry, and place over stain. Wait several minutes, then apply an absorbent pad moistened with ammonia. Alternate alcohol and ammonia pads until stain has been removed. Wipe surface with cloth dampened with clear water and wipe dry with clean cloth.
•Asphalt •Cork **•Linoleum** **•Vinyl Tile**	Wipe up any excess spill with a cloth dipped in warm sudsy water. Rinse well and wipe dry. If a stain remains, cover with an absorbent pad soaked in rubbing alcohol. Let it remain in place for several minutes, then wipe stain with a cloth dampened with ammonia. (Do not use ammonia on linoleum or vinyl floor tile.) Rinse well with a cloth moistened with warm sudsy water, then rewipe with a cloth dampened with clear water. Allow to dry.
•Bluestone •Brick **•Concrete** **•Flagstone** **•Granite** **•Masonry Tile** **•Sandstone •Slate** **•Terrazzo**	Wipe up excess spill and wash with a solution of washing soda or detergent (not soap) and water. Use a cloth or soft-bristled brush to scrub. Rinse thoroughly with clear water and allow to dry.
•Carpet/Synthetic **•Carpet/Wool**	**Spot Shot Carpet Stain Remover** should take care of the stain. If not, sponge **Rit Color Remover** on the stain and blot with an absorbent pad. Rinse and blot up excess liquid.
•Grout	Wipe up excess with a cloth dipped in warm sudsy water. If any stain

(continued)

(continued from preceding page) persists, apply **Afta Tile & Grout Cleaner** or dip a wet toothbrush into baking soda or powdered cleanser and gently scrub. Rinse well with water and wipe dry.

•Leather •Suede

Mercurochrome or merthiolate will immediately discolor leather and suede. Once contact has been made, there is no way to remove the discoloration.

•Wood

Mix dishwashing detergent in hot water and swish to make a great volume of suds. Dip a cloth in only the foam and apply to the stain. Rinse with a clean cloth dampened with clear water. Polish or wax as soon as possible.

Mildew

•Acetate
•Carpet/Synthetic
•Carpet/Wool
•Fiberglass •Rayon
•Silk •Triacetate
•Wool

Brush* off any excess stain gently. Flush* with a dry-cleaning solvent, either **Carbona No. 10 Special Spot Remover/Carbona Cleaning Fluid** or **Afta Cleaning Fluid.** Then apply a Dry Spotter and amyl acetate. Very gently scrape* or pat the stain with an absorbent pad dampened with Dry Spotter. Flush with the dry-cleaning solvent and allow to dry. If stain persists, sponge* with water and apply a Wet Spotter and a few drops of white vinegar. Scrape or use an absorbent pad dampened with Wet Spotter to work the stain. Flush with water and allow to dry. Apply rubbing alcohol and pat the stain with a pad dampened with alcohol. Flush with alcohol and allow to dry. (Do not use alcohol on acetate, rayon, or triacetate.) To remove any final traces of the stain, use an oxygen bleach as directed on the package label. When treating car-

(continued)

*See Chapter 4 for specific technique instructions.

(continued from preceding page) pets, blot all excess liquid, apply an absorbent pad and weight it down until no more moisture is absorbed. **Afta Mildew Stop,** available in aerosol or dry packet forms, is a good preventive measure. Be sure to read directions carefully.

●**Acrylic Fabric**
●**Cotton** ●**Linen**
●**Modacrylic** ●**Nylon**
●**Olefin** ●**Polyester**
●**Spandex**

Usually most mildew stains can be removed during regular laundering if they are moistened beforehand. If any stain remains, test fabric for colorfastness. If color doesn't change, cover stain with a paste of lemon juice and salt. On cotton and linen, make a paste from an oxygen-type bleach, water, and a few drops of ammonia. Let paste cover stain for 15 to 30 minutes. Flush* thoroughly with water and launder again.

●**Bamboo** ●**Cane**
●**Cork** ●**Linoleum**
●**Vinyl Clothing**
●**Vinyl Tile**
●**Vinyl Wallcovering**

Wipe stain with a cloth dipped in warm sudsy water to which a few drops of ammonia have been added. Rinse well with clear water and wipe dry. If stain is stubborn, test on an inconspicuous place, then apply **X-14 Instant Mildew Stain Remover** according to package directions. Do not use the product on fabric or flocked wallcoverings.

●**Ceramic Tile**
●**Grout**

Apply **Carbona Tile and Bath Cleaner** or **X-14 Instant Mildew Stain Remover.** Another effective method is to dampen the stain with water and rub gently with bar soap—not a deodorant soap. Rinse thoroughly. Blot excess liquid and allow to dry.

●**Leather** ●**Suede**

Rub the stain with petroleum jelly. If stain remains, sponge the area gently with equal parts water and

(continued)

---

*See Chapter 4 for specific technique instructions.

(continued from preceding page) rubbing alcohol (be sure to test for colorfastness first). Then, on suede apply **Child Life Suede & Fabric Cleaner.** On leather condition with **The Tannery** or **Fiebing's Saddle Soap.**

● **Wood**

Gently remove excess with a cloth dipped in a solution of 5 tablespoons washing soda per 1 gallon water. Rinse with a clean cloth moistened with clear water and polish or wax as soon as possible.

Milk *(Follow procedures for Cream.)*

Mud/Dirt

● **Acetate** ● **Burlap**
● **Fiberglass** ● **Rayon**
● **Rope** ● **Silk**
● **Triacetate**
● **Wool**

Let mud dry, then brush* off the excess. This should remove the stain, but if any remains sponge* the area with water and apply a few drops Wet Spotter and a few drops white vinegar. Cover with an absorbent pad dampened with Wet Spotter. Let stand as long as any stain is being removed. Change the pad as it picks up the stain. Keep stain and pad moist with Wet Spotter and vinegar. Flush* with water and repeat Wet Spotter/flushing until no more stain is removed. If stain remains, apply rubbing alcohol to the area and cover with an absorbent pad dampened with alcohol. (Do not use alcohol on acetate, rayon, or triacetate.) Let the pad stand as long as any stain is being removed. Change the pad as it picks up the stain. Keep the stain and pad moist with alcohol. If stain persists, moisten the area with a solution

(continued)

*See Chapter 4 for specific technique instructions.

(continued from preceding page) of 1 cup warm water and 1 teaspoon **Axion** enzyme presoak, but do not use on silk or wool. Cover with a clean pad that has been dipped in the solution and wrung almost dry. Let it stand for 30 minutes. Add enough solution to keep the area warm and just moist. When no more stain is being lifted, flush thoroughly with water and allow to dry.

- ●**Acrylic Fabric**
- ●**Cotton** ●**Linen**
- ●**Modacrylic** ●**Nylon**
- ●**Olefin** ●**Polyester**
- ●**Spandex**

Let mud dry, then brush* off excess. Laundering should remove any remaining stain. If more treatment is needed, sponge* the stain with rubbing alcohol. (Do not use alcohol on acrylic or modacrylic.) Flush* with water. If stain persists, sponge it with a dry-cleaning solvent, either **Carbona No. 10 Special Spot Remover/Carbona Cleaning Fluid, K2r Spot-lifter** (aerosol), or **Afta Cleaning Fluid.** Allow to dry, then launder.

- ●**Acrylic Plastic**
- ●**Alabaster**
- ●**Aluminum**
- ●**Asphalt** ●**Bamboo**
- ●**Brass** ●**Bronze**
- ●**Cane**
- ●**Ceramic Glass/Tile**
- ●**Chromium**
- ●**Copper** ●**Cork**
- ●**Enamel** ●**Glass**
- ●**Grout** ●**Iron**
- ●**Linoleum** ●**Marble**
- ●**Paint/Flat**
- ●**Paint/Gloss**
- ●**Plexiglas**
- ●**Polyurethane**
- ●**Porcelain Dishes**
- ●**Porcelain Fixtures**

Scrape* any excess with a dull knife or spatula. Wipe the surface with a cloth or sponge dipped in warm sudsy water. Rinse well and wipe dry.

(continued)

See Chapter 4 for specific technique instructions.

●**Stainless Steel**   *(see base of preceding page)*
●**Tin** ●**Vinyl Clothing**
●**Vinyl Tile**
●**Vinyl Wallcovering**
●**Zinc**

●**Bluestone** ●**Brick**   Carefully remove excess. Wash with
●**Concrete**   a solution of washing soda (not soap)
●**Flagstone**   and water. Use a cloth or soft-bristled
●**Granite**   brush to help clean. Rinse thoroughly
●**Limestone**   with clear water and allow to dry.
●**Masonry Tile**
●**Sandstone** ●**Slate**
●**Terrazzo**

●**Carpet/Synthetic**   To avoid forcing it further into pile,
●**Carpet/Wool**   allow mud to dry before treating it.
                Gently brush* loose soil, then
                vacuum as usual. If a stain remains,
                spray with an aerosol carpet shampoo,
                either **Glory Professional
                Strength Rug Cleaner** or **Carbona 1
                Hour Rug Cleaner.** When the shampoo
                has dried, vacuum.

●**Felt** ●**Fur/Natural**   Allow mud to dry, then gently brush*
●**Fur/Synthetic**   off. Mix a solution of mild soap in
●**Leather** ●**Suede**   lukewarm water. Swish to create a
                great volume of suds. Apply only the
                foam with a sponge. Wipe area with
                clean dry cloth.

●**Silver**   Wash as soon as possible in hot
                sudsy water. Rinse in hot water and
                dry immediately with a soft cloth to
                prevent tarnish.

●**Wallpaper**   Brush* off any excess dirt. With a
                cloth or sponge dampened with cool
                clear water, wipe the stained area.
                Overlap strokes to avoid streaking.
                Gently pat dry.

---

*See Chapter 4 for specific technique instructions.

●**Wood**

Remove any excess dirt with a brush. Mix dishwashing detergent in hot water and swish to make a great volume of suds. Dip a cloth in only the foam and apply to the stain. Rinse with a clean cloth dampened with clear water. Polish or wax as soon as possible.

Mustard

●**Acetate** ●**Burlap**
●**Carpet/Synthetic**
●**Carpet/Wool**
●**Fiberglass** ●**Rayon**
●**Silk** ●**Triacetate**
●**Wool**

Note: Mustard contains turmeric, a yellow dye. If not treated immediately, it can be impossible to remove. Lift off any excess spill with a dull knife or spatula. Flush* the area with a dry-cleaning solvent, either **Carbona No. 10 Special Spot Remover/ Carbona Cleaning Fluid** or **Afta Cleaning Fluid.** If fabric is strong enough, tamp* or scrape* to loosen the stain. Flush with the dry-cleaning solvent. While tamping stain, blot excess material with an absorbent pad. If stain remains, sponge* with water and apply a Wet Spotter and a few drops of white vinegar. Tamp again to loosen stain. Flush with water. If stain persists, moisten area with 3% hydrogen peroxide and add a drop of ammonia (except on silk and wool). Do not let it bleach any longer than 15 minutes, then flush with water and allow to dry. When treating carpets, blot all excess liquid, then weight down an absorbent pad with a heavy object. When all liquid has been absorbed, allow to thoroughly air dry.

●**Acrylic Fabric**
●**Cotton** ●**Linen**
●**Modacrylic** ●**Nylon**
●**Olefin** ●**Polyester**
(continued)

Note: Mustard contains turmeric, a yellow dye. If not treated immediately, it can be impossible to remove. If stain has just occurred, spray

See Chapter 4 for specific technique instructions.

(continued from preceding page)

● **Spandex**

on **Amway Remove Fabric Spot Cleaner.** Or, if stain is older, scrape* as much of the spill as possible. Flush* with water, apply liquid detergent to the stain, and flush again. If the stain remains, presoak* for several hours or overnight in a warm-to-hot solution of detergent. Rinse and launder as soon as possible.

● **Acrylic Plastic**
● **Asphalt**
● **Vinyl Clothing**
● **Vinyl Tile**
● **Vinyl Wallcovering**

Note: Mustard contains turmeric, a yellow dye. If not treated immediately, it can be impossible to remove. Once mustard has set, the stain is almost impossible to remove from plastic materials. Immediately wipe up any spills with a cloth or sponge dipped in warm sudsy water. Rinse thoroughly and wipe dry with a soft cloth.

● **Aluminum**
● **Bamboo** ● **Cane**
● **Ceramic Glass/Tile**
● **Cork** ● **Glass**
● **Linoleum**
● **Paint/Flat**
● **Paint/Gloss**
● **Plexiglas**
● **Polyurethane**
● **Porcelain Dishes**
● **Stainless Steel**
● **Tin** ● **Zinc**

Scrape* to remove any excess spill (except on ceramic glass rangetops). Wipe the area with a cloth or sponge dipped in warm sudsy water. Rinse well with water and wipe dry with a soft cloth.

● **Bluestone** ● **Brick**
● **Concrete**
● **Flagstone**
● **Granite**
● **Limestone**
● **Masonry Tile**
● **Sandstone** ● **Slate**
● **Terrazzo**

Remove any excess spill. Wash stain with a solution of washing soda and water. Use a cloth or soft-bristled brush to help clean. Rinse thoroughly with clear water and allow to air dry.

See Chapter 4 for specific technique instructions.

•Grout

Wipe up any excess with a cloth dipped in warm sudsy water. If any stain remains, apply **Afta Tile & Grout Cleaner** or dip a wet toothbrush into a little baking soda or powdered cleanser and gently scrub the spot. Rinse thoroughly and wipe dry with a soft cloth.

•Leather •Suede

Note: Mustard contains turmeric, a yellow dye. If not treated immediately, it can be impossible to remove. Although mustard usually causes permanent stains on these materials, try mixing a solution of mild soap in lukewarm water, swishing to create a great volume of suds, and applying only the foam with a sponge. Wipe with a clean cloth dampened with clear water. Dry with a soft cloth. On leather only, follow with **The Tannery** or **Fiebing's Saddle Soap** to condition the leather.

•Silver

Wash in hot soapy water as soon as possible. Rinse in hot water and dry with a soft cloth immediately.

•Wallpaper

The turmeric in mustard usually permanently stains wallpaper. If the stain is fresh, gently wipe the stain with a cloth dipped in the suds of a mild detergent and water. Rinse with a clean cloth moistened with cool clear water. Gently pat dry.

•Wood

Immediately mix dishwashing detergent in hot water and swish to make a great volume of suds. Dip a cloth in only the foam and apply to the mustard. Rinse with a clean cloth dampened with cool clear water. Polish or wax when dry.

Nicotine/Cigar, Cigarette, Pipe Smoke

- **Acetate**
- **Fiberglass** • **Rayon**
- **Triacetate**

Spray on **Amway Remove Fabric Spot Cleaner.** Sponge* the stain with water and apply a Wet Spotter and a few drops of white vinegar. Cover with an absorbent pad dampened with Wet Spotter. Let it stand as long as it picks up the stain. Keep the stain and pad moist with Wet Spotter and vinegar. Flush* with water and repeat until no more stain is removed. If stain persists, moisten it with a solution of 1 cup warm water and 1 teaspoon **Axion** enzyme pre-soak. Cover with a clean pad that has been dipped in the solution and wrung almost dry. Let it stand for at least 30 minutes. Add enough solution to keep the stain warm and just moist. When the stain is removed, or no more is being lifted, flush thoroughly with water and allow to dry.

- **Acrylic Fabric**
- **Modacrylic** • **Nylon**
- **Olefin** • **Polyester**
- **Spandex**

Soak the stain in a solution of 1 quart warm water, ½ teaspoon liquid detergent, and 1 tablespoon white vinegar for 15 minutes. Rinse with water. Sponge the remaining stain with rubbing alcohol and launder if possible. If not, presoak* in a solution of 1 quart warm water and 1 tablespoon **Axion** or **Biz** (enzyme presoaks) for 30 minutes. Rinse well with water, allow to dry, and launder as soon as possible.

- **Acrylic Plastic**
- **Aluminum**
- **Asphalt** • **Bamboo**
- **Brass** • **Bronze**
- **Cane**

(continued)

Wipe the surface with a cloth or sponge dipped in warm sudsy water. Rinse well and wipe dry.

See Chapter 4 for specific technique instructions.

●Ceramic Glass/Tile   *(see base of preceding page)*
●Copper ●Cork
●Enamel ●Glass
●Gold ●Grout ●Iron
●Ivory ●Jade
●Linoleum ●Opal
●Paint/Flat
●Paint/Gloss
●Pewter ●Plexiglas
●Polyurethane
●Stainless Steel
●Tin ●Vinyl Clothing
●Vinyl Tile
●Vinyl Wallcovering

●Alabaster ●Marble

Wipe the surface with a cloth dipped in a solution of washing soda and water. Rinse well and wipe dry. If a stain persists, mix a few drops ammonia with 1 cup 3% hydrogen peroxide. Soak a white blotter in the solution and place over the stain. Weight it down with a piece of glass or other heavy object. Continue applying the solution until the stain has been bleached out.

●Bluestone ●Brick
●Concrete
●Flagstone
●Granite
●Limestone
●Masonry Tile
●Slate ●Terrazzo

Mix a solution of washing soda and water. Gently brush the stain away with a cloth or soft-bristled brush. Rinse with clear water and allow to dry.

●Burlap ●Silk
●Wool

Sponge* the stain with water. Spray on **Amway Remove Fabric Spot Cleaner.** If stain persists, apply a Wet Spotter and a few drops of white vinegar. Cover with an absorbent pad dampened with Wet Spotter. Let it stand as long as any stain is being

(continued)

---

*See Chapter 4 for specific technique instructions.

(continued from preceding page) lifted. Change the pad as it picks up the stain. Keep the stain and pad moist with Wet Spotter and vinegar. Flush* with water. Repeat until no more stain is being removed. If any stain remains, test for colorfastness, then apply rubbing alcohol and cover with an absorbent pad dampened with alcohol. Let it stand as long as any stain is being removed. Flush with water.

•Carpet/Synthetic
•Carpet/Wool
•Foam Rubber

Sponge* the area with a solution of 1 quart warm water, ½ teaspoon liquid detergent, and 1 tablespoon white vinegar. Blot with a clean pad and rinse well with water. If stain remains, sponge stain with a solution of 1 quart warm water and 1 tablespoon **Axion** enzyme presoak. Blot and sponge alternately until no more stain is left. Sponge the area with water. Blot up all excess water and place a clean pad over the area weighted down with a heavy object. When no more liquid is being absorbed, allow the area to thoroughly air dry.

•Cotton •Linen

Soak the stain for 15 minutes in a solution of 1 quart warm water and ½ teaspoon liquid detergent. Rinse well with water. Next, sponge* the area with rubbing alcohol, rinse with water, and allow to dry. If the stain remains, presoak* for 30 minutes in a solution of 1 quart warm water and 1 tablespoon **Axion** or **Biz** (enzyme presoak products). Rinse well, dry, and launder as soon as possible.

•Felt •Fur/Natural
•Fur/Synthetic
•Wood

Mix dishwashing detergent in hot water and swish to make a great volume of suds. Dip a cloth in only the foam and apply. Rinse area with a cloth moistened with clear water.
(continued)

See Chapter 4 for specific technique instructions.

(continued from preceding page) Allow felt and fur to air dry, but wipe wood surfaces dry with a clean cloth and wax or polish.

●Leather ●Suede

Mix a solution of mild soap in luke-warm water. Swish to create a great volume of suds. Apply only the foam with a sponge. Rinse area with a cloth moistened with clear water. Wipe with a clean cloth to dry.

●Porcelain Dishes
●Porcelain Fixtures

Remove the stain by washing in warm sudsy water, or wiping with a cloth dipped in warm sudsy water. Rinse well and wipe dry. To remove stubborn stains, dampen a cloth and dip it into baking soda. Wipe away any remaining stain, rinse, and dry with a clean cloth.

●Silver

Wash in hot soapy water. Rinse in hot water and wipe dry with a soft cloth to prevent tarnish.

Oil/Automotive, Hair, Lubricating, Mineral, Vegetable

●Acetate
●Carpet/Synthetic
●Carpet/Wool
●Rayon ●Silk
●Triacetate
●Wool

Blot up as much excess as possible and apply an absorbent such as corn-meal. After letting the absorbent work, brush* the powder off the fab-ric. If a stain remains, sponge* with a dry-cleaning solvent, either **Carbona No. 10 Special Spot Remover/ Carbona Cleaning Fluid** or **Afta Cleaning Fluid.** Apply a Dry Spotter. Cover with an absorbent pad that has been dampened with Dry Spotter. Let it remain in place as long as any stain is being removed. Change the pad as

(continued)

*See Chapter 4 for specific technique instructions.

(continued from preceding page) it picks up the stain. Keep both the stain and pad moist with Dry Spotter. Flush* the area with the dry-cleaning solvent. If a stain persists, sponge the area with water and apply a Wet Spotter with a few drops of white vinegar. Cover the stain with an absorbent pad moistened with Wet Spotter. Let the pad stay in place as long as any stain is being removed. Change the pad as it picks up the stain. Keep both the stain and pad moist with Wet Spotter and vinegar. Flush with water and repeat the procedure until no more stain is removed. Allow to dry.

•Acrylic Fabric •Cotton •Linen •Modacrylic •Nylon •Olefin •Polyester •Spandex

Blot excess spill as soon as possible. Apply an absorbent and allow it to soak up remaining spill. After brushing* out the powder, sponge* the area with a dry-cleaning solvent, either **Carbona No. 10 Special Spot Remover/Carbona Cleaning Fluid, K2r Spot-lifter** (aerosol), or **Afta Cleaning Fluid.** Apply a Dry Spotter and cover with an absorbent pad moistened with Dry Spotter. Let it remain in place until no more stain is removed. Change the pad as it picks up the stain. To help loosen the stain, occasionally tamp* the area, blotting any loosened material. Flush* with one of the liquid dry-cleaning solvents. If any trace of the stain remains, sponge the stain with water and apply a Wet Spotter and a few drops of ammonia. Tamp the stain again, blotting with an absorbent pad. Flush the area with water and repeat until no more stain is removed. Allow to dry.

•Acrylic Plastic •Aluminum

(continued)

Blot up any excess spill. Wipe the surface with a cloth or sponge dipped

---

*See Chapter 4 for specific technique instructions.

(continued from preceding page)

●**Asphalt** ●**Bamboo**
●**Cane**
●**Ceramic Glass/Tile**
●**Cork** ●**Glass**
●**Linoleum**
●**Paint/Gloss**
●**Pewter** ●**Plexiglas**
●**Polyurethane**
●**Porcelain Dishes**
●**Stainless Steel**
●**Vinyl Clothing**
●**Vinyl Tile**
●**Vinyl Wallcovering**

in warm sudsy water. Rinse well and wipe thoroughly dry.

●**Bluestone** ●**Brick**
●**Concrete**
●**Flagstone**
●**Granite**
●**Limestone**
●**Masonry Tile**
●**Sandstone** ●**Slate**
●**Terrazzo**

Wash with a strong solution of washing soda and hot water. If stain remains, make a paste of 1 pound strong powdered cleaner, 2 cups powdered chalk, and 1 gallon water and cover the stain. Or, cover with a paste made from fuller's earth and hot water. Leave the paste on overnight. Rinse with clear water. Repeat if necessary.

●**Leather**

Rub a stain with a thick paste of fuller's earth and water. Allow it to dry, then brush* off the powder. Or apply **The Tannery.** Repeat if necessary. **The Tannery** will also condition the leather, or use **Fiebing's Saddle Soap.**

●**Marble**

Remove any excess, then wipe with a cloth dipped in warm sudsy water. Rinse well and wipe dry with a clean cloth. If any residue remains, mix a poultice of water, powdered detergent, and bleach. Apply to the stain and cover with a dampened cloth to retard evaporation. After the stain has been bleached out and the oil

(continued)

See Chapter 4 for specific technique instructions.

(continued from preceding page) removed, rinse thoroughly with water and allow to dry.

●**Paint/Flat** ●**Wallpaper**	Make a paste of cornstarch and water. Apply to the stain and allow to dry. Brush* off the powder and repeat if necessary. If the stain persists, make a paste of fuller's earth and trichloroethane. **Caution:** Use trichloroethane with care and wear rubber gloves. Apply to stain and allow to dry. Brush off.
●**Silver**	Immediately wash in hot soapy water. Rinse thoroughly in hot water and dry with a soft clean cloth.
●**Suede**	Test any treatment in an inconspicuous place first. On some oil stains, rubbing lightly with **Suede Stone** will remove any residue. Dip a clean cloth into ground cornmeal and rub into the stain with a circular motion. Gently brush* out the powder with a wire brush. Repeat if necessary. If stain persists, brush stain with lemon juice and hold in the steam of a boiling teakettle for a few minutes. Brush with a wire brush.
●**Wood**	Mix dishwashing detergent in hot water and swish to make a great volume of suds. Dip a cloth in only the foam and apply to the stain. Rinse with a clean cloth dampened with clear water. Polish or wax as soon as possible.

Orange

●**Acetate** ●**Carpet/Synthetic**	Spray on **Amway Remove Fabric Spot Cleaner.** If stain remains,

(continued)

*See Chapter 4 for specific technique instructions.

(continued from preceding page)

- **Carpet/Wool**
- **Fiberglass** ● **Rayon**
- **Silk** ● **Triacetate**
- **Wool**

sponge* area with cool water, then apply a Wet Spotter and a few drops of white vinegar. Cover stain with an absorbent pad dampened with Wet Spotter. Let stand as long as any stain is being removed. Keep both the stain and pad moist with Wet Spotter and vinegar. Flush* with water and repeat if necessary. If stain persists, moisten the area with a solution of 1 cup warm water and 1 teaspoon **Axion,** an enzyme presoak product – do not use on silk or wool. Cover with a clean pad moistened with the solution. Let it stand 30 minutes. Add more solution, if needed, to keep the area warm and moist, but do not allow the wet area to spread. When no more stain is being lifted, flush with water.

- **Acrylic Fabric**
- **Cotton** ● **Linen**
- **Modacrylic** ● **Nylon**
- **Olefin** ● **Polyester**
- **Spandex**

Spray on **Amway Remove Fabric Spot Cleaner.** If stain remains, presoak* in a solution of 1 quart warm water, ½ teaspoon liquid dishwashing or laundry detergent, and 1 tablespoon white vinegar for 15 minutes. Rinse with water and launder if possible. If not, presoak in a solution of 1 quart warm water and 1 tablespoon **Axion** or **Biz** (enzyme presoak products) for 30 minutes. Rinse well with water and launder as soon as possible.

- **Acrylic Plastic**
- **Aluminum**
- **Asphalt** ● **Brass**
- **Bronze**
- **Ceramic Glass/Tile**
- **Copper** ● **Cork**
- **Enamel** ● **Glass**

Wipe up the excess spill. Then wipe the surface with a cloth or sponge dipped in warm sudsy water. Rinse well and wipe dry.

(continued)

See Chapter 4 for specific technique instructions.

●Grout ●Iron   *(see base of preceding page)*
●Linoleum
●Masonry Tile
●Paint/Flat
●Paint/Gloss
●Plexiglas
●Polyurethane
●Porcelain Dishes
●Stainless Steel
●Tin ●Vinyl Clothing
●Vinyl Tile
●Vinyl Wallcovering

●Bluestone ●Brick ●Concrete ●Flagstone ●Granite ●Limestone ●Sandstone ●Slate ●Terrazzo	Wipe up any excess. Wash with a solution of washing soda or detergent (never soap) and water. Use a soft cloth or soft-bristled brush. Rinse thoroughly with clear water and allow to dry.
●Leather ●Suede	Blot up any excess spill. Mix a solution of mild soap in lukewarm water. Swish to create a great volume of suds. Apply only the foam with a sponge. Wipe with a clean dry cloth. On leather only, follow with **The Tannery** or **Fiebing's Saddle Soap** to condition the leather.
●Silver	Wash as soon as possible in hot sudsy water. Rinse in hot water and dry immediately with a soft cloth.
●Wood	Mix dishwashing detergent in hot water and swish to make a great volume of suds. Dip a cloth in only the foam and wipe up the excess spill. Rinse with a clean cloth moistened with clear water. Polish or wax as soon as possible.

Oven Cleaner

●Acetate ●Acrylic Fabric ●Carpet/Synthetic ●Carpet/Wool ●Modacrylic ●Nylon ●Olefin ●Polyester ●Rayon ●Silk ●Spandex ●Triacetate ●Wool	Sponge* the stain with cool water. If stain persists, neutralize the spot with a few drops of a mild acid, such as lemon juice, white vinegar, or 10% acetic acid solution. Thoroughly sponge the area with cool water. Silk and wool must be treated promptly, as oven cleaner will destroy these fabrics.
●Acrylic Plastic ●Aluminum ●Asphalt ●Ceramic Glass/Tile ●Cork ●Linoleum ●Paint/Flat ●Paint/Gloss ●Plexiglas ●Polyurethane ●Vinyl Clothing ●Vinyl Tile ●Vinyl Wallcovering	Wipe well with a cloth dipped in cool water. Wipe dry with a clean soft cloth.
●Bluestone ●Brick ●Concrete ●Masonry Tile ●Terrazzo	Because some oven cleaners leave a soap scum that is almost impossible to remove, wash with a strong solution of washing soda and water. Rinse well and wipe dry.
●Cotton ●Linen	Flush* the stain with cool water until all traces are gone. Launder as soon as possible. Do not use acids, such as white vinegar or lemon juice, on these fabrics.
●Leather ●Suede	Mix a solution of mild soap in luke-warm water. Swish to create a great

(continued)

See Chapter 4 for specific technique instructions.

(continued from preceding page) volume of suds. Quickly apply only the foam with a sponge to remove oven cleaner. Gently wipe away all remains of oven cleaner. Rinse in clear water and wipe dry.

•Wallpaper

Treat quickly and carefully, because the chemicals in oven cleaners can dissolve the paste. Wipe with a sponge dampened with clear warm water. Gently rub over the stain to remove it. Overlapping strokes will prevent streaking. Use a clean dry cloth to pat dry.

•Wood

As some oven cleaners can dissolve wood finishes, work quickly. Wipe the area with a cloth or sponge dampened with cool water. Wipe dry with a soft cloth. Polish or wax immediately to prevent permanent wood damage.

Paint/Latex

•Acetate •Burlap
•Carpet/Synthetic
•Carpet/Wool
•Fiberglass •Rayon
•Silk •Triacetate
•Wool

Note: Once latex paint starts to dry, it begins to adhere to the fibers and may become permanent. Treat stain as soon after spill as possible. After scraping* to remove any excess paint, sponge* the stain with a dry-cleaning solvent, either **Carbona No. 10 Special Spot Remover/Carbona Cleaning Fluid** or **Afta Cleaning Fluid.** Then apply a Dry Spotter to the area and cover with an absorbent pad dampened with Dry Spotter. Let it stand as long as any stain is being removed. Change the pad as it picks up any stain. Keep both the pad and stain moist with Dry Spotter. Flush* with dry-cleaning solvent and allow to dry. If any stain remains, sponge the area with water and apply a Wet

(continued)

*See Chapter 4 for specific technique instructions.

(continued from preceding page) Spotter and a few drops of ammonia. (Do not use ammonia on silk or wool.) Cover with an absorbent pad dampened with Wet Spotter. Let it stand as long as any stain is being removed. Change the pad as it picks up the stain. Keep stain and pad moist with Wet Spotter and ammonia. Flush with water and repeat if necessary. Allow to thoroughly dry. When treating carpets, be sure to blot excess liquid with a clean absorbent pad.

- **Acrylic Fabric**
- **Cotton** •**Linen**
- **Modacrylic** •**Nylon**
- **Olefin** •**Polyester**
- **Spandex**

Note: Treat the stain immediately; it may become permanent once the stain has dried. Flush* the stain with warm water to remove as much as possible, then launder immediately. If paint has dried, moisten area with rubbing alcohol (for acrylic and modacrylic dilute alcohol with 2 parts water) to soften paint, then brush* as much as possible from the fibers. Launder the fabric.

- **Acrylic Plastic**
- **Bamboo** •**Cane**
- **Ceramic Tile**
- **Enamel** •**Glass**
- **Paint/Flat**
- **Paint/Gloss**
- **Plexiglas**
- **Polyurethane**
- **Porcelain Dishes**
- **Porcelain Fixtures**
- **Stainless Steel**
- **Vinyl Clothing**
- **Vinyl Wallcovering**

Gently scrape* up any excess spill. Wash the surface with a cloth dipped in warm sudsy water. Rinse thoroughly with clear water and wipe dry. Paint that is absorbed into fibers of some of these surfaces may be impossible to completely remove. On hard surfaces, such as glass or ceramic tile, gently scrape off the dried paint with a razor blade.

- **Asphalt** •**Cork**
- **Linoleum**
- **Vinyl Tile**

Remove any spill immediately, then wash with a cloth dipped in warm sudsy water. If stain remains, cover it with a rubbing alcohol compress. Let

(continued)

See Chapter 4 for specific technique instructions.

(continued from preceding page) the compress remain in place for a few minutes. Wipe the stain with a cloth dampened with ammonia. (Do not use ammonia on linoleum or vinyl floor tile.) To remove any latent traces of stain, try rubbing the area with superfine (number 0000) steel wool dipped in liquid wax. Wash thoroughly with soapy water, wipe dry, then wax.

- **Bluestone**
- **Ceramic Glass**
- **Concrete**
- **Granite**
- **Masonry Tile**
- **Sandstone** • **Slate**
- **Terrazzo**

Immediately wipe up any excess spill. Then wash with a solution of washing soda or detergent (not soap) and water. Scrub with a cloth or soft-bristled brush. Rinse thoroughly with clear water and allow to dry.

- **Brick**

Apply a commercial paint remover to the stain and allow it to dry. Use a wire brush to remove paint. Wash the area with clear water and allow to dry.

- **Grout**

Wipe up excess paint carefully. Wipe remaining stain with a cloth dipped in warm sudsy water. If any stain persists, dip a wet toothbrush into a little baking soda or powdered cleanser and gently scrub spot. Rinse well with clear water and wipe dry.

- **Leather** • **Suede**

Note: Paint stains may be impossible to remove entirely. Carefully scrape* to remove any excess paint. Mix a solution of mild soap in lukewarm water. Swish to create a great volume of suds. Wipe the paint residue with a sponge dipped in only the foam. Wipe with a clean dry cloth. On leather only, follow with **The Tannery** or **Fiebing's Saddle Soap** to condition the leather.

See Chapter 4 for specific technique instructions.

●Wood	Wipe up fresh paint or gently scrape* dried paint with a paint scraper. Then wipe stain with a sponge or cloth dipped in warm sudsy water. Another effective treatment is a mixture of 1 tablespoon oxalic acid and 1 pint water rubbed on the paint with a cloth dampened in the solution. Wipe dry and wax as needed.

Paint/Oil-base

●Acetate ●Burlap **●Fiberglass ●Silk** **●Triacetate** **●Wool**	Gently scrape* to remove the excess paint and sponge* the stain with a dry-cleaning solvent, either **Carbona No. 10 Special Spot Remover/ Carbona Cleaning Fluid** or **Afta Cleaning Fluid.** Apply a Dry Spotter to the area and cover with an absorbent pad dampened with Dry Spotter. Let it stand as long as any stain is being removed. Change the pad as it picks up the stain. Keep both the stain and pad moist with Dry Spotter. Flush* with the dry-cleaning solvent and allow to dry. If stain persists, sponge with water and apply a Wet Spotter and a few drops of ammonia. (Do not use ammonia on wool or silk.) Cover stain with an absorbent pad moistened with Wet Spotter. Let it stand as long as any stain is being removed. Change the pad as it picks up the stain. Keep both the pad and stain moist with Wet Spotter and ammonia. Flush well with water and repeat as necessary.
●Acrylic Fabric **●Cotton ●Linen** **●Modacrylic ●Nylon** **●Olefin ●Polyester** **●Spandex**	Flush* the solvent indicated as a thinner on the paint container through the stain. If none is indicated, use turpentine. Be careful not to spread the stain. Rinse thoroughly

(continued)

See Chapter 4 for specific technique instructions.

(continued from preceding page) with water and repeat if necessary. Rub area with bar soap (not a deodorant-type) or a liquid detergent. Rinse again and launder.

- ●Acrylic Plastic
- ●Plexiglas
- ●Polyurethane
- ●Vinyl Clothing

Wipe excess immediately with a cloth dipped in warm sudsy water. Rinse thoroughly with warm water and wipe dry. Do not use a thinner on these materials, as it will eat through them. If necessary, dip a cloth into a dry-cleaning solvent, **Brush Top Spot Remover,** and quickly but gently dab at the remaining stain. Rinse well and wipe dry.

- ●Asphalt ●Cork
- ●Linoleum
- ●Vinyl Tile

Wipe immediately with a damp cloth. Cover the stain with a rubbing alcohol compress and let it remain in place for a few minutes. Then wipe the area with a cloth moistened with ammonia. (Do not use ammonia on linoleum or vinyl floor tile.) If stain persists, try rubbing very gently with superfine (number 0000) steel wool dipped in liquid wax. Wash area with warm soapy water, rinse, then wax when dry.

- ●Bamboo ●Cane
- ●Paint/Flat
- ●Paint/Gloss
- ●Porcelain Fixtures
- ●Stainless Steel

Scrape* to remove any excess spill. Wipe area immediately with a cloth or sponge dipped in warm sudsy water to which a few drops of ammonia have been added. Rinse thoroughly with clear water and wipe dry.

- ●Bluestone
- ●Concrete
- ●Flagstone
- ●Granite
- ●Limestone
- ●Masonry Tile
- ●Sandstone ●Slate
- ●Terrazzo

Scrape up the excess spill. Wash area with a solution of washing soda or detergent (not soap) and water. Scrub with a cloth or soft-bristled brush. Rinse well with clear water and allow to dry.

See Chapter 4 for specific technique instructions.

●**Brick**

Apply a commercial paint remover to the stain and allow to dry. Use a wire brush to remove the stain, then wash area with clear water. Allow to dry.

●**Carpet/Synthetic**
●**Carpet/Wool**

Gently dab at the stain with a cloth dipped in the solvent indicated on the paint container label or use turpentine. Do not soak the stain, as the solvent will damage the rubber backing and pad. Continue to wipe with a clean, solvent-dampened cloth as long as the stain is picked up. Sponge* with water and wash with a concentrated liquid carpet shampoo. Sponge with water, blot excess liquid, and allow to dry thoroughly.

●**Ceramic Glass/Tile**
●**Glass**

Scrape* to remove any excess. (Do not scrape ceramic glass rangetops—soak to loosen the stain.) Wipe the stain with a cloth or sponge dipped in warm sudsy water. Rinse thoroughly and wipe dry. If any traces remain, allow to dry, then scrape gently with a razor blade.

●**Grout**

Wipe up excess paint. Then wipe area with a cloth dipped in warm sudsy water. If any stain remains, apply **Afta Tile & Grout Cleaner** or dip a wet toothbrush into a little baking soda or powdered cleanser and gently scrub the spot. Rinse well with water and wipe dry.

●**Leather** ●**Suede**

Gently scrape* to remove the excess. Mix a solution of mild soap in lukewarm water. Swish to create a great volume of suds. Apply only the foam with a sponge. Wipe with a clean dry cloth. If any stain remains, try rubbing **The Tannery,** a leather cleaner, into the spot with a clean soft cloth. Allow

(continued)

See Chapter 4 for specific technique instructions.

(continued from preceding page) it to dry. If stain persists, test a dry-cleaning solvent, **Brush Top Spot Remover** or **Carbona No. 10 Special Spot Remover/Carbona Cleaning Fluid,** on an inconspicuous place. If safe to use, gingerly apply to the stained area. Allow to dry. On leather only, follow with **The Tannery** or **Fiebing's Saddle Soap.**

●**Wood**

Wipe immediately with a sponge dampened with warm water. Wipe dry, then wax the wood. Note: This stain may be impossible to remove if not treated immediately.

Paint/Watercolor

●**Acetate**
●**Carpet/Synthetic**
●**Carpet/Wool**
●**Fiberglass** ●**Rayon**
●**Silk** ●**Triacetate**
●**Wool**

Sponge* the area immediately with water to dilute the paint. Spray on **Amway Remove Fabric Spot Cleaner** or apply a Wet Spotter and a few drops of ammonia. (Take care when using ammonia on silk and wool.) Cover with an absorbent pad dampened with the Wet Spotter. Let the pad remain as long as any stain is being removed. Change the pad as it picks up the stain. Keep both the pad and stain moist with Wet Spotter and ammonia. Flush* well with water and repeat if necessary. If, after drying, a stain persists, mix a little **Rit Color Remover** according to package directions. After testing on an inconspicuous place, flush it through the stain to an absorbent pad. On carpets, sponge the color remover on the stain and blot with an absorbent pad. Rinse well with water and dry.

●**Acrylic Fabric**
●**Cotton** ●**Linen**

(continued)

Soak item in a solution of 1 quart warm water, ½ teaspoon liquid detergent,

See Chapter 4 for specific technique instructions.

(continued from preceding page)

●**Modacrylic** ●**Nylon**
●**Olefin** ●**Polyester**
●**Spandex**

and 1 tablespoon ammonia for 30 minutes. Rinse well. If stain persists, soak in a solution of 1 quart warm water and 1 tablespoon white vinegar for 1 hour. (Take care when using vinegar on cotton and linen.) Rinse well with water and allow to dry. If stain is set, apply rubbing alcohol (dilute with 2 parts water for acrylic and modacrylic) to the area and tamp.* As stain loosens, blot excess liquid and stain with an absorbent pad. Keep both stain and pad moist with alcohol and change pad as it picks up the stain. Allow to dry. As a last resort for any remaining traces, mix **Rit Color Remover** according to package directions and test on a hidden place. If safe to use, flush* through the stain. Rinse well with clear water and allow to dry thoroughly.

●**Acrylic Plastic**
●**Aluminum**
●**Bamboo** ●**Cane**
●**Ceramic Glass/Tile**
●**Glass**
●**Paint/Flat**
●**Paint/Gloss**
●**Plexiglas**
●**Polyurethane**
●**Vinyl Clothing**

Immediately wipe up the spill with a cloth or sponge dipped in warm sudsy water. Rinse well and wipe dry.

●**Alabaster** ●**Marble**

Immediately wipe up the spill with a cloth dipped in warm sudsy water. Rinse well and wipe dry. If a stain persists, soak an absorbent pad in rubbing alcohol, wring almost dry, and place over the stain. Wait 5 minutes and apply an absorbent pad soaked in ammonia and squeezed until damp. Alternate alcohol and

(continued)

See Chapter 4 for specific technique instructions.

(continued from preceding page) ammonia pads until stain has been removed. Wipe surface with a cloth moistened with clear water and wipe dry with a clean cloth.

•Asphalt •Cork **•Linoleum** **•Vinyl Tile**	Wipe up any excess spill with a cloth dipped in warm sudsy water. Rinse well and wipe dry. If a stain remains, cover with an absorbent pad soaked in rubbing alcohol. Let it remain in place for several minutes, then wipe the area with a cloth dampened with ammonia. Do not use ammonia on linoleum or vinyl floor tile. Rinse well with a cloth dipped in warm sudsy water, rinse with clear water, and allow to dry.
•Bluestone •Brick **•Concrete** **•Flagstone** **•Granite** **•Masonry Tile** **•Sandstone •Slate** **•Terrazzo**	Wipe up excess paint. Wash with a solution of washing soda or detergent (not soap) and water. Use a cloth or soft-bristled brush to scrub. Rinse thoroughly with clear water and allow to dry.
•Grout	Wipe up excess spill with a cloth dipped in warm sudsy water. If any stain persists, apply **Afta Tile & Grout Cleaner** or dip a wet toothbrush into a little baking soda or powdered cleanser and gently brush* the spot. Rinse well with water and wipe dry.
•Leather •Suede	Paint will immediately act to discolor these fabrics. Once contact has been made, immediately wipe the area with a cloth dampened with clear water. If any stain remains, dab it with a cloth dipped into a dry-cleaning solvent, **Brush Top Spot Remover** or **Carbona No. 10 Special Spot**

(continued)

---

*See Chapter 4 for specific technique instructions.

(continued from preceding page) **Remover/Carbona Cleaning Fluid.** Allow to air dry. On leather only, follow with **The Tannery** or **Fiebing's Saddle Soap** to condition the leather.

●**Wood**

Mix dishwashing detergent in hot water and swish to make a great volume of suds. Dip a cloth in only the foam and apply. Rinse with a cloth dampened with clear water. Polish or wax as soon as possible.

Parafin *(Follow procedures for Candle Wax.)*

Peanut Butter

●**Acetate**
●**Carpet/Synthetic**
●**Carpet/Wool**
●**Rayon** ●**Silk**
●**Triacetate**
●**Wool**

Scrape* any excess spill with a dull knife or spatula. Sponge* the stain with a dry-cleaning solvent, either **Carbona No. 10 Special Spot Remover/Carbona Cleaning Fluid** or **Afta Cleaning Fluid.** Apply a Dry Spotter. Cover the stain with an absorbent pad dampened with Dry Spotter. Let it remain in place as long as any stain is being lifted. Change the pad as it picks up the stain. Keep both the pad and stain moist with Dry Spotter. Flush* with the dry-cleaning solvent and allow to dry. If stain persists, sponge the area with water and apply a Wet Spotter and a few drops of white vinegar. Cover the stain with an absorbent pad moistened with Wet Spotter. Let it stand as long as any stain is being removed. Change the pad as it picks up the stain. Keep the stain and pad moist with Wet Spotter and vinegar. Flush the area with water and repeat until no more stain is removed. Allow to dry.

*See Chapter 4 for specific technique instructions.

- **Acrylic Fabric**
- **Cotton** • **Linen**
- **Modacrylic** • **Olefin**
- **Polyester**
- **Spandex**

Scrape* to remove excess. Sponge* the area with a dry-cleaning solvent, either **Carbona No. 10 Special Spot Remover/Carbona Cleaning Fluid, K2r Spot-lifter** (aerosol), or **Afta Cleaning Fluid.** Apply a Dry Spotter. Cover the stain with an absorbent pad dampened with the Dry Spotter. Let it remain in place as long as any stain is being removed. Change the pad as it picks up the stain. To help loosen the stain, tamp* and blot the area. Flush* with one of the liquid dry-cleaning solvents. To remove a persistent stain, sponge with water, apply a Wet Spotter, and tamp occasionally. Blot up any loosened material with an absorbent pad. Flush* the area with water and repeat until no more stain is removed. Allow to dry.

- **Acrylic Plastic**
- **Aluminum**
- **Asphalt** • **Bamboo**
- **Cane**
- **Ceramic Glass/Tile**
- **Cork** • **Glass**
- **Linoleum**
- **Paint/Flat**
- **Paint/Gloss**
- **Plexiglas**
- **Polyurethane**
- **Porcelain Dishes**
- **Stainless Steel**
- **Vinyl Clothing**
- **Vinyl Tile**
- **Vinyl Wallcovering**

Scrape* up any excess with a dull knife. (Do not scrape ceramic glass rangetops—soak to loosen dried peanut butter.) Wipe the surface with a cloth or sponge dipped in warm sudsy water. Rinse well and wipe dry with a clean cloth.

- **Bluestone** • **Brick**
- **Concrete**
- **Flagstone**
- **Granite**
- **Limestone**

(continued)

Wash the stained area with a solution of washing soda or a detergent (not soap) and water. Rinse well with clear water and allow to dry. Repeat if necessary.

See Chapter 4 for specific technique instructions.

●**Masonry Tile** ●**Sandstone** ●**Slate** ●**Terrazzo**	*(see base of preceding page)*

●**Leather**

Gently scrape* to remove any excess. Wipe the area with a cloth dipped in warm sudsy water. Rinse with a cloth dampened with clear water and gently wipe dry. Follow with **The Tannery** or **Fiebing's Saddle Soap** to condition the leather.

●**Marble**

Scrape* to remove excess peanut butter. Wipe the surface with a cloth or sponge dipped in warm sudsy water. Rinse well and wipe dry with a clean cloth. If any oily residue remains, mix a poultice from water, powdered detergent, and bleach. Apply to the stain and cover with a damp cloth to retard evaporation. After the oil has been drawn out, rinse thoroughly with water and dry.

●**Silver**

Wash immediately in hot soapy water. Rinse thoroughly in hot water and dry with a soft clean cloth.

●**Suede**

Mix a solution of mild soap in lukewarm water. Swish to create a great volume of suds. Apply only the foam with a sponge. Wipe dry with a clean cloth. If an oil stain remains, powder the area with an absorbent such as cornmeal. Allow plenty of time for it to work. Gently brush* it off and repeat if necessary.

●**Wallpaper**

Gently scrape* to remove excess, taking care not to rip the paper. Make a paste of cornstarch and water and apply to the peanut butter residue. After drying, brush* off the powder. Repeat paste application if necessary.

*See Chapter 4 for specific technique instructions.

•Wood	Gently scrape* to remove any excess. Mix dishwashing detergent in hot water and swish to make a great volume of suds. Dip a cloth in only the foam and apply. Rinse with a clean cloth dampened with clear water. Polish or wax as soon as possible.

Pencil Lead

•Acetate •Burlap **•Carpet/Synthetic** **•Carpet/Wool** **•Rayon •Silk** **•Triacetate** **•Wool**	Use a soft eraser to remove the excess stain, being careful not to distort the fabric. Spray on a dry-cleaning solvent, **Carbona Spray Spot Remover,** and apply a Dry Spotter. Rub in the Dry Spotter with an absorbent pad moistened with Dry Spotter. Cover the stain with a pad, also dampened with Dry Spotter, and let stand for 30 minutes. Spray again with the dry-cleaning solvent and allow to dry. If any stain remains, sponge area with water and apply a Wet Spotter plus a few drops of ammonia (do not use ammonia on silk and wool). Tamp* or scrape* the area to loosen the stain. Flush* with water and repeat if necessary. Allow fabric to air dry.
•Acrylic Fabric **•Cotton •Linen** **•Modacrylic •Nylon** **•Olefin •Polyester** **•Spandex**	Use a soft eraser to remove any excess stain. Rub a little liquid detergent into the stain and add a few drops of ammonia. Tamp* gently, then flush* with water to remove all traces of ammonia. Launder as soon as possible.
•Acrylic Plastic **•Aluminum** **•Asphalt •Bamboo** **•Cane** *(continued)*	Remove any excess marks with a soft eraser. Wipe the surface with a cloth or sponge dipped in warm sudsy water. Rinse well with water and wipe dry.

See Chapter 4 for specific technique instructions.

●**Ceramic Glass/Tile**   *(see base of preceding page)*
●**Cork** ●**Ivory**
●**Linoleum** ●**Marble**
●**Paint/Gloss**
●**Plexiglas**
●**Polyurethane**
●**Porcelain Dishes**
●**Porcelain Fixtures**
●**Stainless Steel**
●**Vinyl Clothing**
●**Vinyl Tile**
●**Vinyl Wallcovering**

●**Bluestone** ●**Brick**
●**Concrete**
●**Flagstone**
●**Granite**
●**Limestone**
●**Slate** ●**Terrazzo**

Wash the stain with a solution of washing soda and water. Scrub with a cloth or soft-bristled brush. Rinse thoroughly with clear water and allow to dry.

●**Grout**

Wipe the surface with a cloth dipped in warm sudsy water. If any stain remains, apply **Afta Tile & Grout Cleaner** or dip a wet toothbrush into baking soda or powdered cleanser and gently scrub the spot. Rinse well and wipe dry with a soft cloth.

●**Leather** ●**Suede**

Mix a solution of mild soap in lukewarm water. Swish to create a great volume of suds. Apply only the foam with a sponge. Wipe with a clean dry cloth. On leather only, follow with **The Tannery** or **Fiebing's Saddle Soap**.

●**Paint/Flat**
●**Wallpaper**

Rub the pencil marks with **Crayerase,** a nontoxic dry chemical cleaning bar. Or, use **Suede Stone** or a soft eraser to remove as many marks as possible. With a clean cloth dampened with clear water, wipe the surface with overlapping strokes. Gently pat dry with another soft cloth.

•Silver	Wash as soon as possible in hot sudsy water. Rinse in hot water and dry immediately with a soft cloth to prevent tarnish.
•Wood	Use a soft eraser to remove any excess marks. Mix dishwashing detergent in hot water and swish to make a great volume of suds. Dip a cloth in only the foam and apply to the stain. Rinse with a clean cloth dampened with clear water. Polish or wax as soon as possible.

Perfume (*Follow procedures for* Cologne.)

Perspiration

•Acetate •Rayon •Silk •Wool	Sponge* the area with water, then spray on **Amway Remove Fabric Spot Cleaner.** Follow with an application of Wet Spotter and a few drops of ammonia. (Take care when using ammonia on silk and wool.) Cover with an absorbent pad moistened with Wet Spotter. Let the pad remain in place as long as any stain is being removed. Change the pad as it picks up the stain. Keep both the stain and pad moist with Wet Spotter and ammonia. Flush well with water and allow to dry thoroughly.
•Acrylic Fabric •Cotton •Linen •Modacrylic •Nylon •Olefin •Polyester •Spandex	Presoak* the stained garment in **Axion** or **Biz** (enzyme presoak products) according to package directions. After soaking, launder as usual. For older stains, sponge area with a diluted solution of white vinegar and water, then launder. If fabric color has changed, stretch the *(continued)*

*See Chapter 4 for specific technique instructions.

(continued from preceding page) stained area over a bowl of ammonia so fumes penetrate while the spot is moist. Prompt treatment of perspiration stains is necessary, as they can weaken most fibers. **Caution:** Never iron a garment with perspiration stains—the heat will set them.

•Leather •Suede

Mix a solution of mild soap in luke-warm water. Swish to create a great volume of suds. Apply only the foam with a sponge. Wipe with a clean dry cloth. On leather only, follow with **The Tannery** or **Fiebing's Saddle Soap** to condition the leather.

•Vinyl Clothing

Wipe the stain with a cloth dipped in warm sudsy water to which a few drops of ammonia have been added. Rinse well and wipe dry with a clean cloth.

Pet Stains/Feces

•Acrylic Fabric •Modacrylic •Nylon •Olefin •Polyester

Quickly and gently scrape* to remove the solids. Be careful not to force any stain into the fiber. Sponge* the stain with a solution of 1 quart warm water, 1 teaspoon liquid detergent, and 1 tablespoon ammonia. Tamp* or scrape to help loosen the stain and blot occasionally with an absorbent pad. Rinse thoroughly with water to remove all traces of ammonia. If a stain persists, presoak* stain in a solution of 1 quart warm water and 1 tablespoon **Axion** presoak product for 30 minutes. Rinse well and launder as soon as possible.

•Asphalt •Cork •Linoleum •Vinyl Tile

Gently scrape* up the solids as soon as possible. Wash the area with a cloth dipped in warm sudsy water.

(continued)

See Chapter 4 for specific technique instructions.

(continued from preceding page)	Rinse thoroughly with water and wipe dry with a soft cloth.

•**Bluestone** •**Brick** •**Concrete** •**Flagstone** •**Granite** •**Limestone** •**Masonry Tile** •**Sandstone** •**Slate** •**Terrazzo**	Scrape* to remove the solids, then wash the area with a cloth dipped in a solution of washing soda or detergent (not soap) and water. Rinse well with clear water and allow to dry.
•**Carpet/Synthetic** •**Carpet/Wool**	After removing solids, apply either **Spot Shot Carpet Stain Remover, Stain-X Carpet Stain Remover,** or **Up & Out** (do not use Up & Out on wool). Be sure to follow the label directions for special instructions and any precautions. An alternate method is to scrape* to remove the solids, being careful not to push stain into pile. Sponge* the area with a solution of 1 teaspoon mild non-alkali detergent and 1 pint lukewarm water. Blot the stain with an absorbent pad. Continue the sponging and blotting until no more stain is removed. If any stain persists, sponge the area with a solution of 1 tablespoon ammonia to 1 cup warm water. (Do not use ammonia on wool carpet.) Blot excess liquid, and continue treatment until no more stain is removed. Place an absorbent pad over the damp area and weight it down. When no more liquid is absorbed, remove the pad and allow area to thoroughly air dry.
•**Wood**	Gently scrape* to remove the solids. Wipe the area with a cloth dipped in warm sudsy water. Rinse with a cloth dipped in clear cool water and wipe dry. Wax or polish as usual.

*See Chapter 4 for specific technique instructions.

Pet Stains/Urine
(*Follow procedures for* Urine.)

Preserves
(*See* Apple, Berries, Cherry, Grape, Orange, Prune.)

Prune

●Acetate
●Carpet/Synthetic
●Carpet/Wool
●Fiberglass ●Rayon
●Rope ●Triacetate
●Wool

Sponge* the stain with cool water, then sponge the area with lemon juice or rub a slice of lemon over the stain. Flush* with water, and blot as much liquid as possible. Let dry. If stain persists, apply a Wet Spotter and cover with an absorbent pad moistened with Wet Spotter. Let stand as long as any stain is being removed. Change the pad as it picks up the stain. Keep the stain and pad moist with Wet Spotter. Flush with water. If any trace of the stain remains, moisten the area with a solution of 1 cup warm water and 1 teaspoon **Axion,** an enzyme presoak product—do not use on silk or wool. Cover with a clean pad that has been dipped in the solution and wrung almost dry. Let it stand for 30 minutes. Add enough solution to keep the stain and pad moist and warm, but do not allow the wet area to spread. When no more stain is visible, flush thoroughly with water and allow to air dry.

●Acrylic Fabric
●Modacrylic ●Nylon
●Olefin ●Polyester
●Spandex

Sponge* stain with cool water immediately. Then rub with a lemon slice or sponge lemon juice on stain. Flush* with water, blotting as much liquid as

(continued)

*See Chapter 4 for specific technique instructions.

(continued from preceding page) possible. Allow to dry. If any trace of stain persists, presoak* in a solution of 1 quart warm water, ½ teaspoon dishwashing detergent, and 1 tablespoon white vinegar for 15 minutes. Rinse with water and launder if possible. If not, presoak in a solution of 1 quart water and 1 tablespoon **Axion** or **Biz** (enzyme presoak products). Rinse well with water and launder as soon as possible.

- **Acrylic Plastic**
- **Aluminum**
- **Asphalt** • **Bamboo**
- **Brass** • **Bronze**
- **Cane**
- **Ceramic Glass/Tile**
- **Copper** • **Enamel**
- **Glass** • **Grout**
- **Iron** • **Paint/Flat**
- **Paint/Gloss**
- **Plexiglas**
- **Polyurethane**
- **Porcelain Dishes**
- **Porcelain Fixtures**
- **Stainless Steel**
- **Vinyl Clothing**
- **Vinyl Wallcovering**

Wipe the stain with a cloth or sponge dipped in warm sudsy water. Rinse well and wipe dry.

- **Bluestone** • **Brick**
- **Concrete**
- **Flagstone**
- **Granite**
- **Masonry Tile**
- **Slate** • **Terrazzo**

Wipe up the excess spill and wash the stain with a solution of washing soda or detergent (not soap) and water. Use a cloth or soft-bristled brush to scrub. Rinse thoroughly and allow to dry.

- **Cork** • **Linoleum**
- **Vinyl Tile**

Wipe up the excess spill and wash the area with a solution of washing soda or detergent (not soap) and water. Scrub with a cloth or soft-bristled brush. Rinse thoroughly with

(continued)

---

*See Chapter 4 for specific technique instructions.

(continued from preceding page) clear water and allow to dry. If stain persists, wipe area with cloth dampened in a solution of 1 tablespoon oxalic acid to 1 pint water. Rinse well and wipe dry. Repolish the surface if needed. **Caution:** Oxalic acid is poisonous; use with care and wear rubber gloves.

●**Cotton** ●**Linen**

Test fabric for colorfastness. Stretch the stained fabric over a bowl and fasten in place with a rubber band. Pour boiling water through the fabric from a height of 2 or 3 feet. Avoid splatters. This procedure must be done immediately. If stain persists, soak in a solution of 1 quart warm water and ½ teaspoon detergent for 15 minutes. Then rinse with water. Sponge* area with rubbing alcohol and launder if possible. If not, presoak* for 30 minutes in a solution of 1 quart warm water and 1 tablespoon **Axion** or **Biz** (enzyme presoak products). Rinse well with water and launder.

●**Leather** ●**Suede**

Wipe up any excess juice, then mix a solution of mild soap in lukewarm water. Swish to create a great volume of suds. Apply only the foam with a sponge. Wipe with a clean dry cloth. On leather only, follow with **The Tannery** or **Fiebing's Saddle Soap** to condition the leather.

●**Marble**

After removing any excess liquid, wipe the surface with a cloth dipped in warm sudsy water. Rinse well and wipe dry. If any stain or discoloration remains, mix a poultice of water, powdered detergent, and bleach. Apply a thick paste to the stain and cover with a damp cloth to retard
(continued)

---

*See Chapter 4 for specific technique instructions.

(continued from preceding page) evaporation. Leave in place. When stain has been removed, rinse thoroughly with water and dry.

●**Silver**

Wash silver in hot sudsy water as soon as possible. Rinse in hot water and dry immediately with a soft cloth to prevent tarnish.

●**Wood**

Mix dishwashing detergent in hot water and swish to make a great volume of suds. Dip a cloth in only the foam and apply to the juice. Rinse with a clean cloth moistened with clear water. If any stain remains, rub the area with a cloth dampened with a solution of 1 tablespoon oxalic acid and 1 pint water. Rinse well and wipe dry. Wax or polish as soon as possible. **Caution:** Oxalic acid is poisonous; use with care and wear rubber gloves.

Rouge   *(Follow procedures for* Lipstick.)

Rust

●**Acetate**
●**Fiberglass**
●**Rayon**
●**Silk** ●**Triacetate**
●**Wool**

Because of the degree of difficulty involved in the removal of rust stains, it is best not to try removing this from these delicate fabrics yourself.

●**Acrylic Fabric**
●**Modacrylic** ●**Nylon**
●**Olefin** ●**Polyester**

Apply lemon juice to the stain, but do not let it dry. Rinse thoroughly with water. If possible, launder. If not and the stain remains, test a fabric-safe rust remover, **Bar Keepers Friend Cleanser & Polish,** then apply according to package directions. After

(continued)

(continued from preceding page) using, flush* the area with cool water and launder as soon as possible. **Caution:** Be careful not to spill other brands of rust remover on porcelain or enamel finishes (like those on washing machines), as these products can ruin the finish.

●Asphalt ●Linoleum ●Vinyl Tile

Wipe the stain with a cloth or sponge dipped in warm sudsy water. Rinse well and wipe dry. If any stain remains, use a rust remover, **Bar Keepers Friend Cleanser & Polish,** which is safe for resilient floors when used according to package directions.

●Brick ●Concrete ●Granite

Make a poultice from 7 parts lime-free glycerine, 1 part sodium citrate (available from drug stores), 6 parts lukewarm water, and enough powdered calcium carbonate (chalk) to create a thick paste. Apply this paste to the stain and allow to harden. Remove with a wooden scraper and repeat if necessary. Wash area thoroughly with clear water and let dry.

●Carpet/Synthetic ●Carpet/Wool

Apply lemon juice and salt to the stain. Flush* with water and blot well. If any stain remains, test a fabric-safe rust remover, **Bar Keepers Friend Cleanser & Polish;** if the fabric is not damaged, apply according to label directions. Flush thoroughly with water; blot excess liquid. Allow to dry.

●Ceramic Tile ●Porcelain Dishes ●Porcelain Fixtures

On the tub, sink, ceramic tile, or toilet, wet **Pumie Scouring Stick,** a pumice bar, and rub the iron stain. **Caution:** Do not use this pumice stick on the ceramic glass found on cookware or ceramic cooktops, as it will scratch the surface. A paste of borax and lemon juice also is effective on iron

(continued)

*See Chapter 4 for specific technique instructions.

(continued from preceding page) stains. Rub the paste into the stain and allow it to dry. Rinse with clear water, then repeat if necessary. Rinse again and dry with a clean cloth.

•Cotton •Linen	Rub liquid dishwashing or laundry detergent into the stain, rinse with water, and launder as soon as possible. If stain remains, test fabric for colorfastness, then use a fabric-safe rust remover, **Bar Keepers Friend Cleanser & Polish,** according to package directions.
•Leather •Suede	Iron and rust are chemical stains that should be treated by a professional cleaner.
•Stainless Steel	Rub stainless steel with a damp piece of very fine grade emery paper, followed by rubbing it with a slice of onion. Rinse well with hot water and dry thoroughly with a soft cloth.

Salad Dressing/Creamy

•Acetate
•Carpet/Synthetic
•Carpet/Wool
•Fiberglass •Burlap
•Rayon •Rope
•Silk •Triacetate
•Wool

Blot up any excess spill and sponge* the area with dry-cleaning solvent, either **Carbona No. 10 Special Spot Remover/Carbona Cleaning Fluid** or **Afta Cleaning Fluid.** Apply a Dry Spotter to the stain and cover with an absorbent pad moistened with Dry Spotter. Let it stand as long as any spill is removed. Change the pad as it picks up the stain and keep both the pad and stain moist with Dry Spotter. When no more stain is removed, flush with the dry-cleaning solvent. Allow to dry. If any stain remains, moisten it with a solution of ½ teaspoon **Axion** enzyme presoak and ½

(continued)

*See Chapter 4 for specific technique instructions.

(continued from preceding page) cup warm water—do not use Axion on silk or wool. Cover with a clean pad that has been moistened with the solution. Let it stand for 30 minutes, adding enough solution to keep the area warm and barely moist. Flush* with water and allow to thoroughly dry. When treating carpets, blot up excess liquid. Cover the area with an absorbent pad and weight it down. When no more liquid is being absorbed, allow the area to thoroughly air dry. Or, after blotting up excess dressing, treat the stain with **Stain-X Carpet Stain Remover** or **Up & Out** (do not use Up & Out on wool carpets).

●**Acrylic Fabric**
●**Cotton** ●**Linen**
●**Modacrylic** ●**Nylon**
●**Olefin** ●**Polyester**
●**Spandex**

Remove as much liquid as possible by blotting. Apply a Wet Spotter to the area and work it into the fiber. Rinse thoroughly with water. If stain remains, apply a paste made from **Axion** enzyme presoak and water. Allow the paste to cover the stain for at least 15 minutes, keeping it moist. Rinse the area with water and launder as soon as possible.

●**Acrylic Plastic**
●**Aluminum**
●**Asphalt** ●**Bamboo**
●**Bronze** ●**Cane**
●**Ceramic Glass/Tile**
●**Chromium**
●**Copper** ●**Cork**
●**Enamel** ●**Glass**
●**Gold** ●**Iron** ●**Ivory**
●**Linoleum**
●**Paint/Flat**
●**Paint/Gloss**
●**Pewter** ●**Plexiglas**
●**Polyurethane**
(continued)

Wipe up the excess spill as soon as possible with a cloth dipped in warm sudsy water. Rinse with clear water and allow to dry.

*See Chapter 4 for specific technique instructions.

- **Porcelain Dishes**   *(see base of preceding page)*
- **Porcelain Fixtures**
- **Stainless Steel**
- **Tin** **•Vinyl Clothing**
- **Vinyl Tile**
- **Vinyl Wallcovering**

- **Alabaster**
- **Bluestone**
- **Concrete**
- **Flagstone**
- **Granite**
- **Limestone**
- **Marble**
- **Masonry Tile**
- **Sandstone** **•Slate**
- **Terrazzo**

Wipe up the excess material. Then wipe the stain with a cloth dipped in a solution of washing soda or detergent (not soap) and water. Rinse well with water. If a stain remains, rub it with **Pumie Scouring Stick.** Or mix a poultice from water, bleach, and powdered detergent. Apply a thick paste to the stain and cover with a damp cloth to retard evaporation. When stain is removed, rinse well with water and wipe dry.

- **Leather** **•Suede**

Mix a solution of mild soap in lukewarm water. Swish to create a great volume of suds. Apply only the foam with a sponge. Wipe dry with a clean cloth. On leather only, follow with **The Tannery** or **Fiebing's Saddle Soap** to condition the leather.

- **Silver**

Wash in hot soapy water. Rinse in hot water and wipe dry with a soft clean cloth.

- **Wallpaper**

Blot up any excess material. Wipe area with a cloth moistened with cool clear water. Overlap strokes to prevent streaking. Use a clean cloth to gently pat dry.

- **Wood**

Note: Wooden salad bowls and utensils should not be washed with dishwashing detergent—merely wipe off the dressing with a dishcloth dampened with clear water. Wipe

(continued)

(continued from preceding page) other wood surfaces with a cloth dipped in warm sudsy water. Rinse with water, wipe dry, and polish or wax as usual.

Salad Dressing/Oily

- ●Acetate
- ●Carpet/Synthetic
- ●Carpet/Wool
- ●Rayon ●Silk
- ●Triacetate
- ●Wool

Blot up the excess and sponge* the area with a dry-cleaning solvent, either **Carbona No. 10 Special Spot Remover/Carbona Cleaning Fluid** or **Afta Cleaning Fluid.** Apply a Dry Spotter and cover the stain with an absorbent pad moistened with Dry Spotter. Let the pad remain in place as long as any stain is being removed. Change the pad as it picks up the stain. Keep the pad and stain moist with Dry Spotter. Flush* the area with the dry-cleaning solvent. If the stain persists, sponge the area with water and apply a Wet Spotter and a few drops of white vinegar. Cover the stain with an absorbent pad dampened with Wet Spotter. Let the pad remain in place as long as any stain is being removed, changing the pad as it picks up the stain. Keep both the pad and stain most with Wet Spotter and vinegar. Flush with water and repeat the procedure until no more stain is removed. Allow to dry.

- ●Acrylic Fabric
- ●Cotton ●Linen
- ●Modacrylic ●Nylon
- ●Olefin ●Polyester
- ●Spandex

Blot up the excess spill and sponge* the area with **K2r Spot-lifter** (aerosol), a dry-cleaning solvent. Apply a Dry Spotter and cover with an absorbent pad moistened with Dry Spotter. Let it remain in place as long as any stain is being removed. Change the pad as it picks up the stain. To help loosen any set stains, tamp* the area occasionally, blotting up any loose material. Flush* with a liquid dry-

(continued)

See Chapter 4 for specific technique instructions.

(continued from preceding page) cleaning solvent, **Carbona No. 10 Special Spot Remover/Carbona Cleaning Fluid.** If a trace of the stain remains, sponge with water and apply a Wet Spotter. Tamp the stain again, blotting up any loosened particles. Flush with water and repeat if necessary. Allow to dry.

- ●Acrylic Plastic
- ●Aluminum
- ●Asphalt ●Bamboo
- ●Cane
- ●Ceramic Glass/Tile
- ●Cork ●Glass
- ●Linoleum
- ●Paint/Flat
- ●Paint/Gloss
- ●Pewter ●Plexiglas
- ●Polyurethane
- ●Porcelain Dishes
- ●Stainless Steel
- ●Vinyl Clothing
- ●Vinyl Tile
- ●Vinyl Wallcovering

Blot up any excess dressing. Wipe the surface with a cloth or sponge dipped in warm sudsy water. Rinse well and wipe dry.

- ●Bluestone ●Brick
- ●Concrete
- ●Flagstone
- ●Granite
- ●Limestone
- ●Masonry Tile
- ●Sandstone ●Slate
- ●Terrazzo

Wash with a strong solution of washing soda or detergent (not soap) and warm water. If oily stain remains, cover with a paste made with fuller's earth and hot water. Leave overnight. Rinse with clear water and repeat if necessary.

- ●Leather

Gently blot up the excess. Often, application of **Fiebing's Saddle Soap** will remove any residue. If this doesn't completely remove the stain, rub a thick paste of fuller's earth and water over the stain. Leave it to dry, then brush* the powder off. Repeat

(continued)

---

*See Chapter 4 for specific technique instructions.

(continued from preceding page) application of paste if necessary. Follow with **The Tannery** or **Fiebing's Saddle Soap** to condition the leather.

●**Marble**

Remove any excess spill, then wipe the stain with a cloth dipped in warm sudsy water. Rinse well and wipe dry with a clean cloth. If any residue remains, mix a poultice of water, powdered detergent, and bleach. Apply to the stain and cover with a damp cloth to retard evaporation. After the stain has been bleached out and the oil removed, rinse thoroughly with water and wipe dry.

●**Silver**

Wash immediately after use in hot sudsy water, because silver can be damaged by foods containing acids or egg. Then rinse thoroughly in hot water and wipe dry immediately with a soft cloth to prevent tarnish.

●**Suede**

Blot up the excess dressing. Then dip a cloth into ground cornmeal and rub it into the stain, using a circular motion. When dry, gently brush* off the powder with a wire brush. Repeat cornmeal application if necessary. If stain persists, test lemon juice on an inconspicuous place. If suede isn't damaged, rub the area with lemon juice and hold it in the steam from a boiling teakettle for a few minutes. Brush with a wire brush.

●**Wallpaper**

Make a paste of cornstarch and water. Apply to the stain and allow to dry. Brush* off the powder and repeat if necessary. If the stain persists, make a paste of fuller's earth and a small amount of dry-cleaning solvent, **Carbona No. 10 Special Spot**
(continued)

See Chapter 4 for specific technique instructions.

(continued from preceding page) **Remover/Carbona Cleaning Fluid.** Apply to stain and allow to dry. Brush off.

●**Wood**

Note: Wooden salad bowls and utensils should not be washed with dishwashing detergent—merely wipe off the dressing with a dishcloth dampened with clear water. For other wood surfaces, mix dishwashing detergent in hot water and swish to make a great volume of suds. Dip a cloth in only the foam and apply to the stain. Rinse with a clean cloth moistened with clear water. Polish or wax wood furniture, floors, or woodwork as soon as possible.

Sauce/Barbecue, Spaghetti, Steak

●**Acetate** ●**Burlap**
●**Carpet/Synthetic**
●**Carpet/Wool**
●**Fiberglass**
●**Rayon** ●**Rope**
●**Silk** ●**Triacetate**
●**Wool**

Gently scrape* to remove excess. Sponge* the area with a dry-cleaning solvent, either **Carbona No. 10 Special Spot Remover/Carbona Cleaning Fluid** or **Afta Cleaning Fluid.** Apply a Dry Spotter. Cover the stain with an absorbent pad dampened with Dry Spotter. Let it stand as long as any stain is being removed. Change the pad as it picks up the stain. Keep the stain and pad moist with Dry Spotter. When no more stain is being removed, flush* the area with the dry-cleaning solvent and allow to dry. If any stain remains, moisten it with ½ teaspoon **Axion** enzyme presoak mixed with ½ cup warm water. Cover with an absorbent pad that has been dipped in the solution and wrung nearly dry. Let it stand for 30 minutes, adding enough solution to keep the area warm and barely

(continued)

*See Chapter 4 for specific technique instructions.

(continued from preceding page) moist. Flush the area with water and allow to dry. On carpets, sponge with water to remove the enzyme mixture, then place a clean dry pad over the area and weight it down. When no more liquid is being absorbed, allow it to air dry completely.

- **Acrylic Fabric**
- **Cotton** • **Linen**
- **Modacrylic** • **Nylon**
- **Olefin** • **Polyester**
- **Spandex**

Carefully scrape* to remove as much excess as possible. Spray on **Amway Remove Fabric Spot Cleaner.** If stain remains, apply a Wet Spotter and work into the fabric. Rinse thoroughly with water and launder. If any stain remains, apply an enzyme paste using **Axion** or **Biz** (enzyme presoaks) and water. Let it work for awhile. Keep the paste moist. After about 30 minutes, rinse the area with water thoroughly to remove all traces of enzyme presoak. Launder as soon as possible.

- **Acrylic Plastic**
- **Aluminum**
- **Asphalt**
- **Bamboo**
- **Brass**
- **Bronze**
- **Cane**
- **Ceramic Glass/Tile**
- **Chromium**
- **Copper**
- **Cork**
- **Enamel** • **Glass**
- **Gold** • **Iron**
- **Ivory**
- **Jade** • **Linoleum**
- **Opal** • **Paint/Flat**
- **Paint/Gloss**
- **Pearls** • **Pewter**
- **Platinum**
- **Plexiglas**

(continued)

Note: The tomato sauce contained in these foods can permanently stain some surfaces. Wipe up the excess immediately with a cloth or sponge dipped in warm sudsy water. Rinse with clear water and wipe dry.

See Chapter 4 for specific technique instructions.

- **Polyurethane** *(see base of preceding page)*
- **Porcelain Dishes**
- **Stainless Steel**
- **Vinyl Clothing**
- **Vinyl Tile**
- **Vinyl Wallcovering**

- **Alabaster**
- **Bluestone**
- **Concrete**
- **Flagstone**
- **Granite**
- **Limestone**
- **Marble**
- **Masonry Tile**
- **Sandstone**
- **Slate**
- **Terrazzo**

Carefully remove the excess spill. Wipe stain with a cloth dipped in a solution of washing soda or detergent (not soap) and water. If any stain remains, mix a poultice of water, bleach, and powdered detergent. Apply to the stained area and cover with a damp cloth to retard evaporation. When stain is removed, rinse well and wipe dry with a soft cloth.

- **Leather** **Suede**

Mix a solution of mild soap in luke-warm water. Swish to create a great volume of suds. Apply only the foam with a sponge. Wipe dry with a clean cloth. On leather only, follow with **The Tannery** or **Fiebing's Saddle Soap** to condition the leather.

- **Silver**

Wash silver immediately in hot soapy water as the acids in these sauces can damage the silver. Rinse thoroughly in hot water and wipe dry with a soft cloth to prevent tarnish.

- **Wallpaper**

Wipe immediately with a cloth dampened with clear cool water. Use overlapping strokes to prevent streaking. Gently pat dry with a soft cloth.

- **Wood**

Wipe immediately with a cloth moistened with warm sudsy water. Rinse with a cloth dampened with clear water, wipe dry, and polish or wax as usual.

Sauce/Soy, Worcestershire

●**Acetate**
●**Fiberglass** ●**Rayon**
●**Triacetate**

Blot up the excess. Spray on **Amway Remove Fabric Spot Cleaner** or sponge* the stain with water and apply a Wet Spotter and a few drops of white vinegar. Cover with an absorbent pad dampened with Wet Spotter. Let it stand as long as any stain is being removed. Change the pad as it picks up the stain. Keep the stain and pad moist with Wet Spotter and vinegar. Flush* with water and repeat until no more stain can be removed. If stain still persists, moisten it with a solution of 1 teaspoon **Axion** enzyme presoak and 1 cup warm water. Cover with a clean pad that has been dipped in the solution and wrung nearly dry. Let it stand for at least 30 minutes. Add enough solution to keep the stained area warm and barely moist. When the stain is removed, or no more is being removed, flush with water and allow to dry.

●**Acrylic Fabric**
●**Modacrylic** ●**Nylon**
●**Olefin** ●**Polyester**
●**Spandex**

Blot up any excess sauce with a clean cloth. Then presoak* the stain in a solution of 1 quart warm water, ½ teaspoon liquid detergent, and 1 tablespoon white vinegar for 15 minutes. Rinse with water. Sponge* the remaining stain with rubbing alcohol and launder if possible. If not, presoak in a solution of 1 quart warm water and 1 tablespoon **Axion** or **Biz** (enzyme presoak products) for 30 minutes. Rinse well with water and allow to dry. Launder as soon as possible.

●**Acrylic Plastic**
●**Aluminum**

(continued)

Wipe up any excess spill, then wipe the area with a cloth or sponge

See Chapter 4 for specific technique instructions.

(continued from preceding page)

- Asphalt - Bamboo
- Brass - Bronze
- Cane
- Ceramic Glass/Tile
- Copper - Cork
- Enamel - Glass
- Gold - Grout - Iron
- Ivory - Jade
- Linoleum
- Paint/Flat
- Paint/Gloss
- Pewter
- Plexiglas
- Polyurethane
- Stainless Steel
- Tin - Vinyl Clothing
- Vinyl Tile
- Vinyl Wallcovering
- Zinc

dipped in warm sudsy water. Rinse well with clear water and wipe dry with a soft cloth.

- Alabaster - Marble

Blot up any excess sauce. Wipe the stain with a cloth dipped in a solution of washing soda or detergent (not soap) and water. If a stain remains, mix a few drops ammonia with 1 cup 3% hydrogen peroxide. Soak a white blotter with the solution and place over the stain. Continue applying the solution until all the stain has been bleached out and the oil drawn out. Rinse well and wipe dry with a soft cloth.

- Bluestone - Brick
- Concrete
- Flagstone
- Granite
- Limestone
- Masonry Tile
- Sandstone - Slate
- Terrazzo

Wash stain with a solution of washing soda or detergent (not soap) and warm water. Scrub with a cloth or soft-bristled brush. Rinse with clear water and allow to dry.

●**Burlap** ●**Silk**
●**Wool**

Blot up the excess sauce with a clean pad. Spray on **Amway Remove Fabric Spot Cleaner** or sponge* the stain with water. Apply a Wet Spotter and a few drops of white vinegar. Cover with an absorbent pad moistened with Wet Spotter. Let it stand as long as any stain is being removed. Change the pad as it picks up the stain. Keep both the stain and pad moist with Wet Spotter and vinegar. Flush* with water and repeat until no more stain can be removed. If any stain does remain, apply rubbing alcohol to the area and cover with an absorbent pad dampened with alcohol. Let it stand as long as any stain is being removed. Change the pad as it picks up the stain and keep both the stain and pad moist with alcohol. Flush with water. For stubborn or old stains, moisten the area with a solution of 1 teaspoon alcohol and 1 cup warm water. Cover with a pad dipped in the solution and wrung nearly dry. Let it stand at least 30 minutes. Add enough solution to keep the stained area warm and barely moist. When stain is removed, flush thoroughly with water and allow to dry.

●**Carpet/Synthetic**
●**Carpet/Wool**
●**Foam Rubber**

Blot up what you can with a clean pad. Apply **Spot Shot Carpet Stain Remover** or **Up & Out** (do not use Up & Out on wool carpets). Then flush* the stain with a solution of 1 quart warm water, ½ teaspoon liquid detergent, and 1 tablespoon white vinegar. Blot with a clean absorbent pad and rinse well with water. If any stain remains, flush it with a solution of 1 quart warm water and 1 tablespoon **Axion** enzyme presoak—do not use on wool carpets. Blot and flush alternately until no more stain is left. *(continued)*

*See Chapter 4 for specific technique instructions.

(continued from preceding page) Rinse well with water. Blot all excess liquid and place a clean pad over the area and weight it down. When no more liquid is being absorbed, allow the area to thoroughly air dry.

●Cotton ●Linen

Blot up the excess, then test **Axion** or **Biz** enzyme presoak. If safe to use, presoak* the stain. Or, pretest **Shout Laundry Soil & Stain Remover, Magic Pre-Wash,** or **Miracle White Laundry Soil & Stain Remover** on an inconspicuous place as directed on the package label. If fabric isn't damaged or the color doesn't change, pretreat* the stain. If unable to pretreat or if stain remains, soak stain in a solution of 1 quart warm water and ½ teaspoon liquid detergent for 15 minutes. Rinse well with water, then sponge* stain with rubbing alcohol. Rinse and allow to dry. If stain persists, presoak in a solution of 1 quart warm water and 1 tablespoon enzyme presoak for 30 minutes. Rinse well with water and allow to dry. Launder as soon as possible.

●Leather ●Suede

Carefully blot up excess liquid. Mix a solution of mild soap in lukewarm water. Swish to create a great volume of suds. Apply only the foam with a sponge. Wipe dry with a clean dry cloth. If an oil stain remains, powder the area with an absorbent such as cornmeal. Allow plenty of time for it to work. Gently brush* the powder off. Repeat application of absorbent if necessary. On leather only, follow with **The Tannery** or **Fiebing's Saddle Soap** to condition the leather.

●Porcelain Dishes
●Porcelain Fixtures

Wash the stain in warm sudsy water. Rinse well and wipe dry. If fixture
(continued)

---

*See Chapter 4 for specific technique instructions.

(continued from preceding page) cannot be removed for washing, wipe it with a cloth dipped in warm sudsy water.

●Silver Wash silver in hot soapy water. Rinse in hot water and wipe dry with a soft cloth to prevent tarnish.

●Wood Mix dishwashing detergent in hot water and swish to make a great volume of suds. Dip a cloth in only the foam and apply to the stain. Rinse with a cloth dampened with clear water. Polish or wax as soon as possible.

Shoe Polish (except white)

●Acetate ●Burlap
●Fiberglass ●Rayon
●Rope ●Silk
●Triacetate
●Wool

Sponge* the area with a dry-cleaning solvent, either **Carbona No. 10 Special Spot Remover/Carbona Cleaning Fluid** or **Afta Cleaning Fluid** and apply a Dry Spotter. Cover the stain with an absorbent pad moistened with Dry Spotter. Let the pad remain in place as long as any stain is being removed. Change the pad as it picks up the stain. Keep both the pad and stain moist with Dry Spotter. Flush* the stain with the dry-cleaning fluid. If the stain persists, sponge it with water and apply a Wet Spotter and a few drops of ammonia. (Do not use ammonia on silk or wool.) Cover the stain with an absorbent pad dampened with Wet Spotter and ammonia. Change the pad as it picks up the stain, keeping both the stain and pad moist with Wet Spotter and ammonia. Flush the area with water and repeat if necessary. Allow to dry.

●Acrylic Fabric
●Cotton ●Linen
(continued)

Sponge* the area with a dry-cleaning solvent, either **Carbona No. 10**

*See Chapter 4 for specific technique instructions.

(continued from preceding page)

•Modacrylic	**Special Spot Remover/Carbona Cleaning Fluid, K2r Spot-lifter** (aerosol), or **Afta Cleaning Fluid.** If you apply K2r Spot-lifter, allow it to dry, then brush* off powder. If stain persists, mix a paste of powdered detergent, water, and a few drops of ammonia. Place an absorbent pad beneath the area and apply the paste to the stain. When no more stain is being removed, flush* the area thoroughly with water and launder as soon as possible.
•Acrylic Plastic •Aluminum •Asphalt •Ceramic Glass/Tile •Chromium •Enamel •Glass •Gold •Ivory •Jade •Paint/Flat •Paint/Gloss •Platinum •Plexiglas •Polyurethane •Silver •Stainless Steel •Vinyl Clothing •Vinyl Wallcovering	Wipe the surface with a cloth or sponge dipped in warm sudsy water to which a few drops of ammonia have been added. Rinse well with clear water and wipe dry.
•Alabaster •Marble	Wipe the surface with a cloth dipped in warm sudsy water to which a few drops of ammonia have been added. Rinse well and wipe dry. If a stain persists, mix a poultice from water, bleach, and powdered detergent. Apply to the stain and let it remain until the oil has been drawn out and the stain bleached out. Rinse thoroughly with clear water and wipe dry.

*See Chapter 4 for specific technique instructions.

•Carpet/Synthetic
•Carpet/Wool

Scrape* to remove as much excess as possible. Sponge* the stain with a concentrated solution of carpet shampoo or apply **Spot Shot Carpet Stain Remover.** Continue sponging the area, rinsing the cloth or sponge in clear water as it picks up the stain. Repeat until no more stain is removed.

•Cork •Linoleum
•Vinyl Tile

Cover the stain with a rubbing alcohol compress. Let the compress remain in place for 5 minutes. Wipe the area with a cloth dampened with ammonia. (Do not use ammonia on linoleum or vinyl floor tile.) Rinse well and allow to dry.

•Felt •Fur/Natural
•Fur/Synthetic
•Leather •Suede

Because of the dyes contained in shoe polish, this stain cannot be removed by a nonprofessional.

•Grout

Wipe the stain with a cloth dipped in warm sudsy water. If a stain remains, apply **Afta Tile & Grout Cleaner** or dip a wet toothbrush into a little baking soda or powdered cleanser. Gently scrub the spot. Rinse well and wipe dry with a soft cloth.

•Nylon •Olefin
•Polyester
•Spandex

Immediately sponge* the stain with suds made with dishwashing detergent. Sprinkle lemon juice and salt over the area and allow to penetrate for 1 hour. Rinse thoroughly with water and launder as soon as possible. Repeat treatment if necessary.

•Wallpaper

Note: This stain might permanently dye the paper. Rub the area very gently with a damp cloth sprinkled with a little baking soda. Wipe the area with a cloth dampened with cool clear water. Do not let the wet area

(continued)

See Chapter 4 for specific technique instructions.

(continued from preceding page) spread or run. Overlap strokes to prevent streaking. Use a clean cloth to gently pat dry.

●**Wood**

Wipe the stain with a cloth dipped in warm sudsy water to which a few drops of ammonia have been added. Rinse well with a cloth moistened with clear water and wipe dry. Polish or wax the wood as usual.

Shoe Polish/White

●**Acetate** ●**Burlap**
●**Carpet/Synthetic**
●**Carpet/Wool**
●**Fiberglass** ●**Rayon**
●**Silk** ●**Triacetate**
●**Wool**

Sponge* the stain with a dry-cleaning solvent, either **Carbona No. 10 Special Spot Remover/Carbona Cleaning Fluid** or **Afta Cleaning Fluid.** Apply a Dry Spotter, blotting until no more stain is being lifted. Flush* with the dry-cleaning solvent. Sponge with amyl acetate until no more stain is being lifted, then flush again with the dry-cleaning solvent. Sponge with water and add a few drops of white vinegar if the stain persists. When no more stain is being removed, flush the area with water and allow to dry.

●**Acrylic Fabric**
●**Cotton** ●**Linen**
●**Modacrylic** ●**Nylon**
●**Olefin** ●**Polyester**
●**Spandex**

Sponge* the area with a dry-cleaning solvent, either **Carbona No. 10 Special Spot Remover/Carbona Cleaning Fluid, K2r Spot-lifter** (aerosol), or **Afta Cleaning Fluid.** Apply a Dry Spotter and tamp.* Flush* the area with one of the liquid dry-cleaning solvents. If the stain persists, flush the area with amyl acetate (dilute with water for cotton and linen). Tamp occasionally until no more stain is being lifted. Flush again with the dry-cleaning solvent and allow to dry. If any stain remains,

(continued)

See Chapter 4 for specific technique instructions.

(continued from preceding page) dampen the area with water and add a few drops of white vinegar (dilute for cotton and linen) and tamp until no more stain remains. Flush out the vinegar with water and either allow to dry or launder.

- **Acrylic Plastic**
- **Asphalt**
- **Ceramic Glass/Tile**
- **Chromium** ● **Cork**
- **Enamel** ● **Glass**
- **Gold** ● **Ivory** ● **Jade**
- **Linoleum**
- **Paint/Flat**
- **Paint/Gloss**
- **Platinum**
- **Plexiglas**
- **Polyurethane**
- **Silver**
- **Stainless Steel**
- **Vinyl Clothing**
- **Vinyl Tile**
- **Vinyl Wallcovering**

Wipe the spill with a cloth dipped in warm sudsy water to which a few drops of white vinegar have been added. Rinse well and wipe dry.

- **Alabaster** ● **Marble**

Wipe the surface with a cloth dipped in warm sudsy water to which a few drops of ammonia have been added. Rinse well and wipe dry. If a stain persists, mix a poultice from water, bleach, and powdered detergent. Apply to the stain and let it remain until the oil has been drawn out and the stain bleached out. Rinse thoroughly with clear water and wipe dry.

- **Leather** ● **Suede**

Note: This may be an impossible stain to remove. First apply a leather cleaner, **The Tannery**, to stains on leather. For suede, apply **Child Life Suede & Fabric Cleaner.** Rub it in with a clean soft cloth. Let it dry. If the stain remains, test **Carbona No. 10**

(continued)

(continued from preceding page) **Special Spot Remover/Carbona Cleaning Fluid** in an inconspicuous place. If the surface isn't damaged, gingerly apply the solvent to the stain. Allow the leather or suede to air dry. On leather only, condition with **The Tannery** or **Fiebing's Saddle Soap.**

●**Wallpaper**

Note: This stain might permanently dye the paper. Rub the area very gently with a damp cloth sprinkled with baking soda. Wipe the polish off with a cloth dampened with cool water, but don't let water streaks run down the wall. Overlap strokes. Use a clean cloth to pat dry.

●**Wood**

Gently wipe up the excess with a cloth moistened with the suds of a mild detergent and water to which a few drops of white vinegar have been added. Rinse with a clean cloth moistened with clear water. Polish or wax the wood as soon as possible.

Smoke

●**Acetate**
●**Carpet/Synthetic**
●**Carpet/Wool**
●**Fiberglass** ●**Rayon**
●**Silk** ●**Triacetate**
●**Wool**

Note: Fabrics or carpets that are heavily stained should be laundered or professionally cleaned. For light stains, flush* the area with a dry-cleaning solvent, **Carbona No. 10 Special Spot Remover/Carbona Cleaning Fluid,** taking care not to spread the stain. Apply a Dry Spotter and cover with an absorbent pad dampened with the Dry Spotter. Check the stain every 5 minutes. Before changing pads, press firmly against the stain. Continue the alternate soaking and pressing until no more stain is being lifted. Flush again
(continued)

See Chapter 4 for specific technique instructions.

(continued from preceding page) with the dry-cleaning solvent and allow to dry. If any stain remains, try applying a Wet Spotter with a few drops of ammonia added (do not use ammonia on silk or wool). Cover with an absorbent pad dampened with the Wet Spotter. Let it stand as long as any stain is being lifted. Flush well with water. Repeat if necessary; allow to dry.

- **Acrylic Fabric**
- **Cotton** • **Linen**
- **Modacrylic** • **Nylon**
- **Olefin** • **Polyester**
- **Spandex**

Note: Fabrics that have a smoke residue from a fire are best laundered or professionally cleaned. If the stain is small or laundering immediately is not possible, flush* it with a dry-cleaning solvent—**Carbona No. 10 Special Spot Remover/Carbona Cleaning Fluid** or **Afta Cleaning Fluid.** Apply a Dry Spotter to the stain and cover with an absorbent pad dampened with the Dry Spotter. Check the stain often, tamping* before changing pads. Continue alternate soaking and tamping until the stain is removed. Flush with one of the dry-cleaning solvents and allow to dry. If the stain remains, try the same procedure with a Wet Spotter and a few drops of ammonia. Be sure to flush the area well when the stain is lifted. Allow to dry and launder as soon as possible.

- **Acrylic Plastic**
- **Alabaster**
- **Asphalt** • **Cork**
- **Glass** • **Linoleum**
- **Marble** • **Paint/Flat**
- **Paint/Gloss**
- **Plexiglas**
- **Polyurethane**
- **Vinyl Clothing**
- **Vinyl Wallcovering**

Wipe the stained area with a cloth dipped in warm sudsy water. Rinse well with clear water and wipe dry with a clean cloth.

*See Chapter 4 for specific technique instructions.

●**Bluestone** ●**Brick** ●**Masonry Tile** ●**Sandstone** ●**Slate** ●**Terrazzo**	If stain is small, erase as much smoke as possible with an artgum eraser. Mix ½ cup powdered all-purpose cleaner in 1 gallon water and rub the stain with a sponge dipped in the solution. Rinse well to remove all chemicals and allow to dry.
●**Leather** ●**Suede**	For light stains, mix a solution of mild soap in lukewarm water. Swish to create a great volume of suds. Apply only the foam with a sponge to the smoke residue. Wipe the area dry with a clean, dry, soft cloth. On leather only, follow with **The Tannery** or **Fiebing's Saddle Soap** to condition the leather.
●**Wood**	Wipe the stained surface with a cloth dampened with a solution of mild sudsy water. Rinse well with clear water and wipe it dry immediately, as water will damage most finishes. Polish or wax as soon as possible.

Soap

●**Acetate** ●**Acrylic Fabric** ●**Burlap** ●**Carpet/Synthetic** ●**Carpet/Wool** ●**Modacrylic** ●**Nylon** ●**Olefin** ●**Polyester** ●**Rayon** ●**Silk** ●**Spandex** ●**Triacetate** ●**Wool**	Sponge* with cool water. If stain persists, thoroughly flush* it with cool water. If the color has been altered, or to prevent fading or bleeding, neutralize the spot with a few drops of a mild acid such as lemon juice, white vinegar, or 10% acetic acid solution. Sponge thoroughly with cool water. If soap has a high lye content, the fabric may be damaged permanently. Silk and wool are weakened and sometimes destroyed by strong soap, so be especially prompt in treatment.
●**Acrylic Plastic** ●**Alabaster** ●**Aluminum** (continued)	Rinse well with a sponge dipped in cool water. Wipe dry with a clean soft cloth. Also, baking soda applied with

See Chapter 4 for specific technique instructions.

(continued from preceding page)

- Asphalt ●Bamboo
- Brass ●Bronze
- Cane
- Ceramic Glass/Tile
- Chromium
- Copper ●Coral
- Cork ●Fiberglass
- Glass ●Gold
- Grout ●Iron ●Ivory
- Jade ●Linoleum
- Marble ●Opal
- Paint/Flat
- Paint/Gloss
- Pearls ●Pewter
- Platinum
- Plexiglas
- Polyurethane
- Porcelain ●Rope
- Stainless Steel
- Tin ●Vinyl Clothing
- Vinyl Tile
- Vinyl Wallcovering
- Zinc

a damp cloth should cut soap film. Treat pearls stained with strong soap immediately; they are permanently damaged by strong alkalies.

- Bluestone ●Brick
- Concrete
- Flagstone
- Granite
- Limestone
- Masonry Tile
- Sandstone ●Slate
- Terrazzo

Soap scum may be almost impossible to remove from these surfaces. Scrub with a solution of washing soda or non-alkali all-purpose cleaner and water. Rinse well and dry.

- Cotton ●Linen

Flush* area with cool water until all trace of soap is gone. Launder as soon as possible. The acid treatment recommended for other fabrics cannot be used on cotton or linen, as they may be permanently damaged by acids.

*See Chapter 4 for specific technique instructions.

Stain & Spot Removal Handbook

Proven Procedures And Products For Removing Stains And Spots From Fabrics, Furniture, ~~ors~~, And Much More!

●**Felt**

Brush* in the direction of the nap with a sponge moistened with cool water. If any stain remains, neutralize it with a few drops of lemon juice, white vinegar, or 10% acetic acid solution. Sponge* thoroughly with cool water. Since felt is composed mainly of wool fibers, a strong soap may damage it permanently.

●**Fur/Natural**
●**Fur/Synthetic**

Dip a cloth or sponge in cool water and remove as much of the water as possible. Gently rub with the nap; do not over-wet the pelt or backing. Air dry away from heat.

●**Leather** ●**Suede**

Dip a cloth into the suds of a mild detergent. Gently wipe away any soap film. Rinse with a clean dry cloth. Dry away from heat. Leather may be conditioned with **The Tannery** or **Fiebing's Saddle Soap.** Treat suede with **Child Life Suede & Fabric Cleaner.**

●**Silver**

Wash silver in hot sudsy water with a soft cloth. Rinse in hot water and dry immediately with a soft cloth.

●**Wallpaper**

Take special care, as an alkali like strong soap may dissolve the adhesive behind the paper. Dip a sponge in clear warm water, wring until sponge is damp, then gently stroke the stain, overlapping your strokes. Pat dry with a clean cloth.

●**Wood**

Strong soap may dissolve wood polishes. With a sponge dipped in cool water and wrung out until damp, wipe the area without spreading the stain. Wipe dry with a soft cloth. Polish or wax immediately to prevent permanent wood damage.

*See Chapter 4 for specific technique instructions.

Soft Drinks/Cola

- **Acetate**
- **Fiberglass** • **Rayon**
- **Silk** • **Triacetate**
- **Wool**

Blot up what you can with a clean cloth. Sponge* the remaining stain with water. It is imperative that all the sugar be removed. Usually water will completely remove the stain, but if any remains spray on **Amway Remove Fabric Spot Cleaner** or apply a Wet Spotter and a few drops of white vinegar. Cover with an absorbent pad and let it stand as long as any stain is being lifted. Change the pad as it picks up the stain. Keep the stain and pad moist with the Wet Spotter and vinegar. Flush well with water. Repeat until the stain is lifted. If any sugar remains and turns yellow, it cannot be removed.

- **Acrylic Fabric**
- **Cotton** • **Linen**
- **Modacrylic** • **Nylon**
- **Olefin** • **Polyester**
- **Spandex**

Blot up any excess with a clean cloth and flush* the area thoroughly with water. This is usually enough to remove the stain, but to be certain the sugar is removed, launder immediately. If that is not possible, soak the stain in a solution of 1 quart warm water, ½ teaspoon liquid detergent, and 1 tablespoon white vinegar for 15 minutes. Rinse with water. If it is an old stain, and the sugar has not been carmelized by heat, presoak* the stain in a solution of 1 quart warm water and 1 tablespoon of **Axion** or **Biz** (enzyme presoaks) for 30 minutes. Rinse well with water to remove enzyme and sugar residues. Allow to dry, but launder as soon as possible.

- **Acrylic Plastic**
- **Alabaster**
- **Aluminum**
- **Asphalt**

(continued)

Blot up any excess. Wipe the surface with a cloth or sponge dipped in warm sudsy water. Rinse well and wipe dry.

*See Chapter 4 for specific technique instructions.

- ●Bamboo
- ●Cane
- ●Ceramic Glass/Tile
- ●Chromium
- ●Copper ●Cork
- ●Glass ●Linoleum
- ●Marble ●Paint/Flat
- ●Paint/Gloss
- ●Plexiglas
- ●Polyurethane
- ●Porcelain ●Silver
- ●Stainless Steel
- ●Vinyl Clothing
- ●Vinyl Tile
- ●Vinyl Wallcovering

(see base of preceding page)

- ●Bluestone ●Brick
- ●Concrete
- ●Flagstone
- ●Granite
- ●Limestone
- ●Masonry Tile
- ●Sandstone ●Slate
- ●Terrazzo

Mix a solution of washing soda or detergent (not soap) and water. Gently brush* the stain away. Wash with clear water and allow to dry.

- ●Carpet/Synthetic
- ●Carpet/Wool

Blot up what you can immediately. It is important to remove as much of the sugar as possible. Sponge* the stain with water or flush* area rugs with water. Blot as much liquid as possible and apply **Spot Shot Carpet Stain Remover** or **Stain-X Carpet Stain Remover,** following the directions on the label. If any stain remains, flush it with a solution of 1 quart warm water, ½ teaspoon liquid detergent, and 1 tablespoon white vinegar. Blot with a clean pad and rinse well with water. When no more liquid is being blotted, place an absorbent pad over the area and weight it down. When no more is being absorbed, allow it to thoroughly air dry.

See Chapter 4 for specific technique instructions.

●**Leather** ●**Suede**	Blot up the excess. Mix a solution of mild soap in lukewarm water. Swish to create a great volume of suds. Apply only the foam with a sponge. Rinse well with a clean damp cloth and wipe dry. If suede needs a conditioner, apply **Child Life Suede & Fabric Cleaner.** For leather, condition with **The Tannery** or **Fiebing's Saddle Soap.**
●**Wood**	Mix dishwashing detergent in hot water and swish to make a great volume of suds. Dip a cloth in only the foam and apply to the cola. Rinse well with a clean damp cloth and wipe dry. Do not allow water to remain on the surface. Polish or wax as usual.

Soft Drinks/Noncola

●**Acetate** ●**Carpet/Synthetic** ●**Carpet/Wool** ●**Fiberglass** ●**Rayon** ●**Silk** ●**Triacetate** ●**Wool**	Blot up as much excess as possible and sponge* the area with cool water. Spray on **Amway Remove Fabric Spot Cleaner** or apply a Wet Spotter and a few drops of white vinegar. Cover with an absorbent pad dampened with the Wet Spotter. Let it stand as long as any stain is being removed. Keep both the stain and the pad wet with the Wet Spotter. Flush* with water. Repeat if necessary. If the stain persists, moisten the area with a solution of 1 teaspoon **Axion** enzyme presoak and 1 cup warm water—do not use on silk or wool. Cover with a damp cloth that has been dipped in the solution and wrung almost dry. Let it stand 30 minutes. Add more solution as needed to keep the stain warm and moist, but be careful not to let the wet area spread. When the stain is gone,

(continued)

See Chapter 4 for specific technique instructions.

(continued from preceding page) flush thoroughly with water to remove all sugar residue.

•Acrylic Fabric **•Cotton •Linen** **•Modacrylic •Nylon** **•Olefin •Polyester** **•Spandex**	Blot up as much of the liquid as you can. Launder as soon as possible, as that usually removes all traces of the soft drink. If laundering isn't possible, presoak* the stain in a solution of 1 quart warm water, ½ teaspoon liquid detergent, and 1 tablespoon white vinegar for 15 minutes. Rinse with water, allow to dry, then launder.
•Acrylic Plastic **•Alabaster** **•Aluminum** **•Asphalt •Bamboo** **•Ceramic Glass/Tile** **•Chromium** **•Copper •Cork** **•Glass •Linoleum** **•Marble •Paint/Flat** **•Paint/Gloss** **•Plexiglas** **•Polyurethane** **•Porcelain** **•Stainless Steel** **•Vinyl Clothing** **•Vinyl Tile** **•Vinyl Wallcovering**	Wipe up the excess spill. Then wipe the surface with a cloth or sponge dipped in warm sudsy water. Rinse well and wipe dry.
•Bluestone •Brick **•Concrete** **•Flagstone** **•Granite** **•Limestone** **•Masonry Tile** **•Sandstone •Slate** **•Terrazzo**	Wipe up any excess. Wash with a solution of washing soda or detergent (never soap) and water. Use a soft-bristled brush or sponge. Rinse thoroughly with clear water and allow to dry.
•Leather •Suede	Remove any excess spill. Mix a solution of mild soap in lukewarm water. *(continued)*

*See Chapter 4 for specific technique instructions.

(continued from preceding page) Swish to create a great volume of suds. Apply only the foam with a sponge. Wipe dry with a clean dry cloth. On leather only, follow with **The Tannery** or **Fiebing's Saddle Soap** to condition the leather.

Wood

Wipe the excess spill immediately with a cloth or sponge dipped in warm sudsy water, as soft drinks can damage the finish. Rinse with a clean damp cloth and wipe dry. Polish or wax the wood as soon as possible.

Soup/Creamed
(Follow procedures for Cream.)

Soup/Meat Base

- **Acetate**
- **Carpet/Synthetic**
- **Carpet/Wool**
- **Fiberglass** • **Rayon**
- **Silk** • **Triacetate**
- **Wool**

Treat the stain as soon as possible. Set meat stains can be extremely difficult to remove. Sponge* the stain with cold water. If fresh, this should remove it. If any stain remains, spray on **Amway Remove Fabric Spot Cleaner** or apply a Wet Spotter and a few drops of ammonia (omit ammonia on silk and wool). Cover with an absorbent pad dampened with the Wet Spotter. Let it stand as long as any stain is being lifted, changing the pad as it picks up the stain. Keep the stain and pad moist. Flush* with cool water, making sure to remove all traces of the ammonia. If stain persists, moisten it with a solution of ½ teaspoon **Axion** enzyme presoak and ½ cup warm water—do not use on silk or wool. Cover it with a pad dampened slightly with the enzyme solution. Let it stand for 30 minutes. Add more solution to keep the stain

(continued)

*See Chapter 4 for specific technique instructions.

(continued from preceding page) moist and warm, but do not let the wet area spread. Flush with water and dry thoroughly.

- **Acrylic Fabric**
- **Cotton** • **Linen**
- **Modacrylic** • **Nylon**
- **Olefin** • **Polyester**
- **Spandex**

Fresh meat stains usually can be removed by a thorough washing in cold water. If any stain remains, soak it in a solution of 1 quart warm water, ½ teaspoon liquid detergent, and 1 tablespoon ammonia for 15 minutes. Tamp* or scrape,* blotting occasionally with an absorbent pad. Continue as long as any stain remains. Rinse well with water, making sure to remove all traces of ammonia. If the stain remains, presoak* it in a solution of 1 quart warm water and 1 tablespoon **Axion** or **Biz** enzyme presoak for 30 minutes. Rinse well and dry. Launder as soon as possible.

- **Acrylic Plastic**
- **Alabaster**
- **Aluminum**
- **Asphalt** • **Copper**
- **Cork** • **Linoleum**
- **Marble** • **Paint/Flat**
- **Paint/Gloss**
- **Plexiglas**
- **Polyurethane**
- **Porcelain**
- **Stainless Steel**
- **Vinyl Clothing**
- **Vinyl Tile**
- **Vinyl Wallcovering**

Wipe stain with a sponge dipped in warm sudsy water. Rinse thoroughly and wipe dry.

- **Bluestone** • **Brick**
- **Concrete**
- **Flagstone**
- **Granite**
- **Limestone**
- **Masonry Tile**

(continued)

Wipe up the stain with a sponge dipped in cool water. If any stain remains, wash or brush* the stain with a solution of washing soda or detergent (not soap) in warm water. Rinse well and allow to dry.

See Chapter 4 for specific technique instructions.

●**Sandstone** ●**Slate**   *(see base of preceding page)*
●**Terrazzo**

●**Carpet/Synthetic**
●**Carpet/Wool**

Blot up as much liquid as you can and sponge* the area immediately with cool water. This should remove any stain, but if one remains, apply **Spot Shot Carpet Stain Remover, Stain-X Carpet Stain Remover,** or **Up & Out** (do not use this on wool) according to the package directions. If the stain persists, mix 1 teaspoon mild detergent in ½ pint warm water. Add a small amount to the carpet and blot the liquid. Take care not to force the stain further into the fibers. Continue until no more stain is removed. Flush* thoroughly with water. Place an absorbent pad over the area and weight it down. When no more liquid is drawn out, remove the pad and allow it to air dry thoroughly.

●**Leather** ●**Suede**

Blot up what you can and follow with a leather cleaner, **The Tannery,** according to package directions. Or mix dishwashing detergent in hot water and swish to make a great volume of suds. Dip a cloth in only the foam and wipe the area. Wipe dry with a clean dry cloth. On leather only, follow with **The Tannery** or **Fiebing's Saddle Soap.**

●**Wood**

Wipe the stain with a clean cloth dipped in warm sudsy water. Rinse with a damp cloth and wipe dry. Polish or wax as soon as possible.

Soup/Vegetable Base

●**Acetate**
●**Carpet/Synthetic**

(continued)

Remove any excess immediately. Sponge* the stain with a dry-cleaning

---

See Chapter 4 for specific technique instructions.

(continued from preceding page)

- **Carpet/Wool**
- **Fiberglass** **Rayon**
- **Silk** **Triacetate**
- **Wool**

solvent, either **Carbona No. 10 Special Spot Remover/Carbona Cleaning Fluid** or **Afta Cleaning Fluid.** Apply a Dry Spotter to the stain and cover with an absorbent pad dampened with the Dry Spotter. Let it stand as long as any stain is being removed. Change the pad as it picks up the stain. Keep the stain and pad moist with the Dry Spotter. Flush* with the dry-cleaning solvent. If any stain remains, moisten the area with a solution of 1 teaspoon **Axion** enzyme presoak and 1 cup warm water—do not use enzyme presoaks on silk or wool. Cover the stain with a pad that has been dipped in the solution and wrung almost dry. Let it stand for 30 minutes. Add more solution to keep the area warm and moist, but do not let the wet area spread. When no more stain is being lifted, flush with water and allow to dry.

- **Acrylic Fabric**
- **Cotton** **Linen**
- **Modacrylic** **Nylon**
- **Olefin** **Polyester**
- **Spandex**

Wipe up any excess immediately. Sponge* the stain with a dry-cleaning solvent, either **Carbona No. 10 Special Spot Remover/Carbona Cleaning Fluid, K2r Spot-lifter** (aerosol), or **Afta Cleaning Fluid.** Apply a Dry Spotter and cover with an absorbent pad dampened with the Dry Spotter. Let it stand as long as any stain is being removed. Flush* with one of the liquid dry-cleaning solvents. If any stain remains, apply a few drops dishwashing detergent and a few drops ammonia to the area, then tamp* or scrape* to loosen stain. Keep the stain moist with the detergent and ammonia and blot occasionally with an absorbent pad. Flush well with water to remove all ammonia and launder or allow to dry.

*See Chapter 4 for specific technique instructions.

- Acrylic Plastic
- Aluminum
- Asphalt • Bamboo
- Cane
- Ceramic Glass/Tile
- Copper • Cork
- Glass • Linoleum
- Marble • Paint/Flat
- Paint/Gloss
- Plexiglas
- Polyurethane
- Porcelain
- Stainless Steel
- Vinyl Clothing
- Vinyl Tile
- Vinyl Wallcovering

Wipe up any excess spill immediately. Wipe the surface with a cloth or sponge dipped in warm sudsy water. Rinse well and wipe dry.

- Bluestone • Brick
- Concrete
- Flagstone
- Granite
- Masonry Tile
- Sandstone • Slate
- Terrazzo

Remove any excess. Wash the area with a solution of washing soda or detergent (never soap) and water. Scrub with a sponge or soft-bristled brush. Rinse the area thoroughly and allow to dry.

- Leather • Suede

Carefully blot any excess from the surface. Mix a solution of mild soap in lukewarm water. Swish to create a great volume of suds. Apply only the foam with a sponge. Wipe dry with a clean cloth. If a greasy stain remains, apply an absorbent such as cornmeal. Give it plenty of time to work. Gently brush* or shake the cornmeal off. Repeat if necessary. On leather only, follow with **The Tannery** or **Fiebing's Saddle Soap** to condition the leather.

- Wood

Remove any excess spill immediately. Wipe with a cloth dipped in warm sudsy water. Rinse with a clean

(continued)

See Chapter 4 for specific technique instructions.

(continued from preceding page) cloth dampened with clear water. Polish or wax as soon as possible.

Sour Cream *(Follow procedures for* Cream.*)*

Syrup/Chocolate
(Follow procedures for Chocolate/Cocoa.*)*

Syrup/Corn, Maple, Sugar

- Acetate
- Fiberglass • Rayon
- Silk • Triacetate
- Wool

Sponge* the area with water to help remove the sugar, then apply **Amway Remove Fabric Spot Cleaner.** Or, after sponging apply a Wet Spotter and a few drops of white vinegar. Cover with an absorbent pad moistened with Wet Spotter. Let it stand as long as any stain is being removed. Change the pad as it picks up the stain. Keep the pad and stain moist with Wet Spotter and vinegar. Flush* with water and repeat until no more stain is being removed. If the stain persists, soak in a solution of 1 quart warm water, ½ teaspoon liquid detergent, and 1 tablespoon vinegar for 15 minutes. Rinse well with water and allow to dry.

- Acrylic Fabric
- Modacrylic
- Spandex

Sponge* the area with water and apply a Wet Spotter and a few drops of white vinegar. Cover with an absorbent pad dampened with Wet Spotter. Let it stand as long as any stain is being removed. Tamp* occasionally and change the pad as it picks up the stain. Flush* with water. If a stain persists, presoak* in a solution of 1 quart warm water, ½ tea-
(continued)

*See Chapter 4 for specific technique instructions.

(continued from preceding page) spoon liquid detergent, and 1 table-spoon vinegar for 15 minutes. Rinse well with water and launder if possible. If not, presoak in a solution of 1 quart warm water and 1 tablespoon **Axion** enzyme presoak for 30 minutes. Rinse well with water and launder as soon as possible.

- **Acrylic Plastic**
- **Alabaster**
- **Aluminum**
- **Asphalt** • **Bamboo**
- **Cane**
- **Ceramic Glass/Tile**
- **Cork** • **Glass**
- **Linoleum** • **Marble**
- **Paint/Flat**
- **Paint/Gloss**
- **Plexiglas**
- **Polyurethane**
- **Stainless Steel**
- **Tin** • **Vinyl Tile**
- **Vinyl Wallcovering**
- **Zinc**

Blot up any excess spill. Wipe area with a cloth or sponge dipped in warm sudsy water. Rinse well and wipe dry.

- **Bluestone**
- **Flagstone**
- **Slate**

Wipe up excess spill, then wash with a solution of washing soda or detergent (not soap) and water. Scrub with a cloth or soft-bristled brush. Rinse thoroughly with clear water and allow to dry.

- **Carpet/Synthetic**
- **Carpet/Wool**
- **Cotton** • **Linen**
- **Nylon** • **Olefin**
- **Polyester**

Scrape* to remove the excess spill and sponge* the stain with water. Apply a Wet Spotter and a few drops of white vinegar. (Do not use vinegar on cotton or linen.) Cover with an absorbent pad moistened with the Wet Spotter. Let it stand as long as any stain is being removed. Keep both the pad and stain moist with Wet Spotter and vinegar, changing the pad as it picks up the stain. Flush*

(continued)

---

*See Chapter 4 for specific technique instructions.

(continued from preceding page) with water and repeat until no more stain is being lifted. If a stain persists, apply rubbing alcohol to the area and cover with an absorbent pad dampened with alcohol. Let it stand as long as any stain is being removed. Change the pad as it picks up the stain and keep the stain and pad moist with alcohol. Allow to dry. If a stain still remains, presoak* in a solution of 1 quart warm water, ½ teaspoon liquid detergent, and 1 tablespoon white vinegar for 15 minutes. Rinse with water and sponge stain with alcohol. Launder if possible. If not, presoak in a solution of 1 quart warm water and 1 tablespoon **Axion** enzyme presoak for 30 minutes. Rinse well with water and launder as soon as possible. When treating carpets, apply **Stain-X Carpet Stain Remover** or **Spot Shot Carpet Stain Remover.** Or, thoroughly dampen the spot with the enzyme solution and cover with an absorbent pad moistened with the solution. Keep area covered for 30 minutes. Using an absorbent pad, blot up as much excess moisture as possible, then allow area to thoroughly air dry.

●**Grout**

Wipe up excess immediately with a cloth dipped in warm sudsy water. If any stain remains, apply **Afta Tile & Grout Cleaner** or dip a wet toothbrush into a little baking soda or powdered cleanser and gently scrub the spot. Rinse well and wipe dry.

●**Leather** ●**Suede**

Gently scrape* to remove any excess syrup. Mix a solution of mild soap in lukewarm water. Swish to create a great volume of suds. Apply only the foam with a sponge. Wipe with a dry

(continued)

See Chapter 4 for specific technique instructions.

(continued from preceding page) cloth. On leather only, follow with **The Tannery** or **Fiebing's Saddle Soap** to condition the leather.

●**Wood**

Wipe up any excess spill. Wipe the stain with a cloth dipped in warm sudsy water. Rinse with a cloth dampened with clear water and wipe dry. Polish or wax the wood as soon as possible.

Tea *(Follow procedures for Coffee.)*

Tobacco
(Follow procedures for Nicotine/Cigar, Cigarette, Pipe Smoke.)

Tomato/Tomato Juice/ Tomato Sauce

●**Acetate**
●**Carpet/Synthetic**
●**Carpet/Wool**
●**Fiberglass** ●**Rayon**
●**Rope** ●**Triacetate**
●**Wool**

Sponge* the stain with cool water, then sponge the area with lemon juice or rub a slice of lemon over the stain (use with caution on wool). Flush* with water and blot as much liquid as possible. Let dry. If stain persists, apply a Wet Spotter and cover with an absorbent pad moistened with Wet Spotter. Let stand as long as any stain is being removed. Change the pad as it picks up the stain. Keep the stain and pad moist with Wet Spotter. Flush with water. If any trace of the stain remains, moisten the area with a solution of 1 cup warm water and 1 teaspoon **Axion,** an enzyme presoak product—do not use on silk or wool. Cover with a clean pad dampened
(continued)

*See Chapter 4 for specific technique instructions.

(continued from preceding page) with the solution and wrung almost dry. Let it stand for 30 minutes. Add enough solution to keep the stain and pad moist and warm, but do not allow the wet area to spread. When no more stain is visible, flush thoroughly with water and allow to air dry.

- **Acrylic Fabric**
- **Modacrylic • Nylon**
- **Olefin • Polyester**
- **Spandex**

Sponge* stain with cool water immediately. Then rub with a lemon slice or sponge lemon juice on the stain. Flush* with water, blotting as much liquid as possible. Allow to dry. If any trace of stain persists, presoak* in a solution of 1 quart warm water, ½ teaspoon dishwashing detergent, and 1 tablespoon white vinegar for 15 minutes. Rinse with water and launder if possible. If not, presoak in a solution of 1 quart warm water and 1 tablespoon **Axion** or **Biz** (enzyme presoak products). Rinse well with water and launder as soon as possible.

- **Acrylic Plastic**
- **Aluminum**
- **Asphalt • Bamboo**
- **Brass • Bronze**
- **Cane**
- **Ceramic Glass/Tile**
- **Copper • Enamel**
- **Glass • Grout**
- **Iron**
- **Paint/Flat**
- **Paint/Gloss**
- **Plexiglas**
- **Polyurethane**
- **Porcelain Dishes**
- **Porcelain Fixtures**
- **Stainless Steel**
- **Vinyl Clothing**
- **Vinyl Wallcovering**

Wipe the stain with a cloth or sponge dipped in warm sudsy water. Rinse well and wipe dry.

---

*See Chapter 4 for specific technique instructions.

•Bluestone •Brick •Concrete •Flagstone •Granite •Masonry Tile •Slate •Terrazzo	Wipe up the excess spill and wash the stain with a solution of washing soda or detergent (not soap) and water. Use a cloth or soft-bristled brush to scrub. Rinse thoroughly and allow to dry.
•Cork •Linoleum •Vinyl Tile	Wipe up the excess spill and wash the area with a solution of washing soda or detergent (not soap) and water. Scrub with a cloth or soft-bristled brush. Rinse thoroughly with clear water and allow to dry. If stain persists, wipe area with a cloth dampened in a solution of 1 tablespoon oxalic acid to 1 pint water. Rinse well and wipe dry. Repolish the surface if needed. **Caution:** Oxalic acid is poisonous; use with care and wear rubber gloves.
•Cotton •Linen	Test fabric for colorfastness. If colorfast, stretch the stained fabric over a bowl and fasten in place with a rubber band. Pour boiling water through the fabric from a height of 2 or 3 feet. Avoid splatters. This procedure must be done immediately. If stain persists, soak in a solution of 1 quart warm water and ½ teaspoon detergent for 15 minutes. Rinse with water. Sponge* area with rubbing alcohol and launder if possible. If not, presoak* for 30 minutes in a solution of 1 quart warm water and 1 tablespoon **Axion** or **Biz** (enzyme presoak products). Rinse well with water and launder.
•Leather •Suede	Wipe up any excess juice, then mix a solution of mild soap in lukewarm water. Swish to create a great volume of suds. Apply only the foam with a sponge. Wipe with a clean dry cloth.

(continued)

See Chapter 4 for specific technique instructions.

(continued from preceding page) On leather only, follow with **The Tannery** or **Fiebing's Saddle Soap** to condition the leather.

●**Marble**

After removing any excess liquid, wipe the surface with a cloth dipped in warm sudsy water. Rinse well and wipe dry. If any stain or discoloration remains, mix a poultice of water, powdered detergent, and bleach. Apply a thick paste to the stain and cover with a damp cloth to retard evaporation. Leave in place. When stain has been removed, rinse thoroughly with water and dry.

●**Silver**

Wash silver in hot sudsy water as soon as possible. Rinse in hot water and dry immediately with a soft cloth to prevent tarnish.

●**Wood**

Mix dishwashing detergent in hot water and swish to make a great volume of suds. Dip a cloth in only the foam and apply to the tomato stain. Rinse with a clean cloth moistened with clear water. If any stain remains, rub the area with a cloth dampened with a solution of 1 tablespoon oxalic acid and 1 pint water. Rinse well and wipe dry. Wax or polish as soon as possible. **Caution:** Oxalic acid is poisonous; use with care and wear rubber gloves.

Turmeric *(Follow procedures for Mustard.)*

Unknown Staining Agent

●**Acetate**
●**Carpet/Synthetic**

Sponge* the area with a dry-cleaning solvent, either **Carbona No. 10**

(continued)

---

*See Chapter 4 for specific technique instructions.

(continued from preceding page)

- **Carpet/Wool**
- **Fiberglass** • **Rayon**
- **Silk** • **Triacetate**
- **Wool**

Special Spot Remover/Carbona Cleaning Fluid or **Afta Cleaning Fluid.** Then apply a Dry Spotter. Tamp* or scrape* to help loosen the stain. Flush* with the dry-cleaning solvent. If stain persists, apply amyl acetate and tamp again. Flush with the solvent and allow to dry. If stain still remains, sponge stain with water and apply a few drops of white vinegar. Tamp again. Apply a Wet Spotter and a few drops of ammonia (do not use ammonia on silk or wool). Tamp again. Allow to dry. Sponge with rubbing alcohol and pat with an absorbent pad dampened with alcohol (do not use full-strength alcohol on acetate, rayon, or triacetate). Allow to dry.

- **Acrylic Fabric**
- **Cotton** • **Linen**
- **Modacrylic** • **Nylon**
- **Olefin** • **Polyester**
- **Spandex**

Cover the stain with a rubbing alcohol compress. Let it remain on the stain for a few minutes, then wipe with a cloth moistened with ammonia. If stain persists, sponge* the area with a dry-cleaning solvent, either **Carbona No. 10 Special Spot Remover/Carbona Cleaning Fluid, K2r Spot-lifter** (aerosol), or **Afta Cleaning Fluid.** Apply a Dry Spotter. Tamp* or scrape* to help loosen the stain. Flush* with one of the liquid dry-cleaning solvents. If stain remains, apply amyl acetate and tamp again. Flush with the dry-cleaning solvent. If stain still persists, sponge with water, then apply a Wet Spotter and a few drops of white vinegar. (Do not use vinegar on cotton or linen.) Tamp again and apply a Wet Spotter and a few drops of ammonia. Flush with the dry-cleaning solvent and allow to dry.

See Chapter 4 for specific technique instructions.

- Acrylic Plastic
- Aluminim
- Bamboo • Cane
- Ceramic Glass/Tile
- Chromium
- Copper • Glass
- Gold • Paint/Flat
- Paint/Gloss
- Plexiglas
- Polyurethane
- Vinyl Clothing
- Vinyl Wallcovering

Wipe the stain with a cloth or sponge dipped in warm sudsy water to which a few drops of ammonia have been added. Rinse well and wipe dry with a soft cloth.

- Alabaster • Marble

Wipe the stain with a cloth or sponge dipped in warm sudsy water. Rinse well and wipe dry. If a stain persists, soak an absorbent pad in rubbing alcohol and place it over the stain. Wait 5 minutes, then apply a pad that has been soaked in ammonia and wrung nearly dry. Alternate alcohol and ammonia pads until the stain has been removed. Wipe surface with a damp cloth and wipe dry.

- Asphalt • Cork
- Linoleum
- Vinyl Tile

Wipe the stain with a cloth dipped in a solution of washing soda or detergent and water. Rinse well and wipe dry. If any stain remains, cover with an absorbent pad moistened with rubbing alcohol. Let it remain several minutes, then wipe the area with a cloth dampened with ammonia. (Do not use ammonia on older linoleum or vinyl floor tile.) Wash with a cloth dipped in warm sudsy water. Rinse with clear water and allow to dry.

- Bluestone • Brick
- Concrete
- Flagstone
- Granite
- Limestone

Wash the stained area with a solution of washing soda or detergent (never soap) and water. Scrub with a cloth or soft-bristled brush. Rinse thoroughly with clear water and allow to dry.

(continued)

●**Masonry Tile**	*(see base of preceding page)*
●**Sandstone** ●**Slate**	
●**Terrazzo**	

●**Grout**	Wipe the stain with a cloth dipped in warm sudsy water. If stain remains, apply **Afta Tile & Grout Cleaner,** then, if stain persists, dip a wet toothbrush into a little baking soda or powdered cleanser and gently scrub the spot. Rinse thoroughly with clear water and wipe dry.

●**Leather** ●**Suede**	Mix a solution of mild soap in lukewarm water. Swish to create a great volume of suds. Apply only the foam with a sponge. Rinse with a cloth dampened with clear water. If a greasy or oily residue remains, powder the area with an absorbent such as cornmeal. Allow plenty of time for the absorbent to work. Gently brush* the powder off the hide. Repeat application of absorbent if necessary. If suede has been subjected to intensive stain-removal treatment, condition it with **Child Life Suede & Fabric Cleaner.** On leather, follow with **The Tannery** or **Fiebing's Saddle Soap** to condition the leather.

●**Wallpaper**	Gently rub the stain with an artgum eraser. If stain remains, wipe gently with cloth dampened with lukewarm water. If traces persist, mix a paste of cornmeal (for light colors) or fuller's earth (for dark colors) and press onto stain with the palm of your hand. Let dry, then gently wipe off powder with a soft cloth.

●**Wood**	Mix dishwashing detergent in hot water and swish to make a great vol-

(continued)

---

*See Chapter 4 for specific technique instructions.

(continued from preceding page) ume of suds. Dip a cloth in only the foam and apply to the stain. Rinse with a clean cloth dampened with clear water. Polish or wax the wood as soon as possible.

Urine

- **Acetate**
- **Carpet/Synthetic**
- **Carpet/Wool**
- **Fiberglass** • **Rayon**
- **Silk** • **Triacetate**
- **Wool**

Sponge* the area with water or club soda immediately to dilute the stain. Apply a Wet Spotter and a few drops of ammonia. (Do not use ammonia on silk or wool.) Cover with an absorbent pad moistened with Wet Spotter. Let it stand as long as any stain is being removed. Change the pad as it picks up the stain. Keep both the pad and stain moist with Wet Spotter and ammonia. Flush* with water, then apply Wet Spotter with a few drops of white vinegar. Flush well with water and repeat if necessary. Allow to dry. On carpets, after following these procedures, apply **Lestoil Deodorizing Rug Shampoo, Stain-X Carpet Stain Remover, Up & Out** (not for wool carpets), or **Afta Carpet Stain Remover.**

- **Acrylic Fabric**
- **Cotton** • **Linen**
- **Modacrylic** • **Nylon**
- **Olefin** • **Polyester**
- **Spandex**

Flush* immediately with water or club soda. Soak the stain in a solution of 1 quart warm water, ½ teaspoon liquid detergent, and 1 tablespoon ammonia for 30 minutes. Rinse well with water. If stain persists, soak in a solution of 1 quart warm water and 1 tablespoon white vinegar for 1 hour. (Use white vinegar with care on cotton and linen.) Rinse well and allow to dry. If stain is set, try applying rubbing alcohol to the area and tamping* (do not apply full-strength rubbing alcohol to acrylic or modacrylic—dilute *(continued)*

*See Chapter 4 for specific technique instructions.

(continued from preceding page) with 2 parts water). As stain loosens, blot the liquid and stain with an absorbent pad. Keep both the stain and pad moist with alcohol and change the pad as it picks up the stain. Allow to dry.

●**Acrylic Plastic**
●**Aluminum**
●**Bamboo** ●**Cane**
●**Ceramic Glass/Tile**
●**Glass** ●**Paint/Flat**
●**Paint/Gloss**
●**Plexiglas**
●**Polyurethane**
●**Vinyl Clothing**
●**Vinyl Wallcovering**

Wipe up liquid with a cloth or sponge dipped in warm sudsy water. Rinse well and wipe dry with a soft cloth.

●**Alabaster** ●**Marble**

Wipe the stain with a cloth or sponge dipped in warm sudsy water. Rinse well and wipe dry. If a stain persists, soak an absorbent pad in rubbing alcohol and apply to the stain after wringing nearly dry. Wait 5 minutes, then apply an absorbent pad that has been soaked in ammonia and wrung nearly dry. Alternate alcohol and ammonia pads until stain has been removed. Wipe surface with a cloth dampened with clear water and dry with a soft cloth.

●**Asphalt** ●**Cork**
●**Linoleum**
●**Vinyl Tile**

Wipe the stain with a cloth or sponge dipped in warm sudsy water. Rinse well and wipe dry. If stain remains, cover with an absorbent pad soaked in rubbing alcohol. Let it remain in place for 5 minutes, then wipe the area with a cloth dampened with ammonia. (Do not use ammonia on linoleum or vinyl floor tile.) Rinse well with water and wipe dry with a soft cloth.

●**Bluestone** ●**Brick** ●**Concrete** ●**Flagstone** ●**Granite** ●**Limestone** ●**Masonry Tile** ●**Sandstone**	Wash the stain with a solution of washing soda or detergent (never soap) and water. Scrub with a cloth or soft-bristled brush. Rinse thoroughly with water and allow to dry.
●**Grout**	Wash the stain with a cloth dipped in warm sudsy water. If any stain remains, apply **Afta Tile & Grout Cleaner** or dip a wet toothbrush into baking soda or powdered cleanser and gently scrub the stain. Rinse well and wipe dry.
●**Leather** ●**Suede**	Blot up the excess. Mix a solution of mild soap in lukewarm water. Swish to create a great volume of suds. Apply only the foam with a sponge. Rinse well with a clean damp cloth and wipe dry. if suede needs a conditioner, apply **Child Life Suede & Fabric Cleaner.** For leather, condition with **The Tannery** or **Fiebing's Saddle Soap.**
●**Wood**	Gently wipe the stain with a cloth or sponge dipped in warm sudsy water. Rinse with a clean cloth moistened with clear water and wipe dry. Polish or wax as soon as possible.

Varnish   *(Follow procedures for* Lacquer.*)*

Vegetables/Green, Yellow

●**Acetate** ●**Carpet/Synthetic** ●**Carpet/Wool** *(continued)*	Scrape* to remove any excess. Sponge* the area with a dry-cleaning solvent, either **Carbona No. 10**

See Chapter 4 for specific technique instructions.

(continued from preceding page)

●**Fiberglass** ●**Rayon**
●**Silk** ●**Triacetate**
●**Wool**

Special Spot Remover/Carbona Cleaning Fluid, K2r Spot-lifter (tube), or **Afta Cleaning Fluid.** Apply a Dry Spotter and cover with an absorbent pad moistened with Dry Spotter. Let it stand as long as any stain is being removed. Change the pad as it picks up the stain. Keep the stain and pad moist with Dry Spotter. Flush* with one of the liquid dry-cleaning solvents. If any stain remains, moisten the area with a solution of 1 teaspoon **Axion** enzyme presoak and 1 cup warm water—do not use enzyme presoaks on silk or wool. Cover the stain with a pad that has been dipped in the solution and wrung nearly dry. Let it stand for 30 minutes. Add enough solution to keep the area warm and barely moist. When no more stain is being lifted, flush with water and allow to dry.

●**Acrylic Fabric**
●**Cotton** ●**Linen**
●**Modacrylic** ●**Nylon**
●**Olefin** ●**Polyester**
●**Spandex**

Scrape* to remove the material. Sponge* the area with a dry-cleaning solvent, either **Carbona No. 10 Special Spot Remover/Carbona Cleaning Fluid, K2r Spot-lifter** (aerosol), or **Afta Cleaning Fluid.** Apply a Dry Spotter and cover with an absorbent pad dampened with the Dry Spotter. Let it stand as long as any stain is being removed. Flush* with one of the liquid dry-cleaning solvents. If any stain remains, apply a few drops of dishwashing detergent and a few drops of ammonia to the area. Tamp* or scrape to help loosen the stain. Keep the stain moist with detergent and ammonia and blot occasionally with an absorbent pad. Flush well with water and allow to dry. Launder as soon as possible.

*See Chapter 4 for specific technique instructions.

- Acrylic Plastic
- Aluminum
- Asphalt • Bamboo
- Cane
- Ceramic Glass/Tile
- Chromium
- Copper • Cork
- Glass • Linoleum
- Marble • Paint/Flat
- Paint/Gloss
- Plexiglas
- Polyurethane
- Porcelain
- Stainless Steel
- Vinyl Clothing
- Vinyl Tile
- Vinyl Wallcovering

Note: If not removed immediately, action of vegetables causes "green rust" on uncoated copper. Wipe up any excess material immediately. Wipe the surface with a cloth or sponge dipped in warm sudsy water. Rinse well and wipe dry with a soft cloth.

- Bluestone • Brick
- Concrete
- Flagstone
- Granite
- Limestone
- Masonry Tile
- Sandstone • Slate
- Terrazzo

Wipe up any excess vegetable. Wash the surface with a solution of washing soda or detergent (never soap) and water. Use a sponge or soft-bristled brush to scrub. Rinse thoroughly with water and allow to dry.

- Leather • Suede

Carefully wipe or scrape* to remove the excess spill. Mix a solution of mild soap in lukewarm water. Swish to create a great volume of suds. Apply only the foam with a sponge. Wipe dry with a clean cloth. If a greasy stain remains, apply an absorbent such as cornmeal. Give it plenty of time to work. Gently brush* it off. Repeat if necessary. On leather only, follow with **The Tannery** or **Fiebing's Saddle Soap** to condition the leather.

- Wood

Wipe up any excess material. Wipe the stain with a cloth dipped in warm

(continued)

See Chapter 4 for specific technique instructions.

(continued from preceding page) sudsy water. Rinse with a clean cloth dampened with clear water. Polish or wax as soon as possible after drying.

Vinegar/Cider, Wine

●Acetate ●Burlap ●Cotton ●Fiberglass ●Linen ●Rayon ●Silk ●Triacetate	Note: Acetate will resist mild acids such as vinegar, but cotton and linen can be destroyed or weakened. Immediate treatement is imperative. Thoroughly flush* with water or club soda, taking care not to spread the stain. Neutralize the acid to stop fabric damage and possibly restore any color change by holding the stain over an open bottle of ammonia (do not use for silk) and allowing the fumes to penetrate the fabric. Sponging* with a baking soda solution also neutralizes the acid. Flush the ammonia or baking soda from the fabric with clear water and allow to dry. Launder washable fabrics as soon as possible.
●Acrylic Fabric ●Modacrylic ●Nylon ●Olefin ●Polyester ●Spandex	Sponge* the stain with water to which a few drops of ammonia have been added. Flush* with cool water or club soda. If stain remains, repeat treatment with water and ammonia solution. Thoroughly flush the ammonia from the fabric with cool water and launder as soon as possible.
●Acrylic Plastic ●Alabaster ●Aluminum ●Asphalt ●Bamboo ●Brass ●Bronze ●Cane ●Ceramic Glass/Tile ●Chromium	Wipe spill immediately with a cloth dipped in warm sudsy water to prevent the acid in the vinegar from damaging the surface. Rinse well with clear water and wipe dry.

(continued)

See Chapter 4 for specific technique instructions.

- **Copper** - **Cork**
- **Enamel** - **Glass**
- **Gold** - **Grout** - **Iron**
- **Linoleum** - **Marble**
- **Masonry Tile**
- **Paint/Flat**
- **Paint/Gloss**
- **Pewter** - **Platinum**
- **Plexiglas**
- **Polyurethane**
- **Stainless Steel**
- **Tin** - **Vinyl Clothing**
- **Vinyl Tile**
- **Vinyl Wallcovering**
- **Zinc**

(see base of preceding page)

- **Bluestone** - **Brick**
- **Concrete**
- **Flagstone**
- **Granite**
- **Limestone**
- **Sandstone** - **Slate**
- **Terrazzo**

Mix a solution of washing soda or detergent (not soap) and warm water. Scrub with a soft-bristled brush or cloth. Rinse thoroughly with water and dry.

- **Carpet/Synthetic**
- **Carpet/Wool** - **Felt**
- **Wool**

Blot the excess liquid immediately with an absorbent pad. Sponge* the stain with club soda or a cloth dipped in warm sudsy water. If possible, prevent soaking the carpet. If a stain remains, add a few drops of ammonia to clear water. Sponge into the stain and blot, using great care with wool, as it is sensitive to ammonia. Rinse with clear water. Place an absorbent pad over the stain and blot up as much liquid as possible. Allow to thoroughly air dry.

- **Leather** - **Suede**

Mix a solution of mild soap in luke-warm water. Swish to create a great volume of suds. Apply only the foam with a sponge. Wipe dry with a clean

(continued)

---

*See Chapter 4 for specific technique instructions.

(continued from preceding page) cloth. On leather only, follow with **The Tannery** or **Fiebing's Saddle Soap** to condition the leather.

●**Porcelain Dishes**
●**Porcelain Fixtures**
●**Silver**

Wash in hot soapy water. Rinse in hot water and wipe dry with a soft cloth. Never let acids like vinegar remain on silver as the acid can pit and corrode the metal.

●**Wood**

Mix dishwashing detergent in hot water and swish to make a great volume of suds. Dip a cloth in only the foam and wipe the stain with it. Rinse with a cloth dampened with clear water. Wipe dry and apply a polish or wax.

Vomit

●**Acetate** ●**Burlap**
●**Fiberglass** ●**Rayon**
●**Rope** ●**Silk**
●**Triacetate**
●**Wool**

Gently scrape* up solids. Sponge* the area with water and apply a Wet Spotter and a few drops of ammonia. (Do not use ammonia on silk and wool.) Cover with an absorbent pad moistened with Wet Spotter and ammonia. Let it stand as long as any stain is being picked up. Change the pad as it picks up the stain. Keep the stain and pad moist with Wet Spotter and ammonia. Flush* thoroughly with cool water, making sure to remove all traces of ammonia. If a stain persists, moisten it with a solution of ½ teaspoon **Axion** enzyme presoak and ½ cup warm water—do not use on silk or wool. Cover stain with an absorbent pad dampened with the solution and let it stand for 30 minutes. Add enough solution to keep the area warm and barely moist. Flush with water and dry thoroughly.

See Chapter 4 for specific technique instructions.

- **Acrylic Fabric**
- **Cotton** • **Linen**
- **Modacrylic** • **Nylon**
- **Olefin** • **Polyester**
- **Spandex**

Quickly scrape* to remove solids. Soak the stain in a solution of 1 quart warm water, ½ teaspoon liquid detergent, and 1 tablespoon ammonia. Tamp* or scrape to help loosen the stain. Blot occasionally with an absorbent pad. Rinse well with water, making sure to remove all ammonia traces. If stain persists, presoak* in a solution of 1 quart warm water and 1 tablespoon **Axion** or **Biz** (enzyme presoaks) for 30 minutes. Rinse well and launder as soon as possible.

- **Acrylic Plastic**
- **Aluminum**
- **Asphalt** • **Brass**
- **Bronze**
- **Ceramic Glass/Tile**
- **Chromium**
- **Copper** • **Cork**
- **Enamel** • **Glass**
- **Gold** • **Iron** • **Ivory**
- **Jade** • **Linoleum**
- **Paint/Flat**
- **Paint/Gloss**
- **Pewter** • **Plexiglas**
- **Polyurethane**
- **Porcelain**
- **Stainless Steel**
- **Tin** • **Vinyl Clothing**
- **Vinyl Tile**
- **Vinyl Wallcovering**

Scrape* or wipe up solids, then wash the area with a cloth dipped in warm sudsy water. Rinse thoroughly and wipe dry with a soft cloth.

- **Alabaster** • **Marble**

Wipe up the solids, then wipe the stain with a cloth or sponge dipped in cool water. If stain remains, mix a poultice of water, powdered detergent, and bleach. Apply it to the stain and cover with a damp cloth to retard evaporation. When stain has been bleached out, rinse thoroughly and wipe dry.

*See Chapter 4 for specific technique instructions.

●**Bamboo** ●**Cane**	Scrape* or wipe up solids, then wash stain with a cloth or brush dipped in warm soapy water to which a few drops of ammonia have been added. Rinse with clear water and wipe dry.
●**Bluestone** ●**Brick** ●**Concrete** ●**Flagstone** ●**Granite** ●**Limestone** ●**Masonry Tile** ●**Sandstone** ●**Slate** ●**Terrazzo**	Scrape* or wipe up solids. Then wash the stained area with a cloth dipped in a solution of washing soda or detergent (not soap) and water. Rinse well and allow to dry.
●**Carpet/Synthetic** ●**Carpet/Wool**	On older or fresh stains, scrape* up solids, then apply **Up & Out** (do not use on wool), **Spot Shot Carpet Stain Remover,** or **Stain-X Carpet Stain Remover.** Or, wipe up solids, being careful not to force the stain deeper into the pile. Sponge* the area with a solution of 1 teaspoon mild, non-alkali detergent and ½ pint lukewarm water. Blot the liquid with an absorbent pad. Continue sponging and blotting until no more stain is removed. Sponge the area with a solution of 1 tablespoon ammonia and 1 cup warm water. (Do not use ammonia on wool carpets.) Blot excess liquid. Continue until no more stain is being removed. Place an absorbent pad over the damp area and weight it down with a heavy object. When no more liquid is absorbed, remove the pad and allow carpet to thoroughly air dry.
●**Fur/Natural** ●**Fur/Synthetic**	Carefully wipe up the solids. Wipe stain with a cloth dipped in the suds of a mild detergent and water to which a few drops of ammonia have been added. Rinse with a cloth dampened

(continued)

See Chapter 4 for specific technique instructions.

(continued from preceding page) with clear water. Rub with the nap of the fur; take care not to soak or over-wet the pelt or backing. Air dry away from heat.

●**Grout**

After removing solids, wipe the stain with a cloth dipped in cool water. If any stain remains, apply **Afta Tile & Grout Cleaner** or dip a wet tooth-brush into a little baking soda or pow-dered cleanser and gently scrub the spot. Rinse thoroughly with water and wipe dry.

●**Leather** ●**Suede**

Gently scrape* to remove solids. Mix a solution of mild soap in lukewarm water. Swish to create a great volume of suds. Apply only the foam with a sponge. Rinse well with a clean damp cloth and wipe dry. If suede needs a conditioner, apply **Child Life Suede & Fabric Cleaner.** For leather, condi-tion with **The Tannery** or **Fiebing's Saddle Soap.**

●**Wallpaper**

Gently scrape* up solids. Wipe the stain with a cloth moistened with cool water. Overlap strokes to prevent streaking. Use a clean cloth to gently pat dry.

●**Wood**

Wipe up the solids. Wipe the stain with a cloth dipped in cool clear water. Wipe dry with a soft cloth and polish or wax the wood as usual.

Water Spots

●**Acetate**
●**Acrylic Fabric**
●**Carpet/Synthetic**
●**Carpet/Wool**
(continued)

Water spots on fabrics are caused by the dislodging of sizing or finishing agents found in many garments. Water dislodges these agents and

*See Chapter 4 for specific technique instructions.

(continued from preceding page)

- **Cotton**
- **Fiberglass**
- **Linen**
- **Modacrylic**
- **Nylon**
- **Olefin**
- **Polyester**
- **Rayon** **Silk**
- **Spandex**
- **Triacetate**
- **Wool**

causes them to form rings on the material surface. To remove water spots, dampen the entire area with water and allow to dry. Spots may also be removed by holding the area in the steam from a boiling kettle. If the garment is ironable, press while still damp.

- **Acrylic Plastic**
- **Aluminum**
- **Asphalt**
- **Ceramic Glass/Tile**
- **Chromium**
- **Copper** **Cork**
- **Glass** **Linoleum**
- **Paint/Flat**
- **Paint/Gloss**
- **Plexiglas**
- **Polyurethane**
- **Porcelain Dishes**
- **Porcelain Fixtures**
- **Stainless Steel**
- **Tin** **Vinyl Clothing**
- **Vinyl Tile**
- **Vinyl Wallcovering**

Wipe the stain with a cloth or sponge dipped in warm sudsy water to which a few drops of white vinegar have been added. Rinse well and wipe dry.

- **Alabaster**
- **Bluestone** **Brick**
- **Concrete**
- **Flagstone**
- **Granite**
- **Limestone**
- **Marble**
- **Masonry Tile**
- **Sandstone** **Slate**
- **Terrazzo**

Wash the stain with a solution of washing soda or detergent (not soap) and water. Use a cloth or soft-bristled brush to scrub. Rinse thoroughly with water and allow to dry.

•Leather •Suede

Test denatured alcohol in an inconspicuous area. If safe to use, rub the stain with a cloth dampened with a few drops of alcohol. On leather, follow with **The Tannery** or **Fiebing's Saddle Soap** to condition the leather. To condition suede, apply **Child Life Suede & Fabric Cleaner.**

•Silver

Note: Water spots can tarnish silver. Wash as soon as possible in hot soapy water. Rinse in hot water and dry immediately with a soft cloth.

•Wood

Rub the stain with petroleum jelly or boiled linseed oil. Repeat application until stain vanishes. Use a chamois to finish polishing the surface.

Wine/Red, Rose

•Acetate
•Fiberglass •Rayon
•Triacetate

Blot up the excess with a clean cloth. Spray on **Amway Remove Fabric Spot Cleaner.** Sponge* any remaining stain with water and apply a Wet Spotter and a few drops of white vinegar. Cover with an absorbent pad moistened with Wet Spotter. Let it remain as long as any stain is being removed. Change the pad as it picks up the stain. Keep the stain and pad moist with Wet Spotter and vinegar. Flush* with water. Repeat until no more stain is removed. If a stain remains, moisten it with a solution of 1 teaspoon **Axion** enzyme presoak and 1 cup warm water. Cover with a clean pad that has been dipped in the solution and wrung nearly dry. Let it stand for 30 minutes. Add enough solution to keep the stain warm and barely moist. When no more stain is removed, flush with water and dry.

*See Chapter 4 for specific technique instructions.

- **Acrylic Fabric**
- **Modacrylic** • **Nylon**
- **Olefin** • **Polyester**
- **Spandex**

Note: Be sure to remove the sugar residue or it will cause a permanent stain. Blot up the excess liquid and presoak* the stain in a solution of 1 quart warm water, ½ teaspoon liquid detergent, and 1 tablespoon vinegar for 15 minutes. Rinse with water and sponge* with rubbing alcohol. Launder as soon as possible. If stain remains, presoak stain in a solution of 1 quart warm water and 1 tablespoon **Axion** or **Biz** (enzyme presoaks) for 30 minutes. Rinse well with water and allow to dry. Launder as soon as possible.

- **Acrylic Plastic**
- **Aluminum**
- **Asphalt** • **Bamboo**
- **Brass** • **Bronze**
- **Cane**
- **Ceramic Glass/Tile**
- **Copper** • **Cork**
- **Enamel** • **Glass**
- **Gold** • **Grout** • **Iron**
- **Ivory** • **Jade**
- **Linoleum**
- **Paint/Flat**
- **Paint/Gloss**
- **Pewter** • **Plexiglas**
- **Polyurethane**
- **Stainless Steel**
- **Tin** • **Vinyl Clothing**
- **Vinyl Tile**
- **Vinyl Wallcovering**
- **Zinc**

Blot up any excess spill. Wipe the surface with a cloth or sponge dipped in warm sudsy water. Rinse well and wipe dry.

- **Alabaster** • **Marble**

Blot up the excess. Wipe the surface with a cloth dipped in a solution of washing soda or detergent (not soap) and water. Rinse well and wipe dry. If a stain remains, mix a few drops of ammonia with 1 cup 3% hydrogen

(continued)

See Chapter 4 for specific technique instructions.

(continued from preceding page) peroxide. Soak a white blotter with the solution and place it over the stain. Weight it down with a piece of glass or other heavy object. Continue applying the solution until the stain has been bleached out. Rinse well and wipe dry.

•**Bluestone** •**Brick**
•**Concrete**
•**Flagstone**
•**Granite**
•**Limestone**
•**Masonry Tile**
•**Slate** •**Terrazzo**

Mix a solution of washing soda or detergent and warm water. Gently brush* stain away with cloth or soft-bristled brush dipped in the solution. Rinse with clear water and allow to dry.

•**Burlap** •**Silk**
•**Wool**

Note: Be sure to remove the sugar residue or it will cause a permanent stain. Blot up the excess wine. Spray on **Amway Remove Fabric Spot Cleaner** or sponge* the stain with water and apply a Wet Spotter and a few drops of white vinegar. Cover with an absorbent pad dampened with Wet Spotter and let it stand as long as any stain is being removed. Change the pad as it picks up the stain. Keep the pad and stain moist with Wet Spotter and vinegar. Flush* with water and repeat until no more stain is being lifted. If any stain does remain, sponge with rubbing alcohol and cover with an absorbent pad dampened with alcohol. Let it remain as long as any stain is being lifted. Change the pad as it picks up the stain and keep both the stain and pad moist with alcohol. Flush thoroughly with water. For stubborn or old stains, try moistening the area with a solution of 1 teaspoon liquid laundry detergent safe for silk or wool and 1 cup warm water. Cover with an absorbent pad dipped in the solution

(continued)

---

*See Chapter 4 for specific technique instructions.

(continued from preceding page) and wrung nearly dry. Let it stand for 30 minutes, adding enough solution to keep the area warm and barely moist. When stain is removed, flush thoroughly with water and allow to dry.

●**Carpet/Synthetic**
●**Carpet/Wool**
●**Foam Rubber**

Note: Be sure to remove the sugar residue or it will cause a permanent stain. Blot up what you can with an absorbent pad. Apply **Up & Out** (do not use on wool) or **Stain-X Carpet Stain Remover.** Or, flush* the stain on area rugs or sponge* carpeting with a solution of 1 quart warm water, ½ teaspoon liquid detergent, and 1 tablespoon white vinegar. Blot with a clean pad and rinse well with water. If the stain remains, sponge it with a solution of 1 quart warm water and 1 tablespoon **Axion** enzyme presoak. Blot and flush alternately until no more stain is removed. Rinse with clear water and blot up all the excess liquid with an absorbent pad. Weight down another pad with a piece of glass or other heavy object. When no more liquid is absorbed, allow to thoroughly air dry.

●**Cotton** ●**Linen**

Blot up the excess, then pretreat* with **Shout Laundry Soil & Stain Remover** or **Spray 'n Wash** and launder. If that is not possible, presoak* the stain in a solution of 1 quart warm water and ½ teaspoon liquid detergent and let stand for 15 minutes. Rinse well with water and sponge* area with rubbing alcohol. Rinse again with water and allow to dry. If the stain persists, presoak in a solution of warm water and **Axion** enzyme presoak according to package directions. Rinse with water and launder as soon as possible.

*See Chapter 4 for specific technique instructions.

•Felt •Fur/Natural •Fur/Synthetic	Blot up the excess stain. Mix dishwashing detergent in hot water and swish to make a great volume of suds. Dip a cloth in only the foam and apply. Rinse with a cloth dampened with clear water. Allow to thoroughly air dry.
•Leather •Suede	Blot up the excess wine. Mix a solution of mild soap in lukewarm water. Swish to create a great volume of suds. Apply only the foam with a sponge. Rinse well with a clean damp cloth and wipe dry. If suede needs a conditioner, apply **Child Life Suede & Fabric Cleaner.** For leather, condition with **The Tannery** or **Fiebing's Saddle Soap.**
•Porcelain Dishes •Porcelain Fixtures	Wash the stain with a cloth dipped in warm sudsy water. Rinse well and wipe dry with a soft cloth. To remove any old or set stains in the bottom of dishes, dip a soft damp cloth into a little baking soda and wipe away any remaining residue. Rinse well and wipe dry.
•Silver	Wash silver in hot soapy water. Rinse in hot water and wipe dry with a soft cloth.
•Wood	Mix dishwashing detergent in hot water and swish to make a great volume of suds. Dip a cloth in only the foam and apply to the stain. Rinse well with a clean cloth dampened with cool water. Polish or wax as soon as possible.

Wine/White
(*Follow procedures for* Alcoholic Beverages.)

Yellowing

•Acetate
•Fiberglass •Rayon
•Silk •Triacetate
•Wool

Flush* the spot with water. Test a mild solution of 3% hydrogen peroxide and water in an inconspicuous area—if safe, apply gingerly to the stain. Do not allow the solution to remain on the fabric; flush with water immediately. If any stain remains, it is best not to attempt further cleaning at home.

•Acrylic Fabric
•Modacrylic •Nylon
•Olefin •Polyester

Apply lemon juice to the stain, but do not let it dry. Rinse thoroughly with water. If possible, launder. If you can't launder, test **Whink Rust Stain Remover** on delicate fabrics or **Bar Keepers Friend Cleanser & Polish** on sturdy fabrics. If safe to use, apply according to package directions. Then flush* the area with cool water and launder as soon as possible. Be careful not to spill any rust-remover on porcelain or enamel, as it will ruin the finish.

•Carpet/Synthetic
•Carpet/Wool

Apply lemon juice and salt to the stain. Sponge* the pile with water and blot liquid with an absorbent pad. If any stain remains, test **Bar Keepers Friend Cleanser & Polish** on an inconspicuous area. If safe to use, apply to stain according to package directions. Flush* with water and blot excess liquid. Allow to dry.

•Cotton •Linen

Rub detergent into the stain and rinse well with water. Launder as soon as possible. If the stain remains, test **Bar Keepers Friend Cleanser & Polish** in an inconspicuous place. If safe, apply according to package directions. Flush* thoroughly with water and launder.

*See Chapter 4 for specific technique instructions.

- **Linoleum**
- **Vinyl Tile**

Wipe the stain with a cloth or sponge dipped in warm sudsy water to which a few drops of ammonia have been added. Rinse with a cloth moistened with clear water and wipe dry.

- **Porcelain Dishes**
- **Porcelain Fixtures**

Make a paste of borax and lemon juice. Rub it into the stain and allow to dry. Rinse with clear water and repeat if necessary. Rinse thoroughly and dry with a soft cloth.

Chapter 6
Trademarks of Synthetic Fibers

Trademark	Generic Name	Trademark	Generic Name
A		Courtaulds Nylon	nylon
A.C.E.	nylon or polyester	Crepeset	nylon
Acetate by Avtex	acetate	Crepesoft	polyester
Absorbit	rayon	Creslan	acrylic
Acrilan	acrylic or modacrylic	Cumuloft	nylon
Anso	nylon	**D**	
Antron	nylon	Dacron	polyester
Ariloft	acetate		
Arnel	triacetate	**E**	
Avlin	polyester	Eloquent Luster	nylon
Avril	rayon	Eloquent Touch	nylon
Avsorb	rayon	Encron	polyester
		Enka 10-10	nylon
B		Enkaire	rayon
Beau-Grip	rayon	Enkaloft	nylon
Bi-Loft	acrylic	Enkalure	nylon
Blue "C"	nylon or polyester	Enkasheer	nylon
		Enkrome	rayon
C		Estron	acetate
Cadon	nylon		
Cantrece	nylon	**F**	
Caprolan	nylon	Fibro	rayon
Celanese	nylon or acetate	Fina	acrylic
Chromspun	acetate	Fortrel	polyester
Coloray	rayon		
Cordura	nylon	**G**	
		Golden Glow	polyester

Trademark	Generic Name	Trademark	Generic Name
Golden Touch	polyester	**Q**	
		Qiana	nylon
H			
Herculon	olefin	**R**	
Hollofil	polyester	Rayon by Avtex	rayon
K		**S**	
Kodel	polyester	SEF	modacrylic
KodOfill	polyester	Shareen	nylon
KodOsoff	polyester	Silky Touch	polyester
		Silver Label	nylon
L		Softalon	nylon
Lanese	acetate/ polyester	So-Lara	acrylic
Loftura	acetate	Spectran	polyester
Lusterloff	nylon	Strialine	polyester
Lycra	spandex		
		T	
M		Trevira	polyester
Marquesa	olefin	Twisloc	polyester
Marvess	olefin		
Multisheer	nylon	**U**	
		Ulstron	nylon
N		Ultron	nylon
Natura Luster	nylon		
		V	
		Vectra	olefin
O		Verel	modacrylic
Orlon	acrylic	Vive La Crepe	nylon
P		**Z**	
Patlon	olefin	Zantrel	rayon
Plyloc	polyester	Zeflon	nylon
Polyextra	polyester	Zefran	acrylic or nylon
Polyloom	olefin		

The basic fiber trademarks listed are registered by the member companies of the Man-Made Fiber Producers Association that are currently active. The list does not include service marks, guarantees, warranties or variations of the basic fiber trademark.

Reprinted with permission of the Man-Made Fiber Producers Association, Inc.

Directory of Manufacturers

Afta Solvents Corporation
Express Drive North
Brentwood, NY 11717
516/234-0300

Amway Corp.
7575 E. Fulton Rd.
Ada, MI 49355
616/676-6000

Armour-Dial Inc.
Consumer Services Dept.
Greyhound Tower
Phoenix, AZ 85077
602/248-5557

Canden Company
P.O. Box 161721
Sacramento, CA 95816
916/392-9712

**Carbona Products
Company**
330 Calyer
New York, NY 11107
212/383-5599

**Colgate-Palmolive
Company**
Consumer Affairs
Department
300 Park Ave.
NewYork, NY 10022
212/PL1-1200

The Drackett Company
(Sub. of Bristol Myers Co.)
Consumer Affairs
Department
5020 Spring Grove Ave.
Cincinnati, OH 45232
513/632-1243

Fiebing Company, Inc.
516 S. Second
P.O. Box 041204
Milwaukee, WI 53204
414/271-5011

Herbst Corporation
Merchandising Department
6 Production Drive
Little Rock, AR 72209
501/568-3200

S. C. Johnson & Son, Inc.
Consumer Services
Department
1524 Howe
Racine, WI 53403
414/554-2000

**Magic American Chemical
Corp.**
23700 Mercantile Road
Cleveland, OH 44122
216/464-2353

Missouri Hickory Corp.
410 N. Michigan Ave.
Chicago, IL 60611
312/943-3793

Noxell Corp.
P.O. Box 1799
Baltimore, MD 21203
301/628-7300

**Positive Products
Laboratories, Inc.**
28–11 Astoria Blvd.
Long Island City, NY 11102
212/721-5881

Procter & Gamble
P.O. Box 599
Cincinnati, OH 45201
800/582-0345 (Ohio
residents)
800/543-1745 (other states)

**Scot Laboratories Division
of Scott & Fetzer**
16841 Park Circle Drive
Chagrin Falls, OH 44022
216/543-5119

SerVaas Laboratories, Inc.
P.O. Box 7008
Indianapolis, IN 46207
317/634-1100, ext. 267

Sifers Chemicals, Inc.
P.O. Box 8316
Shawnee Mission, KS 66208
913/648-6644

**Special Products, an
Affiliate of CPC North
America**
Consumer Service
Laboratory
1437 West Morris Street
Indianapolis, IN 46221
317/632-5321

Texize
P.O. Box 368
Greenville, SC 29602
803/963-4261

Trewax Company
11558 South St.
Suite 41
Cerritos, CA 90701
800/421-3823

**United States Pumice
Company**
P.O. Box 6190
Burbank, CA 91510
213/843-8553

Whink Products Company
1901 15th Avenue
Eldora, IA 50627
515/858-3456

White Laboratories, Inc.
P.O. Box 15335
Orlando, FL 32858
800/327-2014

Index